The Politics
of The
European Community

EUROPEAN COMMUNITY STUDIES

General Editor
PROFESSOR ROY PRYCE
Director, Centre for Contemporary European Studies, University of Sussex

A series, written and published in collaboration with the Centre for Contemporary European Studies, designed to provide informed reading about the political, economic, and social aspects of the enlarged European Community and its development towards the goal of European Union.

The Politics
of The
European Community

Roy Pryce

P 21

Rowman and Littlefield
Totowa, New Jersey

11-14-74

First published in the United States, 1973 by
Rowman and Littlefield, Totowa, N.J.

Library of Congress Cataloging in Publication Data

Pryce, Roy.
 The politics of the European Community.

 Bibliography: p.
 1. European federation. 2. European Economic
Community—Great Britain. I. Title.
JN15.P78   382'.9142   73–6697
ISBN 0–87471–199–1

Printed in Great Britain by
Redwood Press Limited, Trowbridge, Wiltshire
and bound by Chapel River Press,
Andover, Hants

Series Preface

The enlargement of the European Community in January 1973 by the entry of Britain, Denmark, and Ireland, marked a major turning point in the post-war history of Western Europe. These countries, together with the original six members, are now working together in a group with a total population of over 250 millions. This represents a major advance towards the achievement of the age-old dream of a united Europe, and provides its members with a framework within which they can together shape the destiny of our part of the world.

At the same time the new Community is one of the most important regional groups on the world scene. It has brought together nine of the economically most advanced and powerful countries in the world whose resources are now comparable in many respects to those of the super-powers. In terms of world trade the Community is indeed far more important than either the United States, the Soviet Union, or China. It is therefore potentially a very powerful element on the international scene, whose policies are likely to be of crucial importance in determining the future economic development of the world as a whole, and in particular the prospects for the developing countries.

How the Community develops in the coming years is therefore of central importance not only for Europe itself but also for all mankind. At the Paris summit meeting held in October 1972, the leaders of its nine member countries set out an ambitious programme for its future. It was then agreed that its ultimate objective should be the achievement by 1980 of a fully-fledged European Union. Although the exact content of this was not spelled out, it is intended that it should include economic and monetary union, and common policies towards the rest of the world covering not only economic but also political and defence issues.

If these ambitions are realised the coming decade will witness not only a major extension of the scope of the Community's work, but also a radical intensification of its impact both within its member countries and also with regard to the rest of the world. This process is unlikely to be smooth: it is likely that there will be constant stresses as the Community seeks to reconcile the differing interests of its members, and to adjust Western Europe's relations with other parts of the world. But of the importance of this process of integration there can be no doubt, not least for the United Kingdom itself, for whom membership involves a major re-casting of policies and attitudes.

The purpose of this series is to provide authoritative studies of the major aspects of the new Community as it moves towards its goal of European Union. This will involve a complex set of political, economic, and social developments. The series aims to describe and analyse these developments; the problems they pose; and the perspectives they offer. In so doing it seeks to help not only those who are undertaking formal studies of the Community, but also the general public, to deepen their knowledge and understanding of the Community and its implications for Europe and the world.

ROY PRYCE

Contents

Introduction

The aim of this book is to provide an introductory study to the politics of the enlarged European Community. Now that the debate about the desirability of entry has been overtaken by the fact of membership, and the fanfares which were sounded on 1 January 1973 have also faded away, a cooler look can be taken at the prospects which lie ahead for the new Community.

About these prospects many questions were raised during the debate which preceded—and accompanied—the decision to join. The protagonists of membership, naturally enough, were inclined to paint a picture of Britian walking hand in hand with her partners into a glorious future; the opponents, on the other hand, conjured up a future full of woes and grief. Whether the hopes of the former or the fears of the latter will be fulfilled must remain largely a matter of conjecture: political scientists for their part are certainly in no position to foretell the future. What they can do, however, is to identify and analyse the factors which are likely to determine the political evolution of the new Community and the problems it is likely to encounter.

This is what this book sets out to do. It is primarily concerned, that is, with the Community as an organised set of political relationships—a political system—and how this system works. It does not attempt to offer a set of prescriptions for its future, either in terms of how that system should develop or which political options it should choose with regard to particular policy issues.* The study does, however, seek to answer a number of questions which were posed during the debate on membership, including those concerned with whether—and to what extent—Britain has 'surrendered' sovereignty by joining, the likeli-

* The author's own views on these issues can be found in an earlier book, written with John Pinder, *Europe after de Gaulle*, Penguin, 1969.

hood (or otherwise) that the Community will develop into a federal United States of Europe, and the political impact of membership on Britain itself.

The book is divided into two parts. The first is devoted to a description and analysis of the Community's political system. For the benefit of those who may not be familiar with the contours of the Community's development, this begins with a historical sketch of events since 1950. Some readers may wish to proceed immediately to the second chapter which analyses the dynamics of the process, and which is followed by a discussion of how the system works, what it has achieved, and what problems it has encountered. The second part examines the major characteristics of the enlarged Community, the problems it is likely to face, and the role of Britain within it.

The book draws on the substantial body of academic work which has been done in recent years on the Community. Footnotes have been kept to a minimum, but references to this literature have been provided in the suggestions for further reading at the end of the book. It is hoped that in this way it will lead some of its readers to further study of the Community which, now that Britain is a member, is of direct concern to us all.

Sussex   ROY PRYCE

Part One The Political system
of
the European Community

I Historical Development

FROM THE SCHUMAN PLAN TO THE TREATY OF PARIS (1950–1951)

The formal initiative which led to the creation of the first European Community was taken by the French Foreign Minister, M. Robert Schuman, on 9 May 1950. He then proposed that French and German production of coal and steel should be placed under a common High Authority 'within the framework of an organisation open to the participation of the other countries of Europe'. But this, he explained, was only the first step towards a much more far-reaching objective:

> In this way there will be realised, simply and speedily, that fusion of interests which is indispensable to the establishment of an economic community; and that will be the leaven from which may grow a wider and deeper community between countries long opposed to one another by bloody conflicts. . . . This proposal will build the first concrete foundation of a European federation which is indispensable to the preservation of peace.

Five other countries—Belgium, the Netherlands, Italy, Luxembourg and West Germany—responded favourably to the proposal, and in April 1951 a treaty was signed in Paris creating the European Coal and Steel Community. This was established, with its headquarters in Luxembourg, in the summer of 1952.

The creation of the six-nation Community marked an important new development in the post-war history of Europe. It took place against a background of a continent which had found itself in the aftermath of that war more divided than ever before as a result of the tensions that had developed among the victorious allies. The positions reached by the Soviet army on the one hand, and that of the western allies on the other, had become an iron curtain on each side of which rival groups, each fearful of the other, had been constructed.

At the same time European countries found themselves overshadowed by the power of their rival protectors, the United States and the Soviet Union, and dependent on them for their security. In the East the dependence was all the greater because of the political needs of the new regimes established by the Communist parties; there, as long as Stalin remained in command, party leaders looked nervously to Moscow for the support they needed to maintain themselves in power. The countries of Western Europe certainly enjoyed a much greater degree of independence vis-à-vis the United States; so that while many of them chose to shelter behind its defensive umbrella as members of the North Atlantic Treaty Organisation (Nato), which was established in 1949, and to accept the offer of Marshall Aid to help in their economic reconstruction, they also took initiatives themselves to work more closely together. Three of them, Belgium, the Netherlands and Luxembourg, had already decided during the war to set up a customs union (Benelux); and the Scandinavian countries soon resumed their own efforts at co-operation. These were to lead in 1952 to the establishment of the Nordic Council, in which parliamentarians joined with governments to promote legal, social and political collaboration.

Parallel with these efforts strong pressures also developed to provide a framework on a wider basis through which the democratic countries of Western Europe could work more closely together. These pressures were by no means wholly related to the Cold War situation. In part they drew their inspiration from the vision of a united Europe which had long been nurtured on the continent, both by visionaries and men of action. More immediately they drew on the determination of many of those who had taken part in the Resistance movements during the war to seek a new framework in which European countries could at last live peacefully together. And to these was added the powerful voice of Winston Churchill who urged the need for reconciliation between former enemies, and the creation—as he put it in his Zurich speech of September 1946—of 'a kind of United States of Europe'. It was as a result of a confluence of these various pressures that the Organisation for European Economic Co-operation (O.E.E.C.) was set up in 1948 by 16 West European countries as a response to the offer of Marshall Aid, and the Council of Europe in the following year. Thirteen countries became members of this body which established a Consultative Assembly and a Committee of Ministers with the general purpose of promoting closer unity between them.

These achievements, however, masked significant differences of purpose between the countries of Western Europe, which had been dramatically expressed at the Congress of Europe held at the Hague in May 1948. This meeting, which brought together some 800 distinguished protagonists of closer unity, had great difficulty in reconciling the demands of some of those from the continental countries for radical measures designed to reduce the role of the nation state with British and Scandinavian attitudes which, while favouring closer unity, wished to see it achieved on the basis of co-operation between national governments.

As far as the British were concerned there were two main reasons for the position they adopted. The first was that their own wartime experience had strengthened, rather than weakened, their sense of national pride and achievement. The second was that they saw themselves as not only a European but also a world power. The Churchillian concept of British influence resting on three overlapping circles of relationships —with the United States, the Commonwealth, and Europe—neatly summed up what the overwhelming majority of the British political elite instinctively felt: we were with Europe, but not of it. It followed that a condition for British participation in moves towards closer unity in Europe was that it should not constrain her freedom of action in other directions.

It was this view which lay at the heart of the policy vigorously pursued in the immediate post-war years by the Labour Government, and which largely conditioned the content and shape of the European organisations which were created. Britain was then in a position to call the tune.

The French initiative of 1950 was the first major challenge to the British position. For if the forms of intergovernmental co-operation which had been developed up to that point suited the United Kingdom very well, they were distinctly less satisfactory for France. That country was above all concerned about relations with her eastern neighbour, Germany, at whose hands she had suffered defeat, or near defeat, on three successive occasions in the recent past. Although Germany was now divided and West Germany had not yet regained the status of an independent state, (though the Federal Republic had been recognised by the West in 1949), French leaders were nevertheless concerned by the rapid economic recovery which had taken place and the change in United States policy which now saw a revived West Germany not as a pastoral no-man's-land, but as a potential bulwark against the Soviet Union. In this situation there was a risk, from the French point of view, of yet again being confronted by a very powerful neighbour on her eastern frontier. There was matter enough for dispute between the two, not least the uncertain future fate of the Ruhr and the Saar whose mineral resources and heavy industries were a major concern to both countries. As relations between them began to deteriorate, fears also began to revive (and not only in France) that history might again be repeated unless action was taken.

Traditionally France had sought to deal with the German problem by alliance with Britain. This policy had not, however, prevented France being invaded, and although in 1947 the treaty of Dunkirk was concluded with Britain which pledged her support against the danger of a revival of a military threat from Germany, the general British stance towards Europe gave little ground for French confidence in her ally. Some greater guarantee was therefore needed. The answer eventually arrived at was the novel and radical solution of embracing her historical enemy.

This step required both courage and imagination. The imagination was largely supplied by Jean Monnet, then head of the French Commissariat au Plan. He had had a long experience of co-operative international ventures, and had reached the conclusion that a bold step forward was the only way of providing an effective new framework for common action in Western Europe. It was he who already in 1940 had proposed a Franco-British political union: together with a number of his associates, he now worked out an equally bold plan. The idea of some type of international control over those heavy industries which alone could provide the sinews of war was not in itself new; but what was new in the scheme which Monnet drew up was the coupling of this idea with the notion of an eventual United States of Europe. It was this plan—still little more than the germ of an idea—which Monnet succeeded in selling to Schuman, and he in turn (by what seems to have been sleight of hand) to the French cabinet. Before anyone could change their minds, and before the full implications had been realised by more than a handful of people, Schuman announced the new initiative to a crowded press conference.

The tactic of surprise paid off handsomely, but it still required courage and determination to translate the Schuman Plan into reality. One big hazard was the British refusal to take part in the negotiations: a decision which was reached after an intensive and rather agonised exchange of messages across the Channel in the weeks immediately following Schuman's announcement. On the British side there was a good deal of irritation at being confronted by what was considered to be a *fait accompli* and resistance to the French concern that there should be a prior commitment to the type of organisation they proposed. The Labour Government, having recently nationalised the coal industry in Britain, and being committed (if somewhat more hesitantly) to the similar treatment of the steel industry, was understandably opposed to the transfer of authority to some rather ill-defined body over which it would not have direct control. By this time, too, the configuration of political forces which had emerged on the continent had made it clear that there was no immediate prospect of socialist parties gaining power in the countries of the proposed Community. The idea of a socialist United States of Europe—which had originally been espoused by some leading figures on the left-wing of the British Labour Party—was now regarded as a chimera. But in addition to all these objections, there was fundamentally little sympathy with the idea of any deep British commitment to continental Western Europe, and opposition to—and little belief in the practicability of—a federal union which was mentioned in the Schuman Plan as its ultimate objective.

The British refusal to join in negotiations did not, however, prevent other countries going ahead on the basis of the French plan. There was little expectation in Britain at the time that they would get very far, and few who realised how significant a turning point had been reached. The main factor in the situation was the willingness of the Federal Republic to respond to the French initiative. This was due primarily to Konrad Adenauer, who shared with Schuman, (a fellow Catholic) a conviction of the necessity of overcoming traditional Franco-German rivalry. He was also intent on binding the new German nation into the West, fearing the consequences of a policy of flirtation with the Soviet Union both for his own country and Europe as a whole. In Italy the Austrian-born premier Alcide de Gasperi was equally anxious to find a framework in which Italy could resume its position among the nations of Western Europe, and one which would offer a stable economic background in which the country could deal with its own internal problems. The trio of Benelux countries, for their part, were already committed to a customs union and looking beyond this to a closer economic union. Once their larger neighbours moved in the same direction, they could not afford to stay outside; in any case, there were many among their leaders who were determined supporters of closer European unity.

In a remarkably short period of time—less than a year—these six were able to agree on a treaty setting up a European Coal and Steel Community (E.C.S.C.). Their basic decision was to establish a common market for coal and steel, to establish a series of rules for the conduct and regulation of the common market, and to create a set of institutions to supervise its development. Relatively few serious problems were encountered in the course of the negotiations, though those countries which feared the impact of freer competition on either the coal or steel sector pressed for special measures which would allow them to alleviate any resulting problems. Such measures were in fact provided for the Belgian coal industry and Italian steel. One important issue which proved somewhat more difficult was the extent of the powers of the High Authority proposed by the French. This was conceived of as an independent body which would regulate the common market in the interests of all its members free from direction from individual member governments. Although the French had made agreement to the principle of such a 'supranational' body a pre-condition for participation in negotiations, it emerged from the negotiations in a somewhat modified form. All the other countries were understandably hesitant to give such a body *carte blanche*. What they did therefore was to construct a treaty which laid down in very considerable detail the rules which were to govern the operation of the common market for coal and steel. There was clearly much less risk in a supranational body administering such rules, than in allowing it to establish the rules itself. Under pressure from the Netherlands in particular, a body representing the national governments was also created: a Council of Ministers to which the High Authority had to refer various types of proposed decisions, and whose other main task was to see that the actions of the High Authority did not conflict with other areas of national economic policy. A Court of Justice was also provided, to which governments, firms and individuals, as well as the High Authority itself, could appeal. And in an attempt to ensure that the High Authority was responsible to someone, a parliamentary assembly was to be set up, to which the High Authority would report annually, and by whom it could be dismissed.

Under the energetic leadership of Jean Monnet, who was appointed president of the first nine-man High Authority, the task of implementing the treaty began in August 1952, shortly after it had been approved by the six national parliaments. Luxembourg had reluctantly agreed to provide the site for the institutions of the new Community, and it was from there that first decisions of the High Authority began to flow in the autumn of that year. The common market for coal was opened in February 1953, that for steel a little later in May. Arrangements were also put in hand for price publicity, and a start was made on implementing the agreed rules of competition and the other provisions of the treaty. Somewhat to the surprise of the men in Luxembourg, the decisions were accepted, even if it was not long before issues arose in which the High Authority found itself in conflict both with individual member governments and firms.

The early years of the new Community were nevertheless relatively smooth. This was a period when economic growth was proceeding apace; the problems that arose were mainly technical in nature; and the fears that had been expressed in some quarters during the negotiations of wholesale unemployment or bankruptcies proved quite unfounded.

It was not in fact until 1958 that the Community found itself confronted by a major crisis: stocks of unsold coal began to accumulate as the industry found itself unable to compete with imports of cheaper American coal and the increasing use of oil. The High Authority sought the agreements of the member governments to the declaration of a state of 'manifest crisis' which under the treaty would have allowed it to fix production quotas and take other measures to deal with the situation. In May 1959, however, the Council of Ministers refused its agreement, and although subsequently it allowed the High Authority to take a series of piecemeal measures (including the temporary isolation of the Belgian coal market), national governments increasingly began to take unilateral action to safeguard the interests of their domestic industries. This development coincided both with a marked decline in the political leadership of the High Authority itself and the creation of two new Communities. Several of the senior officials who, with Monnet, had played a major part in establishing the Community now moved to Brussels, and it was there that the political spotlight was now focused. The Community continued to exist, but in a minor key. In July 1967 its executive was merged with that of the other two Communities. Although juridically the E.C.S.C. remains a separate entity it has ceased to have a clear positive identity of its own. Its most important work was accomplished early in its history when it succeeded quite remarkably in the task set for it by those who conceived it: a pilot project and first step along the road towards eventual economic and political union.

TWO ABORTIVE PROJECTS: THE EUROPEAN DEFENCE COMMUNITY AND THE EUROPEAN POLITICAL COMMUNITY (1952–1954)

Although two new Communities were created alongside the E.C.S.C. in less than eight years after the first announcement of the Schuman Plan, this was only after the Six had suffered a severe set-back in the intervening period. This was due to the failure of a project for a Defence Community, for which a treaty was signed in May 1952, and with which was associated a complementary proposal for a Political Community.

The proposal for a Defence Community was again made by the French, and, like the Schuman Plan, was largely inspired by Monnet. But unlike the Schuman Plan its content and timing was not determined by Monnet or the French Government so much as by external pressures. The initiative was the result of the outbreak of the Korean War in June 1950 and American fears that this might bring in its train a Soviet move against Western Europe. They therefore decided that it was now a matter of urgency that the Federal Republic should make a military contribution to Nato. Monnet's reaction was to see in this proposal both a threat and an opportunity: a threat because German contingents in Nato might lead in the direction of a new German army and the creation of a new road-block on the way towards a political union; an opportunity because the proposal could perhaps be diverted to increase the scope of integration by extending it to defence and military matters.

He therefore proposed that a limited rearmament of West Germany should take place within the framework of a European army under the aegis of a European Defence Community (E.D.C.) modelled on the proposed Coal and Steel Community (negotiations for which were then under way under his chairmanship). With some difficulty he succeeded in selling the idea to the French Government, whose prime minister, René Pleven, presented it to the French National Assembly in October 1950. This plan—the 'Pleven Plan'—was approved in outline at that stage by 343 votes to 225.

Once again the British were invited to take part in negotiations, but refused to do so; and although there was a change of government in Britain in 1951 while the negotiations were still proceeding the incoming Conservative administration also decided not to take part, although proffering external support for it. Within the Six themselves opinion was much more divided on the proposal than it had been on the Schuman Plan, and a particularly bitter conflict developed in France itself. There was strong opposition both to the rearmament of West Germany and to placing French military forces under European control. The Communists and Gaullists (then a rising political force) both opposed the project, as did also a substantial body of opinion in the Socialist party. Together they made a formidable body of dissent. The negotiators themselves had considerable difficulty in resolving the complex political and technical problems which the proposal presented, though they succeeded in reaching agreement on a treaty for the new Community in Paris in May 1952.

Before it could come into effect, however, it required ratification by the six national parliaments. In each of them there were heated and lengthy debates: after almost two years only four of them had done so. In the meantime the Korean War had come to an end and Stalin had died: the immediate pressures that had given rise to the proposal had ceased to operate. Italy and France still hesitated to press ratification of the treaty to a vote. In both, the ruling governmental coalitions were highly unstable and fearful of provoking defeat by bringing the matter to a vote. Eventually Pierre Mendès-France decided to put the matter to the test, after an abortive attempt to alter the treaty in order to gain more support for it. The critical vote took place in the National Assembly in Paris on 30 August 1954: on a procedural issue it was

rejected by a vote of 319 to 264, with 43 abstentions.
This vote spelled the end of the project, and with it a parallel and related proposal for a European Political Community. The need for an effective political authority at the Community level had become apparent during the E.D.C. negotiations: article 43 of the E.D.C. treaty provided that an assembly of parliamentarians should work out proposals for submission to the ministers. On the initiative of Schuman and De Gasperi action was taken in September 1952 on this proposal in advance of ratification, and an enlarged version of the Coal and Steel Community's assembly (which had by that time just come into being) was charged with drawing up proposals by March 1953. This it duly did, in a document which proposed a bicameral Parliament (consisting of a directly-elected Peoples' Chamber, and an indirectly-elected Senate), a European Executive Council whose president was to be elected by the Senate and which would be collectively responsible to (and dismissable by) the Parliament, a Council of Ministers and a Court of Justice. The proposal, however, was never seriously considered by the ministers, and after the failure of the E.D.C. it was consigned to the archives. One of the pillars on which this ambitious edifice was to have been built had collapsed. All that now remained was the Coal and Steel Community.

RELANCE: FROM MESSINA TO ROME (1955–1957)

This failure was a bitter blow to those who had staked their hopes on the six-nation Community: it called into question the whole strategy which Monnet had conceived of advancing from one sector to another in pursuit of eventual economic and political union. The viability of the Six as a group was also at stake, for in the aftermath of the E.D.C. it was the British who reasserted themselves and succeeded swiftly in picking up the pieces. They proposed that a German military contribution to Nato should be organised within the framework of an expanded Brussels Treaty Organisation, a body originally set up in 1948 by Britain, France and the Benelux countries for their military defence and the promotion of political and cultural co-operation. This proposal, though it contained provisions for majority voting on certain issues, effectively left control of military forces in the hands of each national government; it therefore avoided the most controversial feature of the now-defunct E.D.C. At the same time, however, it contained provisions restricting the Germans to twelve divisions, banning the production on West German soil of atomic, biological and chemical weapons, and instituting an inspection system. It therefore contained safeguards against an uncontrolled German military expansion.

These proposals speedily found acceptance on the part of the govern-ments of the Six[1] and a treaty was signed in Paris in October 1954 set-ting up the new organisation: Western European Union (W.E.U.).

There were some who hoped that the W.E.U. might provide a springboard from which Britain and the Six might together go for-ward. This however, was not the British intention. The initiative remained across the Channel, and again it was Jean Monnet who played a considerable part in relaunching the Six along the road towards a further instalment of integration. The strength of the politi-cal will to undertake this can be judged by the speed with which recovery from the deep depression and disappointment of the frustrat-ing fight for the E.D.C. was achieved.

Very rapidly there was a proliferation of plans for a *relance*. There was general agreement that the way forward lay through extending the experience of the E.C.S.C. in the realm of economic integration. There was considerable disagreement, however, on how this could best be attempted. Monnet himself was strongly in favour of another venture in sector integration, and his own preference went to nuclear power. Here was a realm apparently free from entrenched national interests: it promised to be an expanding and forward-looking area of technology, and one in which the high cost of research and development would make closer co-operation highly desirable if not essential. At the same time Monnet hoped that joint action could be accompanied by a common decision to forswear the production of nuclear weapons; in other words, integration could be released from the unfortunate con-nection it had acquired with weapons of war during the period of the E.D.C. and once again become identified (as it had been with the Schuman Plan) with images of peace.

This idea, however, met with a less than enthusiastic response in the other five. Both the Federal Republic and the Benelux countries, for their part, were much more interested in a general common market than a purely nuclear agency. They were willing to accept the latter, however, as long as it was accompanied by more general economic integration. It was on this basis that they were prepared to go forward, and it was this compromise which provided the essential basis for the formal steps which were now taken to explore the possibilities of a new move forward.

In June 1955 the foreign ministers of the Six met in Messina and there agreed to set up an intergovernmental committee to study ways in which 'a fresh advance towards the building of Europe' could be achieved. The meeting itself reached no decision on the various differ-ing strategies which had been suggested, but the nomination shortly

[1] Italy was also included as a partner in the new organisation.

afterwards of the Belgian foreign minister, Paul-Henri Spaak, to head the Committee meant that a powerful new impulse was given to the Messina resolution.

Once again, the British were invited to take part, and an official of the Board of Trade was this time despatched to the outskirts of Brussels where in the Château de Val Duchesse the Spaak Committee worked intensively on the problem it had been given. One of its critical decisions was that the next stage in economic integration should take the form of a customs union rather than a free trade area; in other words, the aim should be not only the removal of internal customs duties, but also the erection of a common tariff round the enlarged market, and the development within it of a range of common policies. The arguments put forward in favour of this course were both economic and political—but they were not of a sort to appeal to the British Government. It was certainly in favour of easier access to continental markets, but the price at the time appeared too high. One of the most serious objections was that a common tariff would run counter to trading arrangements with the Commonwealth, and the British did not stay to see whether some compromise arrangement might have been possible—unlike the French who had a not dissimilar problem with regard to their overseas possessions, and who succeeded handsomely at a later stage in persuading their partners to accept a very favourable set of arrangements.

So it was left for the Six to labour on. The Spaak Report, which was presented to the ministers in April 1956, came out in favour of a compromise solution between those who sought further instalments of sector integration and those who favoured a general common market. It suggested that action should be taken on both fronts, singling out the peaceful uses of nuclear energy as a priority area for sector integration. The ministers acted rapidly. Meeting in Venice at the end of May they adopted the report as a basis for formal negotiations, and charged the Spaak Committee with the task of drawing up the necessary draft treaties.

The major problem during the subsequent negotiations was to devise a package that would not run the risk of a second rejection by the French assembly. The French negotiators found themselves therefore in a strong diplomatic position. Fearing that French industry, which had traditionally sheltered behind high protective barriers, might find itself in difficulties in a common market they sought—and were largely successful in obtaining—a series of provisions designed to safeguard their position. At the same time they insisted (against German wishes) that the new Community should adopt a common agricultural policy. The commitment was not spelled out in any detail, but it was to prove a sufficient basis for the

French subsequently to exploit in the interests of their farmers.

The successful outcome of the negotiations rested essentially on a bargain struck between the French and the Germans, the latter being willing to make a series of concessions to the French, including—at a late stage—the conclusion of a special association agreement for their overseas possessions (mainly in West Africa) in return for the prospect of a greatly expanded tariff-free market for their industrial goods. A complex series of other bargains and side payments was also struck to accommodate the interests of the other members. In many cases these were only achieved with considerable difficulty, and many informed observers in Britain were very dubious whether the treaties would be concluded and ratified.

But this time, there was no hitch. In a ceremony in Rome on 27 March 1957—while the rain poured down outside—the six foreign ministers signed treaties establishing two new Communities, the European Economic Community (E.E.C.) and the European Atomic Energy Community (Euratom). Ratification was speedily achieved, and the new institutions were able to set to work in Brussels on 1 January 1958.

THE NEW COMMUNITIES IN ACTION (1958–1962)

Contrary to many expectations it was the Economic Community rather than Euratom that led the way in the new phase of integration, and which in its first four years of existence astonished almost everyone by the rapidity with which it made progress in carrying out the tasks allotted to it.

Unlike the treaty setting up the E.C.S.C., the Common Market Treaty was for the most part a framework for action rather than a detailed set of rules. The one major exception to this was the provisions it laid down for the achievement of a customs union. Customs duties between members were to be gradually abolished over a 12 to 15 year transition period divided into three stages. At the same time, differences between national tariffs towards the outside world were gradually to be aligned to produce a common external tariff. The other provisions relating to the free movement of workers, capital, the right of establishment, and the creation of common or harmonised policies in certain crucial areas, such as agriculture, transport, external trade and competition, were much more imprecise. For the most part the treaty confined itself to general statements of objectives, and indications of the instruments that were to be used to achieve the desired goals. This lack of precision was in part due to the fact of the very wide range of problems which had to be tackled: the negotiators had not had time, nor had they been in a position, to examine many of them in detail. But imprecision was also due to disagreements on many issues between the partners; this was particularly the case with regard to the thorny problem of agriculture.

A great deal therefore depended on the institutions of the new Community, and in particular on the ability of its nine-man Commission to find ways of reconciling these divergent interests. In both of the new Communities the name Commission had been preferred to High Authority; but the change was not simply one of nomenclature. Enthusiasm for 'supranationality' had waned; it had not been possible to agree on the detailed rules for the operation of the Community; and the national governments were anxious to keep as much power as possible in their own hands, at least in the early stages of the development of the general common market. The main task given to the E.E.C. Commission therefore was that of making proposals: decisions were to be taken by the Council of Ministers. The right—virtually an exclusive right—to initiate policy proposals was nevertheless a very important function, and under its first president, Walter Hallstein, the new Commission speedily made its impact. It was helped in its task by a number of favourable factors. One of these was the continuing rapid pace of economic growth in the member countries; industrial producers were for the most part in an expansionist frame of mind, and they responded positively to the prospect of the common market, and were soon to urge a more rapid rate of tariff dismantlement than had originally been envisaged. There were also a number of favourable political factors. Externally the United States continued to give its support to the Communities: this was particularly important in preventing the British from attempting to intervene to trouble its early development. The British government, after its withdrawal from the Spaak Committee, was certainly not pleased to see the Six succeed in setting up the new Communities. It undertook a major reappraisal of its policy and—having decided against any direct attempt to wreck the Communities—came up with the idea of a wider Free Trade Area of which both Britain, the Community and other O.E.E.C. countries could be part. The British argued that it would be in everyone's interest to extend the area of free trade in industrial goods and that this indeed had been one of the early objectives of the O.E.E.C.[1] From the British point of view it was a splendid idea: it reconciled a continuation of preferential arrangements with the Commonwealth with open access to European markets, avoided the difficult problem of agriculture (which was initially omitted altogether from the scheme) and politically offered at least the possibility of containing the development of the Communities.

---

[1] The British did not dwell on the fact that at that stage they had opposed the idea.

There was initially sufficient support from the free-trade minded members of the Six—notably the Germans and the Dutch—to make it appear a viable project. Agreement was reached in the O.E.E.C. to undertake negotiations, which eventually got under way in 1958 under the chairmanship of Reginald Maudling. There was little in the scheme, however, to appeal to the French. To them all it offered was increased competition in their industrial markets: hardly a welcome prospect. Nevertheless, for some time they were uncertain of the policy which they should follow.

In May 1958 the Fourth Republic was plunged into its final crisis over Algeria, a crisis which was resolved by the return to power of de Gaulle. At this point prospects seemed distinctly gloomy for the new Community. Disagreements between its members over the British proposal were reflected even in the Commission—and now it was faced by a French Head of State who had consistently and vehemently opposed the creation of the Communities. De Gaulle, however, decided to throw his weight against the Free Trade Area proposal. In retrospect it is not difficult to see why. From his point of view it offered a series of economic disadvantages and no countervailing political gains. It could well lead the British and their friends to a position from which they could dictate the future economic and political development of Western Europe. And although de Gaulle admired the British, he had no reason—particularly in the light of his wartime experiences—to play a subordinate role to them once again. The French put forward a series of counter proposals and rallied (with the aid of the Commission) the support of their partners in the Community. In November 1958 the negotiations broke down. Subsequently the British, under pressure from the Scandinavian countries, decided to go ahead with the construction of a smaller industrial free trade area. This led in 1960 to the setting up of the European Free Trade Association (E.F.T.A.) with seven members—Britain, Denmark, Norway, Sweden, Switzerland, Portugal and Ireland—with its headquarters in Geneva. Its aim was both to demonstrate that a free trade area could work and, hopefully, to exert pressure on the Community to arrive at an agreement with its members.

Its immediate effect, however, was to remove British pressure on the Community. This, coupled with the decision of de Gaulle to maintain French obligations under the Rome treaties and the measures he took at the end of 1958 to strengthen the French economy, paved the way for the early success of the E.E.C.

The first set of internal tariff cuts—a modest 10%—was duly carried out on 1 January 1959, and by the end of the following year the Council of Ministers agreed to a first move towards a common agricultural policy. In devising a strategy to develop such a policy the Commission, and in particular its Member with a special responsibility for agriculture, the Dutchman Sicco Mansholt, played a critical part. It was he who decided that priority should be given to the organisation of markets and the establishment of common prices; who devised the mechanism by which these were to be achieved; and who steered the Commission's proposals through the Council of Ministers.

In this process a series of bargains was struck between the member states, sometimes within the agricultural sector itself, sometimes between that sector and other policy areas. Such bargains involved the careful construction and negotiation of elaborate 'packages' which from time to time became the object of marathon sessions of the Council of Ministers. One such notable package was the outcome of a series of ministerial meetings which went on almost without interuption from 4 December 1961 until the early hours of 14 January 1962. This feat of endurance involved 45 separate meetings (seven of them at night), 137 hours of discussion, with 214 hours in sub-committee: 582 000 pages of documents—and three heart attacks.[1] Out of it came a series of agreements detailing the first substantial measures laying the foundations of the common marketing arrangements for agriculture, an agreement on how the early stages of the common market agricultural policy were to be financed, and on the regulation of competition between firms in the Community. As a result the Six agreed to move to the second stage of the E.E.C.'s transitional period.

With the speeding up of the timetable for tariff reductions on industrial goods (agreed during 1960) and considerable progress towards a common policy for agriculture, the E.E.C. began to assume an air of success. This was increased by an initiative taken by de Gaulle late in 1959 which led to negotiations designed to lead to a treaty of political union, that is, the extension of the scope of integration to matters of defence, foreign policy and culture. The French leader had now come round to the view that the Community of the Six was not only a useful economic grouping but one which could serve French political interests. He instinctively believed that French leadership (certainly as long as it remained in his hands) would predominate: he was confident that he could deal with the Germans, and had a low opinion of the other members of the Community. The proposal for negotiations on political union was nevertheless welcomed by the other governments: it accorded with the aims to which they had agreed in the preamble to the treaties of Rome—'an ever closer union among the European peoples'—and the other five no doubt considered that they could contain any French ambitions to dictate policy within such a union, though from the beginning the Dutch were distinctly nervous. A

[1] Walter Hallstein, quoted in Leon Lindberg, *The Political Dynamics of European Integration*, Stanford (1963), p. 273.

15

'summit' about the proposal meeting was held in Paris in February 1961 and again in Bonn in July of that year: agreement was then reached on the creation of a special committee under the chairmanship of M. Christian Fouchet (then French ambassador to Denmark) to work out proposals to 'give shape to the desire for political union'.

That same month (July 1961) Mr. Macmillan announced to the House of Commons his Government's decision to apply for membership of the Community, a move which was shortly followed by formal application being lodged with the Community not only by Britain but also by Denmark, Ireland and Norway. The British had now realised that the dangers of remaining outside the Community—which showed at this stage every sign of success—outweighed the risks of joining. The attempt to exert pressure from outside through E.F.T.A. showed no sign of success and United States support for the Six precluded any further attempts to press alternative strategies on the lines of the defunct European free trade area.

These developments seemed to underline the success of the Community and to offer the prospect of it being expanded into a framework within which most of the countries of Western Europe could move forward to more far-reaching economic and political integration.

CONFLICT, CRISIS AND STAGNATION (1963–1969)

Success, however, brought new tensions into the life of the Community which were to usher in a new and distinctly more troubled period in its development. The projected moves towards both geographical extension and political union both failed, and although in the next six years the customs union was completed and some common policies agreed, the influence exerted by de Gaulle over its affairs during this period—and the hostility his policies aroused within it—eventually produced an impasse out of which the Community was only able to move after his departure from the French presidency in April 1969.

The first signs of major trouble appeared in the early part of 1962 when the negotiations on political union ran into difficulties. In January that year a revised draft treaty was put forward by the French (apparently on the initiative of de Gaulle himself) to which several of the other members of the Community raised serious objections. Although none of them was prepared to put decision-making in such delicate areas of policy as defence and foreign affairs into the hands of a Commission, they were anxious both to safeguard the role of the existing Community institutions in the spheres covered by the three treaties, and to make provision for a move towards at least some type of Commission-type body after an initial three-year period. The institutions which de Gaulle proposed, on the other hand, were firmly intergovernmental in character; it was feared moreover that they would in practice tend to undermine the Commission in Brussels. The other members of the Community were also concerned about de Gaulle's attitude to Nato, and wished to have reassurance that the new Community organisation would not weaken it, or lead to conflict with the United States.

The decisive opposition, however, came from the Dutch. They were anxious at all costs to have the British by their side, believing that the interests of the two countries were likely to be very close on all major issues, and fearing that otherwise they might be squeezed between the French and the Germans. They argued that as Britain was currently negotiating entry into the existing Communities she should take part also in the talks on political union. The French refused: at which point the Dutch effectively vetoed further negotiations within the Fouchet Committee.

This was no doubt a great relief to the British government which was having difficulty enough in convincing opinion in the country of the desirability of entry without the additional complications that a new treaty would have brought. But for de Gaulle it was further evidence of the dangers of allowing the British to join. In January the following year, he, in turn, abruptly put an end to the negotiations on entry. There can be little doubt that he did so primarily because of his wish to exclude a potentially dangerous rival from the Community. At the time other reasons were given, and in particular the 'non-European' character and interests of Britain. There was sufficient truth in this for it to be a useful line of argument with at least some sections of opinions within the Six, and de Gaulle had to be careful to ensure that in saying no to the British he did not risk breaking up the Community itself.

The critical element in the situation was the Federal Republic: had Adenauer sided with the British de Gaulle would have been virtually isolated. But in fact the Federal Chancellor attached more importance to reconciliation with France; between de Gaulle's press conference and the decisive meeting of the negotiators in Brussels he went to Paris to sign a treaty of co-operation with France. This signalled the choice he had made, and it meant that once the dust had settled the Federal Republic took a leading part, together with the Commission, in urging that the Community should continue towards the objectives set out in the Rome treaties.

There was nevertheless a period of several months during which the other members of the Community showed their strong disapproval of de Gaulle's unilateral action by bringing the Brussels decision-making machinery to a halt. And although by mid-1963 a formula had been found to get it moving again, the French veto left a legacy of distrust among their partners which weighed heavily on subsequent developments. The style of bargaining changed, especially when after Adenauer's retirement from office later in 1963, de Gaulle found himself faced by an unsympathetic Chancellor in the person of Ludwig Erhard. For the latter the relationship with the United States was of capital importance, and he showed considerable support for the American proposal for a Multilateral Nuclear Force (M.L.F.) within the framework of Nato which cut right across de Gaulle's attempts to get German support for the French *force de frappe*. De Gaulle retaliated by threatening to walk out of the Common Market unless the Germans agreed to the Commission's proposals for a common grain price, proposals which (the Commission argued) had to be settled before the Community could play a positive part in the mutual tariff-cutting negotiations which had been proposed by President Kennedy and which were due to take place within the framework of G.A.T.T. The German interest in the success of these negotiations was substantial, as industry in the Federal Republic was anxious to obtain easier access to the United States domestic market.

In December 1964 Erhard gave way, and agreement was reached on the level of the future common grain price. This was the first major decision reached by the Community since the collapse of the negotiations with Britain, and to some it seemed to usher in a new period of rapid forward movement. The Germans had also agreed to take part in evolving a medium-term economic programme for the Community: a first modest step which the Commission hoped would lead beyond the customs union towards closer economic integration. Emboldened by these developments, the Commission decided in the Spring of 1965 to attempt to force the pace. It proposed that the terminal date for the customs union should be brought forward to 1 July 1967 to coincide with the coming into effect of common prices for agricultural products; that from the same date the Community should be financed directly from the proceeds of the common external tariff and the agricultural levies on imports of foodstuffs; and that some budgetary powers should be given to the European Parliament.

This was a bold package which aimed at strengthening the authority of the Commission and the Parliament at the same time as it pushed forward the process of economic integration. De Gaulle reacted angrily: to him it was a threat to the continued predominance of the national governments in the decision-making machinery of the Community. When his negotiators failed to 'untie' the package his response was to boycott the Community; and in the following months he widened his attack on the Commission which he scathingly dismissed as a group of *apatrides* (stateless persons).

For seven months the Community came to a virtually complete halt. Some routine business was transacted by correspondence, but otherwise there was complete paralysis. On this occasion de Gaulle was isolated, for although there were some differences between the other Five, they contrived to maintain a united front. In the December presidential election in France there was a significant volume of opposition to de Gaulle's European policy, and this may have contributed to his failure to win a clear majority on the first ballot. At all events, de Gaulle —who had already withdrawn French forces from the integrated Nato command—now sought to withdraw from what had become a dangerously exposed position. At the end of January 1966, in Luxembourg, a compromise was reached. The institutional role of the Commission was confirmed (accompanied by a rather anodyne set of recommendations with regard to certain procedural aspects of its work) and the members agreed to disagree about the use of majority voting in the Council of Ministers, France insisting that on matters of 'vital national importance', it would maintain a veto. At the same time, the Commission's original package of measures was dropped.

The Luxembourg compromise, while it blocked the institutional development of the Community, also marked the end of de Gaulle's hopes of being able to shape it according to his wishes. For the time being a rather uneasy truce had been accepted by both sides, a truce which in May 1966 allowed the Council to fix 1 July 1968 as the date for the completion of the customs union and the common farm policy. But any hope of more far-reaching developments had to be indefinitely postponed.

It was in this situation that the Labour Government in Britain decided to make a second application to join. A majority of members in the cabinet had decided, like Mr. MacMillan's Government before them, that Britain was no longer able to sustain a world role on her own, and that the development of the Commonwealth did not offer a viable alternative. After a reconnaissance of the Community capitals early in 1967, the decision to apply was taken by the Government and approved by an overwhelming majority in the House of Commons. This time, however, the negotiations did not even get to first base. In December, after another press conference given by the French president in which he made it clear that his objections to British entry remained, the Council of Ministers failed to agree on the British request for the opening of talks.

On this occasion, as in 1965, the French were isolated. And again the Five, backed by the Commission, stood firm. A series of proposals were put forward with the aim of associating Britain with various aspects of the work of the Communities, and preparing the ground for later membership. Attempts were also made to revivify the Western European Union, and use this as a forum where issues of common foreign policy could be discussed with Britain, a move which led to conflict with France in that body and its temporary withdrawal from active participation in it.

Although the Six were able to make some further progress in carrying out the programme of work set in the E.E.C. treaty—the customs union, for instance, was formally completed on 1 July 1968 as previously agreed, and some advances were made towards a common transport and foreign trade policy—disagreement over its enlargement, and distrust of de Gaulle, cast a heavy shadow over its work. The French president, for his part, while continuing to seek to extract the maximum of economic benefit from the Community for France (particularly with regard to agriculture) was casting around for some alternative political framework for French policy. He courted the Soviet Union and a number of the East European states on the one hand; on the other he began to toy with the idea of constructing a new type of political directorate for Western Europe with Britain, the Federal Republic and Italy.

The British, however, maintained their application to join the existing Communities. Relations with France became glacial as, together with the Five, they maintained their pressure for the opening of negotiations. At this point an impasse had been reached: it was only ended when de Gaulle resigned from the French presidency in April 1969, having failed to obtain a majority in a referendum on a set of proposals which included the abolition of the Senate and the creation of new regional institutions in France.

THE SECOND RELANCE: FROM THE HAGUE TO THE PARIS SUMMIT (1969–1972)

It took only a short time for the Community to regain its impetus. At the suggestion of the new French president, Georges Pompidou, a summit meeting of the leaders of the Six was held in the Hague in early December 1969 and there agreement was reached on the outlines of a far-reaching programme for future action. This was summed up in three words: completion, deepening, and enlargement.

The new impetus derived from several sources. In the first place, there was the desire of the new French government to restore relations with their partners in the Community. Although their policy statements retained a Gaullist intonation, they were clearly anxious to break out of the isolation into which de Gaulle had led the country. At the same time their willingness to open negotiations with Britain suggested that they were beginning to feel uneasy about the economic and political strength of the Federal Republic, and viewed British membership as providing a guarantee against undue German influence in the Community. The Federal Republic, for its part, now had a chancellor —Willy Brandt—who was genuinely committed to furthering the economic and political development of the Community, which he believed provided the right framework for the Federal Republic and a necessary basis for its new *Ostpolitik* of seeking improved relations with the countries of Eastern Europe.

The Germans, for their part, came to the meeting determined as a first priority to obtain agreement to the opening of negotiations with the applicant countries; the French, on the other hand, appeared to give priority to the development of the existing Community. A balance had therefore to be struck between the two, and this was incorporated in the three-part package.

The first element in this was agreement on what needed to be done to complete the transition period as laid down in the E.E.C. Treaty. The French insisted that an essential part of this were definitive arrangements for the financing of the common agricultural policy; it was agreed that these would be coupled with the direct financing of the Community from its own resources rather than by annual grants from national governments. Once agreement on this had been reached, the end of the Community's transition period would be reached; in this sense, the initial tasks laid down in the E.E.C. treaty would have been completed.

But although the Community would have then reached its 'final stage' with the entry into force of all the measures required for the establishment of the Common Market, it was agreed that a series of further actions would be required to strengthen the Community and promote its development into an economic union. This is what was entailed by 'deepening'. The ministers agreed that in the first place during the course of 1970 they would take decisions on proposals already presented by the Commission for the achievement of an economic and monetary union. Other action was to be taken to increase technological co-operation between the member countries, to give a new impetus to Euratom, to reform the Social Fund, and to renew discussion on the establishment of a European university.

As far as enlargement was concerned, the ministers re-affirmed their agreement in principle that this should happen, and that negotiations should be opened with the applicant states as well as with the other members of E.F.T.A. Finally, they added an instruction to their foreign ministers 'to study the best way of achieving progress in the matter of political unification, within the context of enlargement', and asked them to report before the end of July 1970.

These decisions marked the opening of a new and much more creative phase in the development of the Community. They opened up the twin prospects of geographical enlargement and a far-reaching set of new objectives going well beyond the existing treaties which were implied by economic and monetary union. Taken together these made the Hague meeting at least as important as that held in Messina in 1955, and showed, as that earlier meeting had also done, the extraordinary powers of recovery of the Six after a period of frustration and disappointment.

Negotiations with the applicants were duly opened on 30 June 1970 in Luxembourg with Britain, Denmark, Ireland and Norway. All the major issues in the British case were settled within a year: astonishingly rapid progress in comparison with previous attempts. In the meantime significant developments in other directions had also taken place. Already in December 1970 the Council of Ministers agreed both on the final form of financing for the common agricultural policy; the method by which the Community was to be financed by its own resources (primarily the proceeds of the external tariff and levies) and some budgetary powers for the European Parliament. In other words, they now settled the issues which had caused the crisis in 1965–1966, and on lines not dissimilar from those originally proposed at that time by the Commission. As a result, the transition period of the E.E.C. was formally ended on 31 December 1969, exactly 12 years after its establishment.

Progress towards economic and monetary union, on the other hand, was much more difficult. Early in 1970 steps were taken to strengthen the work being done on the elaboration of a medium-term economic programme, and agreement was reached on a short-term mutual aid system by which their central banks established a $2 billion fund to help each other in case of temporary balance of payments difficulties. In June the Council agreed in principle on the main recommendations of a committee set up under the Luxembourg Prime Minister, M. Pierre Werner, with regard to the achievement of economic and monetary union. They endorsed the view that this could be attained by 1980 'provided it enjoys the permanent political support of the governments', and that the first three-year stage towards it should open on 1 January 1971.

When it came to making more specific decisions on what exactly was to be done, however, the ministers ran into difficulties. They were unable to agree in December 1970 on a formal commitment to 1980 as the target date for the achievement of economic and monetary union, the Germans and the Dutch stressing the importance of giving the Community greater powers for the effective co-ordination of national economic policies, while the French insisted on the importance of the prior co-ordination of some aspects of monetary policy and the need to concentrate on the steps needed for the first stage of the process. In February 1971, however, a compromise was reached. No binding commitment to 1980 as the terminal date was entered into, and the ministers indicated only in general terms the new institutional requirements which economic and monetary union would demand. They did specify, however, the policy areas where common action would be required, including internal monetary and credit policy, monetary policy with regard to the rest of the world, certain aspects of budgetary and taxation policy, and regional policy. They also agreed on the need for a unified capital market and a common policy on capital movements to and from non-member countries. In addition, they agreed in more detail on a programme of work for the first phase of the transition period extending for a three-year period up to December 1974. They also decided to set up machinery for medium-term financial aid to members faced with balance of payments difficulties, establishing a fund with a ceiling of $2 billion for this purpose, so complementing the similar arrangements already in force for short-term monetary assistance.

Hardly had these decisions been taken, however, when severe strains were placed on the Community by an inflow of 'hot' money into the Federal Republic in expectation of a revaluation of the Deutschmark, and the subsequent German decision taken in May 1971 to let the Mark 'float'. This ran contrary to the Community's recent decision to narrow exchange rates margins as a step on the long road to monetary union, and—after a lengthy and heated debate—the Council only assented to this move for a limited period of time, observing that it was incompatible with the smooth functioning of the Community. The French, for their part, then announced that they saw no point in participating in the meetings of expert groups working on economic and monetary union as long as this situation continued. This was a sharp reminder of the type of problem that was likely to present itself as the Community moved into these highly sensitive areas of national sovereignty, as well as the continued vulnerability of the Community's economic and monetary system to external factors (in this case, those generated by the United States).

It was, however, only a foretaste of worse to come. In August 1971 President Nixon announced a package of monetary and trade measures designed to strengthen the dollar, and plunged the whole of the world's monetary system into a prolonged period of stress and uncertainty. The members of the Community once again found themselves in disarray when they sought to establish a common position vis-à-vis the United States, and the following months were spent in agitated discussions both within the Community and between its members and the other major members of the International Monetary Fund. It was only in December that agreement was reached in Washington—the so-called 'Smithsonian agreement'—on a series of measures to be taken, of which the most important were a realignment of exchange rates and a widening from 2·25% to 4·5% of the permissable margin of fluctuation of other currencies against the dollar.

This, however, threatened to take the members of the Community further away from their own stated goal of narrower exchange rate margins. In March 1972 they responded to this by agreement to limit these within the Community currencies to 2·25%, and at the same time to strengthen short-term economic co-ordination and to take steps to counteract regional disparities. At the time this was hailed as an important new step towards the goal of economic and monetary union and as giving a new impetus to it after a year of frustration. Additional significance was given to the decision by a commitment made by the British also to observe it.

On 23 June, however, pressure on sterling forced the British government to allow sterling to float and—together with Ireland and Denmark—to withdraw from their monetary commitment to the Community. Italy also sought, and was granted, a partial exception for a three-month period. So, once again the fragility of the Community's attempts to move towards their goal was made painfully apparent.

During this period only very cautious progress was made towards the parallel goal of political union—that is, measures to enable the Community to acquire a common foreign policy. Following the Hague Summit, a high-level committee of officials under the Belgian diplomat, Vicomte Davignon, was set up to review the situation and make proposals. But its report suggested only modest measures: twice-yearly meetings of foreign ministers to be serviced by quarterly meetings of a political committee consisting of senior foreign office officials. This was a far cry from the bolder proposals which had been considered in the early sixties at the time of the Fouchet negotiations. The new machinery was however set up, and the applicant countries also began to take an active part in its work.

As 1972 progressed attention was focused primarily on the preparations for a further Summit meeting which, it was hoped, might set a new set of objectives for the enlarged Community. In an intensive series of discussions, which was pursued both at the level of heads of state and government and also in the Council of Ministers, general agreement emerged that there should be three main items on the agenda: economic and monetary union, political co-operation, and institutional questions. The preparation for the meeting, however, proved arduous. One major bone of contention was a French proposal that a political secretariat should be set up in Paris to promote foreign policy co-ordination. Once again fears were aroused that this might prove to be a device to by-pass the existing Community institutions, and at one stage disagreement on the issue seemed to threaten a postponement of the Summit.

In the end the issue was resolved by an agreement to drop the proposal, and the Summit meeting duly took place in Paris on 19–20 October. The outcome of the meeting was a lengthy communiqué which was a good deal more positive than had been originally anticipated.[1] It showed clearly that the Community had moved into a distinctly new phase of its evolution, not only in terms of its size, but also in terms of its ambitions. Two things were particularly striking about the preamble to the communiqué: its emphasis on the role of the Community in the world at large, and the recognition of its authors that 'economic expansion is not an end in itself' and that in future the Community should pay far more attention to its social goals, including the quality of life to be achieved for its citizens.

The detailed substantive part of the communiqué then reviewed the major areas of the future work of the Community, which it said should aim to transform itself, before the end of the decade, into a 'European Union'. Pride of place among the specific objectives to be achieved within this framework was given to economic and monetary union, the terminal date for which was confirmed as being not later than the end of 1980. Steps were to be taken during the course of 1973 to enable transition to the second stage of this union on 1 January 1974; these would include: the setting up of a European Monetary Co-operation Fund, to be administered by the Committee of the Central Banks of the Community countries; concerted action to narrow exchange rate fluctuations; the creation of a European monetary unit of account; and new measures for short-term monetary support. Parallel with these measures, further steps were to be taken to strengthen and intensify the co-ordination of economic policies, with priority being given to the fight against inflation. It was also agreed that the Community should take up a common position on international monetary issues and seek a reform of the existing system, the criteria for which were also specified in the communiqué.

A new emphasis was also given by the meeting to regional policy —on which Mr. Heath had laid particular insistence. It was agreed that the Commission should be asked to prepare a report on the situation and to formulate specific proposals, that the member governments would in future co-ordinate their national policies, and that at the Community level a Regional Development Fund would be established before the end of 1973, to be financed from Community funds in the second stage of the transition towards economic and monetary union.

[1] For the full text, see Appendix.

Its term of reference would cover not only help for agricultural regions but also those suffering from 'industrial change and structural under-employment'.

Further sections of the communiqué dealt with social, industrial (including scientific and technological), environmental and also energy policies, with a set of timetables for action specified in each case. With regard to the Community's external relations the section devoted to the developing countries struck a careful balance between French and British interests in its statement that 'the Community must, without detracting from the advantages enjoyed by countries with which it has special relations, respond even more than in the past to the expectations of all the developing countries'. It also emphasised (no doubt at French insistence) 'the essential importance' which it attached to the association agreements and Mediterranean policy—while adding references to its U.N.C.T.A.D.-inspired scheme of generalised preferences, market stabilisation schemes for primary products and an (unspecified) increase in government aid to the developing world. All these matters, the communiqué added, would be the subject of studies and decisions 'in good time' during 1973.

With regard to other aspects of its foreign trade policy, the Summit made particular reference to the United States, Canada, and Japan with whom it said it was anxious to maintain 'a constructive dialogue'. It also committed the Community to making decisions on a global approach to all aspects of foreign trade policy by the middle of 1973, and to participate in the new round of negotiations being proposed within the framework of the General Agreement on Tariffs and Trade (G.A.T.T.). It also reaffirmed the Community's intention of following a common commercial policy towards the countries of Eastern Europe from 1 January 1973.

On the more specifically political aspects of external relations, the Summit called on its members to make 'a concerted and constructive contribution' to the Conference on Security and Co-operation in Europe, agreed that in future its foreign ministers would meet four times a year (rather than twice as in the past) to foster co-ordination of their policies in this sphere, and that by mid-1973 they would present a report on how their co-operation could be further improved.

The two final sections of the communiqué deal respectively with institutional reform and the achievement of a 'European union', both in notably generalised terms. Any significant institutional reform (other than an agreement that in future, national Cabinet meetings should be held on the same day of the week) was in fact postponed—in spite of Dutch insistence that a firm date should be fixed for the introduction of direct elections to the European Parliament. Instead, the Commission was asked to submit proposals for changes before 1 May 1973, and the ministers undertook to take decisions before the end of the first stage of the transitional period for economic and monetary union. But no specific reforms were mentioned nor were any specific dates fixed for their introduction. A rather ambiguous paragraph invited the Commission and the Council to take some practical steps to strengthen the powers of the Parliament and to improve their own relations with it, without indicating what precisely was to be done. Similarly the notion of the projected 'European union' was not spelled out, though it was agreed that a report on it would be drawn up before the end of 1975 for submission to a new Summit meeting.

This lengthy statement of future intentions was not achieved without a good deal of hard bargaining, and it left most of the detail of future policies to be hammered out by the Community institutions. Nevertheless, it was a comparatively clear statement of priorities for the future and an impressive confirmation that with enlargement a new impetus was to be given to the Community's search for 'a closer unity among the European peoples'.

In the meantime, the treaty of accession had been submitted for approval both in the existing member countries and the four applicant countries. Britain was the only one not to hold a referendum, the decision in favour of membership taking the form of the passage through Parliament of the European Communities Bill to give legal force to the treaty. This was finally achieved in the early autumn, in the face of strong opposition from a majority of the Labour party. By an overwhelming majority the Irish people approved of accession in a referendum held in May 1972; and the Danes by a majority of 63·5% to 36·5%. The Norwegians on the other hand rejected entry; the result of the referendum in that country produced a negative majority of 53% to 47%. As a result, only three of the four intending new members ratified the treaty of accession, and the new Community which came into existence on 1 January 1973 has nine rather than ten members.

2 The Political Dynamics of Integration

One of the most striking features of the Community has been the way in which, in spite of setbacks, it has clearly moved a substantial distance along the road originally indicated in the Schuman Plan. In the first place the scope of integration has greatly increased: from a modest start with the coal and steel sector it has been extended to a general common market both for industrial and agricultural products. At the same time the process has penetrated further and further into the details of economic and social organisation in the member countries. Its aim of removing not only the barriers to the free movement of goods, but also the obstacles inhibiting the movement of people, services and capital, has led the Community institutions to become concerned with such apparently esoteric matters as the methods by which beer is brewed, the definition of what constitutes a midwife, and the transport of corpses across national frontiers. But at the same time the Community has also increasingly moved into areas of high policy, previously the jealously guarded domain of national governments, where major decisions affecting the direction of the economy are taken.

This increase in the scope and intensity of the process of economic integration is one aspect of its highly dynamic political nature: the Community has constantly set itself new and more far-reaching objectives. A second aspect of this dynamic quality is the way in which it has not only been able to survive a succession of crises and failures, but also to rally support to enable it to proceed with renewed vigour after each set-back. The process has in addition proved very dynamic in the sense that it has had a major impact on many neighbouring states, and has led a number of them—including Britain—to make major changes in their own policy and eventually to seek to join it. Others have concluded association or trade agreements with it. And, on the world scene, the emergence of the Community has began to have a significant impact on the operation of several major international institutions—those, for instance, concerned with the organisation of world trade, monetary affairs and development policy—as well as impinging on Europe's relations both with the super-powers and other regions.

These are not inconsiderable achievements. They have been accompanied, however, by periods of considerable stress and a number of setbacks. Progress has been neither smooth nor easy. Nor, if one examines the different policy areas in which the Community is involved, has the achievement been at all even. In some, such as agriculture, common policies have been erected; in others, only hesitant progress towards them been made. And even where such policies do exist their impact has given rise in several cases to violent controversy and demands—as in the case of the common agricultural policy—that they should be drastically reformed.

The major question we are concerned with here is the lessons to be derived from this experience as far as the new Community is concerned: in particular the factors which are likely to condition its capacity successfully to pursue its quest for 'a closer union among the European peoples'.

In posing, and in seeking to answer, this question it is important to bear in mind that what the members of the Community are aiming to achieve, that is a substantial measure of economic and political unity, is extremely difficult for any group of countries to attain. Until recently, comparatively few groups of countries even attempted it, and of those that did even fewer succeeded. And although in the post-war period there has been a proliferation of such attempts in various parts of the world, almost all have encountered great difficulties. Several have had to abandon the attempt, and others—such as Nigeria—have only maintained a union at the cost of bitter civil war. The experience of Western Europe, so far at least, has been quite exceptional for the rapidity of the process of integration, the extent of its achievements, and the capacity for recovery it has demonstrated after periods of difficulty and failure.

Political scientists in recent years have spent a great deal of time in trying to identify the factors which are crucial in determining success or failure in voluntary attempts at union. To the uninitiated some of the literature on the subject will appear to be highly abstract, and not a little obscure. Nor can it be said that as yet any generally-accepted overall theory of integration has emerged. Partial theories abound, but frequently seem to have little connection one with another; there are also significant differences in the assumptions on which they rest, particularly those advanced by Marxist writers and others—the bulk of them Americans—who do not accept a Marxist interpretation of the relationship between economic, social and political phenomena.

Whichever view one takes, however, a number of major elements can be singled out as relevant for an understanding of the dynamics of the process of integration. For our purposes, attention will be concentrated on four of these.[1] In the first place, as a preliminary step, we need to examine how far the major economic, political and social characteristics of the member countries of the Community have provided favourable conditions for the process to develop. Secondly, we have to analyse how strong the political will to unite has been, the motives behind that will, and the factors which have influenced both its strength and direction over time. Thirdly, the extent of the support which has been generated for the Community; and, finally, the role of political leadership. Together these four constitute the major components which have impinged on the development of the Community: by examining the experience of the Six we can lay the foundations for an analysis of how these various elements are likely to operate within the enlarged Community.

STRUCTURAL FACTORS

As far as the first of these factors is concerned, most students of integration agree that, given the inherent difficulties attendant upon a process of integration, it is desirable that a group wishing to embark on such a venture should possess a number of structural characteristics which are likely to provide a favourable background to their efforts. Some of the more obvious of these are geographical propinquity; a common cultural background; a roughly comparable level of economic development; a similar set of economic and political values; and compatible political systems. The number and relative size of the component units of the group are also important variables—though with regard to the first of these the experience of the United States has led some to question whether a union consisting of a relatively large number of small units may not be easier to maintain than one in which the units are fewer but larger.

As far as comparability of size is concerned, on the other hand, there is less disagreement: it is generally assumed that a group consisting of roughly equal units is likely to enjoy more favourable conditions than one in which one country has resources wholly disproportionate to those of its partners. This, for instance, is the situation with regard to the Council for Mutual Economic Assistance (Comecon) where the

[1] For a more detailed and elaborate analysis see Leon N. Lindberg and Stuart A. Scheingold, *Europe's Would-Be Polity*, New Jersey (1970).

resources of the Soviet Union clearly far outstrip those of the other member countries. This example shows, however, the danger of reaching over-hasty conclusions on the basis of the list of criteria which has just been suggested, for although the degree of integration achieved by Comecon is certainly much less in most respects than in the case of the E.E.C., the group has persisted over the years and shows many signs of developing still closer links.

As a rough guide to the likely integrative potential of a group the check-list nevertheless has its value. If we apply it to the Six we see that from the outset they benefited from a set of relatively favourable conditions, even if these were by no means so overwhelmingly positive that success was guaranteed in advance. It is true, for instance, that they shared a common cultural heritage—but this was characterised by many divisive elements, including religious sectarianism; it was true that they were at much the same level of economic development—but it was precisely because of this that France feared being overtaken by a revived Germany; they also shared similar economic and political values—though the prevailing values were being challenged by significant political forces in several of the countries concerned; and they had similar political institutions, though in three of the major countries these had only recently been established. In short, they were faced with a number of obstacles to the achievement of a harmonious group as well as being provided with a number of relatively favourable background conditions.

One of their most serious disadvantages undoubtedly derived from the fact that together they constituted neither a natural geographical unit nor corresponded to any recent political unit. References to Charlemagne's empire— the nearest historical parallel that could be found—underlined this. For a great deal of the intervening period the peoples involved had been in conflict with one another, and in the more recent past the two main countries, France and Germany, had through bitter experience come to regard each other with intense suspicion and hostility. And, although the new Community gave itself the name 'European' it was in fact a mini-Europe; a truncated, partial realisation of the old dream of unity. It is hardly surprising, therefore, that the problem of relations with its neighbours in Western Europe —particularly Britain—came to assume such importance, and proved to be so serious a source of stress within the group.

We shall need later on to consider in what respects the structural characteristics of the enlarged Community differ from those of the Six, and whether or not they are likely to provide a set of conditions for its development which are more, or less favourable, than those of the original group. But we now need to turn to the second major element which was earlier identified as a major component in the process of integration, namely, political will. For however favourable a given set of background conditions may be they need to be accompanied by a strong urge to unite if a new political grouping is to emerge.

POLITICAL WILL

We are here concerned with one of the most fundamental aspects of the whole process; the origins, strength and direction of its driving force and motive power. At this point the focus of our attention must necessarily switch from the type of relatively objective data which has been mentioned in the preceding discussion of background conditions, to the much more difficult and complex sphere of subjective perceptions—for it is these which provide the motivation for the individuals and groups who, by their attitudes and actions, provide the constituent elements of a will to unite. The mechanism by which any given individual or group arrives at a particular perception of a given set of data, and how these perceptions change over time, are both critical to an understanding of any political process. Here, however, we have only space to discuss the visible end-product of that process and to indicate the main factors which appear to have contributed to the creation and maintenance of a political will to unite which has been so marked a feature of the development of the Community over the years.

The basic element in the creation of such a political will is clearly dissatisfaction with the existing state of affairs, and the expectation of benefits to be derived from union. These benefits are not necessarily confined to those of a wholly material and tangible nature, but they are necessarily related—if they are to provide a basis for significant political pressure—to the central purposes of any organised political community, namely, security (internal and external) and welfare. The strength of the political will, based on such expectations, that a group develops will clearly be a major component in its capacity to move towards union. Equally important, however, is the question of whether or not the various demands that contribute to it converge on a similar set of objectives, or are in conflict with one another. Similarly, the way in which the flow of demands for union evolves over time is also of critical importance. It cannot be assumed that they will necessarily remain constant either in strength or direction, and should they weaken or be focused on increasingly divergent objectives the process of integration is likely either to come to a halt or experience serious tensions.

In the case of the Community the flow of demands for union has been characterised both by its strength and persistence over time. One important feature to be noted in this context is the way in which pressure for integration has been maintained in spite of the fact that some of the original concerns which gave birth to the process have now receded into the background. The threat of renewed conflict between France and Germany, which was so potent an argument in the early days is, for instance, now no longer regarded by most West Europeans as a threat. Fear of aggression from the East has also waned. Nevertheless, support for the pursuit of integration has grown rather than diminished. How do we explain this?

Part of the answer undoubtedly lies in the fact that the formation of the customs union has given more and more individuals and groups a stake in the Community: they see it as necessary in terms of their own welfare. In more general terms, the evolution of modern industry has underlined the need for a larger home market with the security that only an absence of tariff barriers can give. In short, the Community is now widely regarded as an essential instrument for the achievement and maintenance of a prosperous economy and a necessary precondition for a rising standard of living. In more political terms it has also come to be seen by many as an instrument through which its member countries, all of whom are acutely conscious of the limitations of their own power in comparison with that of the super-powers, can collectively express and pursue more effectively their interests in the world at large. Many of the protagonists of integration see the Community as making a positive contribution to a more peaceful and better-ordered world through, for instance, the establishment of improved relations with the Soviet Union and the countries of Eastern Europe; helping the less-developed countries; and as an essentially pacific element in a world which has recently been characterised by ideological conflict between the super-powers.

All these considerations have contributed to maintain, and indeed to strengthen, the pressures in favour of integration within the original member states of the Community. One result is that the process has now become very much less dependent than it was in the early stages on the external support of the United States. So although that support has tended to weaken over the years, and indeed to have evolved into a policy which, while still fundamentally friendly, is nevertheless more critical of certain aspects of the Community's policies, this has not had a negative effect on the pace of integration itself. Indeed, the need to assert specifically European interests in negotiations with the United States has increasingly been stressed as part of the objectives of the process.[1]

The various types of demands advanced in favour of closer unity have up to now on the whole not proved to be difficult to reconcile, at least at the level of the overall objectives of the Community. There has

[1] See, for instance, J. J. Servan-Schreiber, *The American Challenge,* London (1968).

been a very large measure of agreement that the initial objective should be a customs union, accompanied by a limited number of common economic policies. There has also been a substantial body of opinion that the Community should aim to move towards political union —which in the Community jargon means a common posture towards the outside world. In the early stages of the process the slogan of *il faut faire l'Europe* was a whole programme in itself, and there was a very large measure of agreement on the type of measures that had to be taken to remove some of the more obvious and irritating barriers to the free movement of persons, goods, services and capital which had been inherited from the past. Differences in ultimate objectives did not therefore impinge very noticeably in the early stages of the process which is frequently referred to as that of 'negative integration'.

The further the six-nation Community developed, however, the more it became necessary to define in terms of specific policies a series of more precise objectives. At this point—and the question was raised with regard to political union in 1960–1962 and with regard to the Community's institutional development in 1965–1966—quite marked divergences became apparent. More recently this has also been the case with regard to economic and monetary union. In other words, the further the process develops the more significant becomes the degree of convergence or divergence between the various strands that compose the political will to advance further on the path towards union. This is an important consideration in terms of the enlarged Community, and will be considered later alongside the question of the factors likely to affect the strength of the demands for further instalments of integration.

So far we have discussed demand-flows as they affect the maintenance and development of the Community's political system as a whole. But similar considerations also need to be applied at the level of individual policy sectors. Here the experience of the Six shows quite clearly that in each individual sector there has been a different constellation of demands. In some they have been both strong and relatively easy to reconcile; in others strong, but divergent; and others again so weak that there has been little incentive for action to be taken. Patterns of demand have also fluctuated over time and have been influenced by how successfully the Community has responded to them. In the case of Euratom, for instance, a set of relatively strong if divergent demands at the outset was gradually transformed—as a result of the Community's failure to bring the expected benefits to its members—into a reluctance to grant it funds, a preference for individual national nuclear programmes, and a downgrading of the Community's functions.

With regard to agriculture, on the other hand, a set of strong and apparently irreconcilable demands was successfully transformed into a common policy and in a way which, by linking advances in the agricultural sector to agreements in other policy areas, provided the central mechanism by which the Community advanced through its transitional period. Whatever one may think about the content of the common agricultural policy, this was clearly a major success for the leadership of the Community, and underlined the crucial nature of the role that such leadership plays in the ongoing process.

PATTERNS OF SUPPORT

Before turning to a closer examination of that role, however, we should next consider the third major component in that process: the factors which generate support for the Community as it develops. Analytically such support can be distinguished from the demands made on the system, for we are here concerned with attitudes towards the Community as an instrument for the achievement of union, rather than the nature and direction of the pressures for such union.

We can conceive a situation, for instance, in which although there are strong pressures for collective action these are accompanied by hostility towards, or lack of confidence in, some of the existing members of the union or in the political system set up to promote common action. To put the matter in a more positive way, we can say that the successful pursuit of economic and political union requires a high degree of mutual trust on the part of the members of the group concerned, and the successful generation of support for the political system —in this case the Community—which they establish as the instrument of their union.[1]

In examining the experience of the Six in these respects we have first to recall the relevance of a number of the structural features of the group mentioned earlier. These did not automatically provide the basis for a sense of loyalty to the new Community: indeed, among the mass of the population there were strong currents of mutual diffidence and hostility. Nor among substantial sections of the economic and political elites in the various countries were there close ties. Such international links as existed between the various political parties were on the whole weak (paradoxically they were probably strongest in the case of the Communist parties who opposed the creation of the Communities) and very limited in their impact. Some sectors of the economy had given rise to more substantial relationships, but very few of them coincided with the frontiers of the six-member Community. As the debates in the

---

[1] This distinction corresponds to that between 'identitive' and 'systematic' support made by Lindberg and Scheingold (*op. cit.*, pp. 38–63). They also make a further distinction, applicable to both categories, between 'utilitarian' and 'affective' supports.

various countries about the E.C.S.C. and E.E.C. showed, many groups of producers—accustomed to operate within heavily-protected national markets—were fearful of their new partners whom they regarded as dangerous competitors.

Initially, therefore, there was little sense of solidarity or mutual trust among the overwhelming majority of the people of the six-member Community. What there was, on the other hand, was a widespread—if essentially passive—desire for peace and also for better living conditions. It was this desire which provided the basis for the 'diffuse support' on which the pro-integration elites were able to count when they first launched the Community, and which has subsequently grown to a very substantial measure of popular support for the Community as it has developed.

The existence of this support has been attested by a number of studies of mass opinion in the six countries, among which two—undertaken in 1962 and 1970 respectively—merit particular attention. The first of these was undertaken at the request of the Communities' Press and Information Service and carried out by Gallup International between January and March 1962, in the six member countries on the basis of a total sample of 6334 adults over the age of 20. In reply to a general question on European unity the results shown in *Table 2.1* were obtained.

The general picture which emerged from this was that between six and eight citizens out of every ten in the member countries were in favour of European unity, with only a small minority opposed to it. It

Table 2.1 ATTITUDES TO EUROPEAN UNIFICATION, 1962

Attitude	Belg.	Fr.	Ger.	It.	Neths.	Lux.*	E.E.C.
Very fav.	31	28	50	36	62	(11)	40
Rather fav.	34	44	31	24	25	(16)	32
Total 'fav.'	(65)	(72)	(81)	(60)	(87)	(27)	(72)
Rather unfav.	4	6	3	3	3	(3)	4
Very unfav.	1	2	1	1	1	(2)	1
Total 'unfav.'	(5)	(8)	(4)	(4)	(4)	(5)	(5)
Don't know	30	20	15	36	9	(68)	23

Source: *Sondages*, Revue Française de l'opinion publique No. 1. (1963) Reproduced in J.-R. Rabier, *L'Information des Européens et l'intégration de l'Europe*, Institut d'Etudes Européennes de l'Université libre de Bruxelles (1965) p. 44.

*Figures unreliable

should be added, however, that at this stage there was a substantial body of 'don't know's', a rather low level of factual information about the Community itself, and only a small proportion among the population that gave a high priority to the quest for unity or gave it much of their attention.[1]

The 1970 survey, carried out again at the request of the Communities' Information Service by Gallup International and International Research Associates—this time on the basis of a representative sample of the population over 16, covering 8725 persons in the six countries —showed a continuing high level of support for the process of integration (Table 2.2).

Table 2.2 ATTITUDES TO EUROPEAN UNIFICATION, 1970

Attitude	Belg.	Fr.	Ger.	It.	Neths.	Lux.	E.E.C.
Very fav.	31	24	39	40	30	52	34
Rather fav.	35	46	37	38	44	24	40
Total 'fav.'	(66)	(70)	(76)	(78)	(74)	(76)	(74)
Indif.	16	11	13	7	11	14	11
Rather unfav.	3	6	4	4	7	2	4
Very unfav.	2	2	1	1	3	2	2
Total 'unfav.'	(5)	(8)	(5)	(5)	(10)	(4)	(6)
Don't Know.	13	11	6	10	10	6	9

Source: Reported in J.-R. Rabier, 'Europeans and the unification of Europe', Government and Opposition (Autumn 1971) p. 487.

Both polls showed, not unexpectedly, that there were considerable differences in the spread of opinion when it was analysed in more detail. In general terms, young people were more favourable than their elders, for instance, and the more educated and better-off sections of the population more favourable than the less-well educated and poorer groups in society. But of the substantial and sustained support for the process of integration there can be no doubt.

Nevertheless, the actual development of the Community has been due to the work of the political elites in the various member countries, and in the early days a critical role was played by a relatively small minority of politicians, civil servants, businessmen and trade unionists who set out, whether working within the Communities' institutions or in their national context, to make the new machinery work. Their task

[1] J. R. Rabier, L'Information des Européens et l'intégration de l'Europe, Institut d'Etudes Européenes de l'Université libre de Bruxelles (1965) pp. 46–50.

was eased by several helpful factors. One was the relative political stability which Western Europe experienced in the 1950s and 1960s. It was only in France during this period that there was a change of regime and even there, though the Fifth Republic certainly brought significant constitutional and political changes, they were not of a type to raise serious doubts about the country's acceptability as a member of the Community. This was also a period when the ideological element in party politics appeared to have waned, not, it is true, as far as the Communist parties were concerned, but markedly so with regard to relationships between Liberals, Christian Democrats, and Social Democrats. In several of the member countries they were to be found in coalition with one another; and even where they disagreed on domestic matters they found a large measure of common ground with regard to support for the Community process. It was largely on the basis of support from such parties that the Community was launched and subsequently sustained.

At the centre of this broadly-based coalition which first emerged at the time of the Schuman Plan were the strong Christian Democrat parties in the Federal Republic and Italy and the smaller, but strategically important *Mouvement Républicain Populaire* (M.R.P.) in France. From the beginning some of the more moderate right-wing parties also gave their support: these included the Radicals in France, the F.D.P. in the Federal Republic (a partner in government both with the Christian Democrats and also subsequently the Social Democrats), and the Liberals and Monarchists in Italy. To the left of these parties there were also some groups which rallied to the Schuman Plan: the Social Democrats in the Benelux countries, France and Italy and also in the last country the small Republican party. At this stage both the German S.P.D. and the Nenni Socialists in Italy were opposed to it, but though both maintained their opposition to the E.D.C., by the time of the Rome treaties the former were prepared to vote in favour and the latter to abstain.

The fact that as it developed the Community was able to secure this accretion of support from the moderate left was of critical importance. Had it failed to do so it could have been fatal, especially as by 1965 the S.P.D. had moved into a governmental coalition with the C.D.U. in the Federal Republic, and at about the same time (in 1963) the *apertura a sinistra* in Italy brought the Nenni Socialists into government. In both cases useful influence was exerted by the trade unions connected with the two parties, a number of influential leaders of both the Christian and Free Trade unions in the Community countries having from an early point decided that economic integration was likely to be in their interests.

This support given by the Centre parties in the various countries was sufficient to guarantee, in all except France, that successive governmental coalitions would support integration. The opposition of the Communists, numerically strong in both France and Italy, was neutralised by their exclusion from office. The major threat was therefore posed by the Gaullists in France who fought a bitter campaign against the successive proposals for the creation of the Communities. In 1950 the fact that they were not a member of the governing coalition meant that they were not able to prevent a decision in favour of the Schuman Plan. In 1954, however, they played an important part in the rejection of the E.D.C. The continued instability of governments in the Fourth Republic also meant that it was touch or go whether or not the 1957 Rome treaties would be approved: this was a major factor which allowed the Mollet Government to exert such successful pressure on its partners during the negotiations. As it was, they were only approved by the Assembly a few months before the Gaullists came back to power in the wake of the insurrection in Algeria and the threat of civil war in France. The return of de Gaulle to power in May 1958 seemed then to pose a major threat to the whole construction; it was only when he decided to accept the obligations assumed by the Fourth Republic that the survival of the new Communities was secured.

This decision was in itself an indication that the Communities had begun to take root; as the process developed it gradually generated its own sources of support. The changing attitude of the Italian Communist Party, for instance, was significant in this context. On the basis of the experience of the E.C.S.C. it began to moderate its initial outright opposition, and move towards a position in which, today, it accepts the existence of the Community, and takes part in a number of its institutions, even if it remains very critical of the Community's political structure and many of its policies. A similar, if much slower evolution, has also taken place in the case of the French communists.

The mechanisms through which the Community has built up support have attracted much attention on the part of academic students of integration. Some of them have stressed in particular the role played by the increasing level of transactions of various sorts triggered off by the process of integration; they point in particular to the enormous increase in intra-Community trade which has occurred (amounting to 600% over the period 1958–1970); the increased social interchange which this has brought in its train; and the corresponding processes of political socialistation which involvement in the affairs of the Community has triggered off as more and more individuals have been caught up in meetings with their opposite numbers from other countries.

Some of the statistical data relating to transaction flows within the Community has, however, given rise to considerable dispute. The conclusion reached in one study carried out by Karl Deutsch and a number of colleagues and published in 1967 that 'European integration has slowed down since 1957–1958' has been hotly disputed.[1] Both its statistical base and the interpretation to be placed on the data have been questioned, and—as the debate has widened—so has the role to be assigned to transactions as a generator of supports for the process of integration.[2] What is certainly the case is that while many types of social interchange have been rising within the Community, the flows in many cases have not been directly related to its activities, nor have they been confined to the Community alone. The mass media, for instance, have been relatively little affected by its existence; the vast increase in flows of tourists has also obeyed the logic of sea and sunshine rather than anything else. To the extent that these phenomena have had a political impact, and the nature of this impact is in itself a matter of dispute, they have served rather to create and strengthen a generic sense of 'being European' rather than a specific attachment to the Community as such. They may indeed have played some part in underlining the incomplete nature of a Community limited to six countries, and have contributed in this way to preparing the way for its enlargement.

There is no doubt, nevertheless, that during the 1950s and 1960s a new set of loyalties began to develop to the Community and its institutions. There was, in the first place, a general acceptance on the part of those involved in its day-to-day activities of its decisions and the procedures which it evolved to arrive at them. A set of new structures came into existence, both within national administrations and also those created to serve the needs of such groups as farmers, trade unionists and industrial producers. A new political infrastructure was created to serve the need of the Community's political system. It was, however, primarily bureaucratic in nature: one notable absentee was any genuinely Community-wide political party. Some forms of transnational co-operation between like-minded parties did develop, but in all cases they were weak and ineffective. This is still the case today. The Community as it is constituted at present lacks the support that such a new party structure could give it, and this is a serious weakness.[3]

There have also been some signs in recent years that a number of the values on which the Community has so far been based are now being questioned, especially by the younger generation. The May 1968 events

[1] Karl W. Deutsch et al., *France, Germany and the Western Alliance*, New York (1967) p. 218.

[2] See Donald J. Puchala, 'International transactions and regional integration' in Leon N. Lindberg and Stuart A. Scheingold (eds.), *Regional integration: theory and research*, Harvard (1971).

[3] See H. Vredeling, 'The common market of political parties' in *Government and Opposition* (Autumn 1971).

in Paris made it apparent that a significant section of the politically-active students there rejected many of the values of contemporary society, including the virtues of a mixed economy, economic growth, and a competitive society. When the Commission of the Communities, in response to the calls for increased participation to which those events gave rise, sought to enter into a dialogue with representatives of that younger generation it encountered a set of markedly hostile attitudes.[1] And a few years later even the Commission's own president, then the Dutchman Sicco Mansholt, himself publicly questioned the conventional wisdom of making economic growth a major objective of the Community's activities.[2]

Although the student left has in the meantime fallen into disarray these were all signs that a new type of debate about the Community had begun—and is likely to continue in the future. How that debate will proceed, and how far it will lead to divisions within the enlarged Community about both its general aims and also specific policies, are both questions which need to be asked in the context of assessing how much support it is likely to continue to enjoy in the future. We shall also need to examine the likely impact on the pattern of support for the Community of the current attitude of the Labour Party, and its implications. For if the enlarged Community is to succeed in pursuing further the path towards closer union it will need at least to maintain existing levels of support, and if possible to generate a stronger pattern of loyalties to it.

POLITICAL LEADERSHIP

So far we have been considering a range of variables which affect the flow of inputs into the Community's political system: the pressures generated in favour of union and the nature and extent of the support which it has enjoyed. Without a high level of both types of input the Community would have had much greater difficulty in moving forward at the pace which it achieved over its first 20 years, and might indeed have collapsed. But, important though these are, they constitute only part of the explanation of the dynamics of the process. Equally important is the role that has been played by political leadership.

Such leadership is of course a vital element in any political system, but it is particularly crucial when a group of countries embarks on a process of integration. For this involves not merely the maintenance of an existing status quo, but a series of creative acts for which courage

[1] See *Quelle Europe voulons-nous?* Secretariat Européen de liaison des organisations de jeunesse, Bruxelles (1969).

[2] See below, pp. 105–106.

and imagination are required as well as the normal political skills of reconciling and resolving conflicts between different sections of society. In guiding a process of integration, three functions are of particular importance if it is to maintain its momentum: a strategic function, which involves decisions about the general direction the process is to take; a tactical function, which is concerned with the selection of specific steps within that overall strategy; and a continuous negotiating function which is directed at building up the coalitions of interests and arriving at the compromises necessary to maintain a steady flow of decisions on individual policy issues. Without the successful accomplishment of these tasks the projected union is likely to fail, for it will lack a sense of direction, a clearly defined set of immediate objectives, and a capacity to maintain confidence in its ability to fulfil the expectation focused on it. Should such an 'output failure' occur, and continue for any appreciable period of time, the results can be quite disastrous. In such a situation individual members or particular groups within the Community may threaten to withdraw their support and the process, having come to a halt, may face a major crisis of confidence.

As we have already seen, the European Community has itself not wholly avoided such a situation, though its leadership has succeeded at critical moments in mitigating the effects of this type of stress and after a while in finding a basis for a renewal of its forward movement. One of the characteristics of this process, and indeed of the leadership of the Community in general, is the interaction which has taken place between two different types of leaders. The most prominent have naturally been national leaders: heads of state or government and their ministers, backed up by their civil servants. But alongside them a very important role has also been played by a smaller group of individuals whom we may call 'supranational leaders'. By this is meant those who have either occupied positions of authority in the Community's own institutions, particularly the Commission, or who have been able to exercise leadership in a Community rather than a purely national context.

Pre-eminent among those in this second category has been Jean Monnet, the father of the Schuman Plan, sometime president of the High Authority of the E.C.S.C., and, from 1955, the president of the Action Committee for the United States of Europe. This he established on his resignation from the E.C.S.C. as an unofficial body grouping the major democratic parties and trade unions of the member countries in favour of integration to discuss and promote the process. During the late 1950s and early 1960s this proved to be a very influential pressure group, its occasional meetings and resolutions underpinning what became a very intensive network of contacts at the highest levels of the political systems of the member countries. The one major exception to this was in France itself where, as long as de Gaulle was in power, the influence of the Committee on the direction of French policy was very limited. It did, however, serve an important function in maintaining the cohesion of the other five when conflict occurred between de Gaulle and his partners and also in sustaining pressure for the enlargement of the Community.

At an earlier stage in its development Monnet also played a crucial role as a catalyst with regard to the creation of the six-nation group and in helping to devise the strategy which carried it forward. As the main author of the ideas which appeared in the guise of the Schuman and Pleven Plans he conceived—and also acted as midwife for—the Coal and Steel and Defence Communities. Behind the scenes he was extremely active, once the plans had been launched, in seeking to build up support for them in the various member countries. And when the E.D.C. project collapsed, he played an equally important part in preventing a complete collapse of the Community movement. It was he and the group around him which formulated, and also helped again to mobilise support for, the ideas which led to the relaunching of the process at the Messina Conference in 1955.

In all these cases, which were the times when the major strategic decisions about the early development of the Communities were taken, there was a very close interaction between Monnet and his circle and the various leaders of the member countries. This was crucial for success: the same has also been true of the way in which the Community has arrived at decisions with regard to the specific steps to be taken within the framework of its agreed overall strategy.

In this process other factors have come into play to exercise leadership functions, in particular the Commission. It has regularly formulated programmes of work and deadlines both for itself and the Council of Ministers. Examples of these include the 1962 Memorandum of the E.E.C. Commission for an *Action Programme for the second stage* (of the E.E.C.'s transition period); another set of ideas incorporated in a document from the same source known as *Initiative '64;* and a whole series of similar programmes for specific policy fields, including such matters as the free movement of labour, the free offering of services and the right of establishment, the harmonisation of certain forms of indirect taxation, and so on.

Several of these have been adopted in due course by the Council of Ministers which independently has also set itself its own targets. Sometimes, as in the Spring of 1963, these have covered several sectors of its work; in other cases they have been time-tables for individual policy areas (this has frequently been the case for the common agricultural policy, for instance). A more recent example was the decision in June 1971 on a set of proposals to be worked out and agreed for the first three-year stage of the monetary and economic union.

This constant self-imposition of tasks and time-tables has proved to be a very fruitful method of maintaining momentum, even if on many occasions the time-tables have not been rigorously respected. They have served to give the institutions of the Community a clear sense of purpose coupled with a spirit of urgency. In some cases sanctions for non-fulfilment have also been built into these programmes. Several examples of this are to be found in the E.E.C. Treaty where it was provided that if a certain decision (for instance, on transition from one stage to another) has not been taken by a particular date by unanimity, it could subsequently be taken by majority vote. Such instances have been, however, comparatively rare: for the most part the psychological pressures exerted on the ministers by their own decision, of which they are then constantly reminded by the Commission and the mass-media, has sufficed to create a situation in which everyone tries hard to carry it out. As a former French minister of agriculture, Pisani, once remarked during a particularly hard-fought meeting: 'We are condemned to succeed'.

The role assigned within the Community's institutional structure to the Commission of initiating policy proposals has also been of the utmost importance in maintaining forward movement. As the first president of the E.E.C. Commission frequently said, one of its most important tasks is to act as the motor of integration. It acts as a permanent spur and goad to action, identifying problems and assigning priorities within the various policy areas, and maintaining a constant flow of proposals for various types of legislative and other action on the part of the Council. At the same time it is also able, particularly through its information activities, to alert the political elites in the member countries (and, indirectly, the general public) to what it considers necessary, and via the European Parliament, the Economic and Social Committee, and other non-governmental bodies, to build up a climate of opinion and a series of pressures which can—if it is successful—help to prod the Council into action.

In selecting issues for decision the Commission has, of course, to exercise careful judgement. There have been occasions—most notably in the proposals it put forward in the Spring of 1965—when it has badly misjudged its chances of success. If an issue is not 'ripe' its proposals can as they did on that occasion, meet with a refusal on the part of the Council. On the other hand, if it fails to take an initiative, it may find the Council usurping its role.

In recent years there has in fact been an increasing tendency for this to happen, and for the leadership function—particularly at the strategic level—to be exercised more and more by the national governments.

This has important implications for the future, should the trend continue, for it places a very heavy premium on the capacity of a limited number of individuals—the heads of state or of government—to agree among themselves. During the 1960s it was precisely this problem that created such stresses within the Community. Although the commitment of de Gaulle to closer unity with his partners was not in doubt, both the forms he proposed it should take and the pre-eminent role he claimed for France within the group created serious tensions. Initially, the understanding he was able to establish with Adenauer was on the whole a positive element in the life of the Community even though it meant the continued exclusion of the British. Once the Chancellor had left the scene however, relations between the two countries began to deteriorate, and amity was replaced by a succession of French threats designed to bludgeon the Federal Republic into accepting French leadership. When de Gaulle subsequently, in 1965–1966, made a bid to weaken the role of the Commission and to recast the institutions of the Community into a mould which more closely corresponded with the way in which he wished to see its business transacted, he found himself isolated. When he then failed to achieve his objectives he soon began to search round for alternative solutions—including a reversion to something on the lines of the free trade area which the British had originally proposed, within which the Community would have been superseded by looser forms of organisation.

The threat which de Gaulle posed to the Community was particularly acute because of the combination of his own personal prestige, the determination with which he pursued his strategy, his dramatic style, and the fact that he was the undisputed leader of one of the major states of the Community. Since he left the scene there has been no similar threat, and although there have certainly been strong Gaullist intonations about the policies being pursued by President Pompidou it has proved far easier for France's partners to reach an accommodation with that country. The pragmatic bargaining styles which characterised relations between them in the three years leading up to the entry of the new members marked a reversion to an earlier pattern of leadership, and one which is more consonant with the needs of the successful pursuit of integration. The tasks which lie ahead for the Community's leaders are nevertheless very considerable, not least because the decisions which have to be taken at this stage of the process will necessarily impinge more and more directly on the heartland of national sovereignty. As the Community has developed the stakes for each of the partners have steadily risen. It is to this aspect of the process, together with some other general features of it, which we now turn.

THEORIES AND PRACTICE

So far we have been dealing one by one with the four major components which contribute to the dynamics of the process of integration in Western Europe. It is now time to take a brief overview of the process as a whole, and to identify in particular a number of aspects of it which it is necessary to bear in mind in considering the prospects for the new Community. In order to do this we first need to consider what light the actual experience of the Community has so far shed on various theories about the dynamics of a process of union.

In the immediate post-war period there were those, not large in numbers but by no means wholly without political influence, who believed that instant federation was possible. Their proposal was that a constituent assembly should be summoned to work out a constitution for a new political framework, together with the other measures necessary to arrive at an advanced form of economic and political union. The ad hoc assembly that met in Strasbourg in 1952–1953 to work on proposals for a treaty for a political community to complement the E.C.S.C. and the E.D.C. owed much to this federalist thinking. It was not, however, an approach which commanded any wide measure of support, and the work of that assembly was speedily pigeon-holed.

Federalist thinking has nevertheless remained influential, and has continued to insist on the need to construct, as a matter of priority, the political institutions of a democratic Europe which would derive their legitimacy 'from the consent directly expressed by European citizens and would exercise their powers directly on European citizens without intereference from the member states'.[1] Federalists disagree fundamentally with those who believe that an effective Community can be built on a confederal basis with power remaining essentially in the hands of national governments[2] and also doubt whether it can be built by the sleight of hand of bureaucratic elites operating through an institution like the Commission, which lacks a popular power base.

This latter view—to which the label 'neo-functionalist' has been attached—is nevertheless one which has had a great influence on the strategy pursued by the Community. It owes a good deal to the functionalist school of thought which originated with the writings of David Mitrany and several other prominent writers—including Leon-

[1] Altiero Spinelli, *The Eurocrats*, Baltimore (1966) p.11.

[2] For a powerful statement of this case see Stanley Hoffmann, 'Obstinate or obsolete? The fate of the nation state and the case of Western Europe', *Daedalus*, (Summer 1966). (Reproduced in L. J. Cantori and S. L. Spiegel, *The International Politics of Regions: A Comparative Approach*, New Jersey 1970).

ard Woolf, Norman Angell, Robert Cecil and G.D.H. Cole—in the inter-war period. They were concerned with devising a strategy in a world-wide context that could gradually lead in the direction of some better-ordered set of relations for international society as a whole. Although these writers were not unduly optimistic about human nature and human behaviour they believed that the latter, at least, could be amended by a process of learning if the environment in which men live was changed. That environment, they thought, was being poisoned by an exclusive loyalty to the nation state. The starting point for the construction of a better world in their view could be provided by men's concern with welfare:[1]

> If welfare needs are the most important, argue the Functionalists, then surely men can be persuaded by education and experience to switch their loyalties from national governments, which in the long term can give them only second best, and redirect them to agencies which best administer to those needs.

This approach therefore advocated the establishment of a number of international functional agencies to perform specific welfare tasks, and conceived of a future world order—if only in rather general terms—as one characterised by a series of such agencies with overlapping membership and hence a diffusion on the part of the individuals affected by them of their previously exclusive sense of loyalty to a single political community.

The impact of this school of thought can certainly be detected in several of the projects which were put forward in Western Europe in the immediate post-war period; and it continues to be influential not least among certain critics of the Community who believe that it would have been preferable to deal with Western Europe's own problems in this way, rather than construct what they fear will become a new super-state having all the bad characteristics of the smaller ones it replaces, but on a larger and more dangerous scale.[2]

Functionalist thinking certainly contributed to the ideas which were incorporated in the Schuman Plan, but the general strategy adopted by the Six was of another kind. The Schuman Plan, for instance, made it quite plain that the Coal and Steel Community was conceived not just as an isolated welfare agency but as the nucleus of a new political community. The strategy in this case was that successful integration in one sector of the economy would lead to demands for integration in other sectors and that in this way an economic and political union could

[1] Paul Taylor, *International Cooperation Today: the European and the Universal Pattern*, London (1971) p. 55.

[2] This is the thesis developed by Frans Alting von Geusau, *Beyond the European Community*, Leiden (1969).

gradually be constructed. It was wholly in keeping with this strategy that a second functional agency—the Defence Community—was proposed alongside the E.C.S.C., and that later on Euratom and the E.E.C. were set up to extend the functional scope of the process. The central objective throughout the process was, however, political in nature; a functionalist technique was being applied to a federalist objective. There was, however, one crucial difference: the protagonists of the Community approach did not propose to make a frontal assault on national sovereignty, but rather gradually to erode it. Their chosen instrument was 'an integrated European bureaucracy . . . more far-sighted and rational that the national bureaucracies':[1] they believed that a united Europe could be built by a process of gradual accretion.

Theories related to this type of approach to the problems of achieving union have been given the name 'neo-functionalism', and are particularly identified with a group of American scholars, among whom Ernst B. Haas, Leon Lindberg and Joseph Nye have been prominent. There is no space here to go into the details of the theories they have constructed—and which have evolved over time—but it should be noted that, like the older functionalists, they too lay great stress on the learning function and the cumulative nature of the process. Early versions of their theories gave particular prominence to what was called 'spill-over' mechanisms and the inherently expansive logic of integration. At the same time they also emphasised, unlike the Mitrany school, the importance of the role of central institutions. Reflecting on the early years of the E.E.C. Leon Lindberg wrote in 1963:[2]

> What is striking about the Treaty of Rome and the first years of the E.E.C. is the scope of the tasks assigned to the central institutions, and the extent to which these tasks appear to be inherently expansive; that is, the extent to which integrative steps in one functional context spill over into another. An ever-widening circle of actors finds this system to be an effective, logical and appropriate framework in which to pursue its goals, and this is one essential feature of the Community.

In more recent years some of the original rather optimistic assumptions about the development of the process have been modified by this group of writers, some of whom also sought to construct more complex, rigorous and quantifiable models to describe and explain it. This work has contributed a great deal to our knowledge of the process; it has, for instance, identified the major variables which affect it, and also analysed the varying patterns of bargaining which accompany it. It has

---

[1] Altiero Spinelli, *op. cit.*, p. 13.

[2] Leon N. Lindberg, *The Political dynamics of European Economic Integration*, Stanford (1963) p. 293.

been more successful in describing and classifying these variables, however, than in explaining how they occur; for while a distinction has been made between those which have pushed the Community forward through a step-by-step process ('forward linkages') and those which lead to a quantitative or qualitative change ('systems transformations') they have not been able to account for the relative incidence of the two.[1] Also, although they have noted that progress in one policy area may not lead to progress in another, and conversely that failure in one may not automatically lead to a general breakdown—a phenomenon which has been called 'the autonomy of functional contexts'—the reasons for this also remain rather elusive. Some of these writers have also undoubtedly tended to attach too positive a role to crises within the system, for although it is true that many of the positive bargains which have been reached have only emerged after a period of stress within the Community, there have been some periods of stress (and notably that between 1965 and 1969) which have had a wholly negative impact on the functioning of the system, and which indeed began to threaten it with some measure of disintegration. Neo-functionalist writers have also been forced to concede that there is an area of 'high politics' which may not be susceptible to erosion by a process of accretion and certain political actors—the discovery followed the impact of de Gaulle on the Community—who disdain pragmatic bargaining and are concerned above all with the fight for the retention of national sovereignty.[2]

The academic writings of the neo-functionalist school, though they have greatly added to our knowledge of the process of integration, have therefore certainly not been able to provide a wholly convincing set of explanations for the vagaries of its internal dynamics. Nor have they been much concerned with the actual impact of the process, for in their attempt to remain value-free they have remained loftily remote from the arguments which have accompanied the process about the direction it should take and the content of particular policy decisions.[3] The direction which academic theorizing about the process of integration has recently taken has indeed tended to restrict interest in it to within the academic community itself: those who have been engaged actively in the process have proceeded on a highly pragmatic basis. To

[1] See L. N. Lindberg and S. A. Scheingold, *Europe's Would-be Polity*, New Jersey (1971) Ch. 4.

[2] For a recent criticism of neo-functionalism see Ronn D. Kaiser, 'Toward the Copernican phase of regional integration theory', *Journal of Common Market Studies* (March 1972).

[3] This point has been forcibly made by Stuart Scheingold, 'Domestic and international consequences of regional integration' in Lindberg and Scheingold (eds.) *Regional Integration: Theory and Research*, Harvard (1971).

them abstract theories about the dynamics of the process are only of marginal interest; what they have to concern themselves with in their daily activities is the resolution of conflicting pressures and objectives with regard to the actual content of Community decisions.

There are a number of the features of the process in which they are engaged, however, which have either not conformed to prevailing theories about it, or which the theories have not taken properly into account, which deserve to be underlined. One of the most striking of these is the way it has consolidated and reinforced rather than weakened the role of the individual national states and their governments. This will be discussed at greater length in the following chapter: here it is sufficient to note that the early assumptions of Monnet and his colleagues that there would be a gradual accretion of authority by the supranational element in the Community's institutional structure have not been fulfilled. On the contrary, the member states—and in particular the Federal Republic—have acquired a new confidence as the Community has developed, and have taken steps to assert their authority within it. The increasing functional scope of its activities has not been accompanied by an increase in the powers of the Commission but rather by a consolidation and extension of those of the national elements within the decision-making structure.

A second important phenomenon is what may be called the dialectical nature of the process. Stated simply, this is that each step forward has generated not only new supports and demands for further action, but also contrary pressures of various sorts. Each new proposal for common action, for instance, has triggered off a defensive reaction on the part of the national governments, each determined to assert their national interest in the ensuing bargaining process. There are significant parallels here with the economics of the process. There have been far more mergers, for instance, between firms in the same country than genuine trans-national mergers. And with regard to the outside world, the more the Community has constructed common policies, the more pressure it has come under from those affected by them. The British reaction is the prime example; convinced of the success of the Community, the British Government, by seeking to join, was for a long time a source of serious internal stress. The evolution of attitudes in the United States towards the Community is also significant in this context: as the Community has asserted its own interests, support for it from across the Atlantic has gradually waned. In short, the repercussions of the process have been far more complex than had originally been anticipated; spillover has indeed occurred, but so to has what in the jargon is known as 'negative feedback'; in other words, each achievement has triggered off reactions within and without which have not necessarily been conducive to the harmonious development of the Community.

Finally, there is a third feature of the overall process which also deserves to be underlined. This is that it has proved to be cumulative not only in scope, but also in difficulty. It was relatively easy for the Six originally to agree to merge control over one sector of their economies; it was much more difficult for them to agree on the construction of a general common market. And recent experience with regard to both economic and monetary union and also political union show that, as the Community has moved closer to the heartlands of national sovereignty, so the issues involved have become more difficult to handle, and progress more slow.

The whole process can perhaps best be compared with a Himalayan expedition. As they toil upwards the members may indeed be encouraged by the progress they have made, even if this has involved occasional falls and pauses for breath. But ahead of them lie the higher slopes; and to conquer these a strong will is required and much skill and determination. It is precisely on these higher slopes that Britain and the other new members now find themselves, along with the original members of the party.

3 How the System Works

We now turn to a consideration of a different range of issues about the Community's political system: those concerned with the scope of its activities and how it carries them out. This involves, among other things, a discussion of the question of implications of membership for the exercise of national sovereignty; the range of issues over which Britain, together with the other members, is now committed to taking decisions within the framework of the Community; the mechanisms by which such decisions are taken and the forms they take; the financing of the Community's activities; and how decisions are implemented and subjected to judicial review.

THE ISSUE OF SOVEREIGNTY

During the debate about entry, one of the issues most frequently raised was that of sovereignty. The usual starting point for the discussion was the assertion put forward by the opponents of entry that membership would involve a very substantial—and in their view, unacceptable—'surrender' of sovereignty. As one member of Parliament put it: 'If we enter this union we shall lose control over our whole national life as we have known it up to the present day'.[1] The loss of sovereignty, it was asserted, would in fact be two-fold. In the first place the Government itself would no longer be able to decide many issues on its own: it would be obliged to discuss them with its partners in the Council of Ministers in Brussels and fall in with the decisions taken in this body. Its loss of authority would be exacerbated by the

[1] Mr. Raphael Tuck, House of Commons, 17 February 1972.

fact that it would not be it but rather the Commission that would formulate the proposals for discussion: it would therefore not only have lost the power of autonomous decision, but also the right of initiative. And although it might be argued—as in fact Government spokesmen did argue—that, Britain, like the other members, would retain a right of veto where she felt her own national interests were at stake, this would also mean that others would have a similar veto to frustrate Britain's own wishes where they considered that their interests were in jeopardy.

Secondly, and as a consequence of this situation, the sovereignty of Parliament would also be gravely compromised. It would no longer be in a position, over a wide range of policy issues, effectively to control the actions of the Government. It would be confronted with a series of decisions emanating from Brussels in the elaboration and scrutiny of which it had no part; which it could neither amend or throw out; and concerning the execution of which it would be virtually powerless. Moreover, it would have no power of the purse with regard to the Community and so would lack one of its principal traditional weapons for bringing its influence to bear.

The protagonists of membership, for their part, sought to answer by insisting in the first place that there was no question of a 'surrender' of sovereignty. This word, they argued, had emotional connotations implying coercion on the part of the Community which was wholly untrue. What was involved was a voluntary process in which Britain, by her own free decision, would in the future be exercising sovereignty in association with her partners: pooling it, rather than giving it away or being forced to abandon it. There was nothing new in this: by her existing membership of a large number of international organisations Britain had already accepted a series of constraints upon her freedom of action, and had pooled her sovereignty to achieve certain objectives which on her own she could not hope to attain. The realities of the modern world made this absolutely necessary. Joining the Community would involve an extension of this process; a difference in degree, perhaps, but not of kind. In such a situation the Government would indeed forego the right to make certain decisions on its own, but this was necessary in order to achieve the benefits of membership. And as the Community as a voluntary association could only survive if it dealt equitably with the interests of its members, we should not anticipate having to accept decisions which ran counter to our interests. It was true, the argument continued, that there would be important repercussions on Parliament, but the answer to these lay on the one hand in devising ways in which the two Houses could be given an opportunity to discuss relevant Community business, and on the other, by strengthening the Community's own parliament.

So the argument went back and forward, with learned legal opinion being mobilised in support of the two positions. But if one strips away the polemics which it generated and examines the two positions with care, what emerges is less a disagreement about the facts of the case than the political conclusion to be drawn from these facts. There was relatively little disagreement about the nature of the constraints which membership would involve for both government and parliament. But whereas some concluded that those constraints were intolerable, those in favour of membership saw them as an acceptable and necessary part of entry.

Now that entry has taken place and those constraints are operating, the issue may appear to be somewhat academic. This, however, is not the case, even for those who have no wish to see the question of membership re-opened. For in a slightly different form the issue is one that has remained open throughout the development of the Community. It is indeed one that is bound to remain a central concern of any group of countries involved in a process of integration. This is the question of states' rights; in other words, how far the pooling of sovereignty should go and whether or not authority should be transferred by and from the constituent member states to an independent authority acting on their behalf.

In the following pages it should become clear how far that pooling has taken place up to the present time and the nature of the debate which has taken place on the issue within the founder members. As far as they are concerned, there are very few individuals or groups who reject the present arrangements though there are certainly those, and in particular the Gaullists and Communists, who insist very strongly that national governments should maintain ultimate sovereignty within the Community. That this is the case today is indisputable. The rules which the member countries have agreed to accept are self-imposed and national governments remain free to change the rules or unilaterally to declare them no longer operative. It is only if they had explicitly handed over power of amendment and abrogation or divested themselves of authority to make or unmake such agreements in the future that it would be legitimate to say that a 'surrender of sovereignty' had taken place.

This is far from being the case in the Community. The existing treaties contain no such provisions. They establish a substantial body of rules by which the members have agreed to abide, but there is no suggestion at any point that the member states have divested themselves of authority to change, rescind or abrogate these rules. There are indeed specific provisions in each of the treaties that any changes in the rules shall require a decision by the member states and also ratification by them. The question of unilateral withdrawal is not dealt with in any of them—for the good reason that none of the partners was willing to tie its own hands with regard to this matter. The absence of provisions, which has so alarmed some critics in this country, should on the contrary be a source of comfort to all those who are concerned about sovereignty. The silence on this means quite clearly that each of the signatories maintains absolute authority to take such a decision at any point in the future. The fact that the Treaty of Paris was concluded for a 50-year period and the other two for an unlimited period is irrelevant in this context.

The members of the Community are all free to withdraw from it at any point: it is because this is the case that such great care has to be exercised to obtain their agreement as each step is taken. There is no power within the Community that can force them to continue along this path: there is no army to coerce a reluctant partner.

There is therefore a clear distinction between a 'surrender' of sovereignty and the voluntary acceptance of self-imposed rules of conduct governing the exercise of sovereignty by a group of states. The former has not taken place in the Community: the latter has. The distinction is a very important one, and neither in theory nor practice is it diminished by the fact that the development of a process of integration may well create a situation in which the volume and intensity of the constraints increase along with the practical disadvantages of withdrawal. If the Community develops in a way that is considered satisfactory from the point of view of the security and welfare interests of each of its members they will have no incentive to withdraw. If, on the contrary, a member or group of members become dissatisfied and are unable to change it to suit their own objectives, they will still be able, in the last analysis, to withdraw from it. There is no doubt that before reaching this point every effort would be made to avoid so drastic a step, and that it would not happen unless an individual state or group of states had very powerful reasons for doing so. But of the right of each member to take such action, there can be absolutely no doubt.

DECISION-MAKING IN THE COMMUNITIES: SCOPE AND FORM

Before examining in some detail how the processes of decision-making are carried on within the Community it is first necessary to establish the scope of such decisions and their legal characteristics.

As we have seen in the last chapter, the scope of the Community has been significantly expanded since it first began in 1950. There are still, however, many significant policy areas which belong wholly to the sphere of each national government or in which the degree of intervention by the Community is slight. A useful checklist illustrating these points is provided by a table drawn up by two American political scientists *(Table 3.1)*. They have sought to construct a list covering all the policy areas in which modern states have become involved, and to assess the extent to which these have been affected by the evolving scope of the Community. The figures they give are essentially subjective, but nevertheless serve as an indicator of the evolving situation.

As one would expect, all the higher scores are concentrated in the area of economic functions (including economic aspects of external relations), but even here there is no single major policy area where all choices are made at the Community level. The figures in fact tend greatly to exaggerate the degree of 'Europeanisation' of decision-making because the ordinal rankings give no indication of the political distance that has to be travelled between for instance, points 3 and 4 on the scale. Nor does this type of listing attempt to distinguish the relative importance of the various policy sectors: if one were to attempt to show the relative weight of Community and national decision-making in terms of the saliency of policy areas for the performance of a state's primary security and welfare functions, the continued overwhelming predominance of the nation state would emerge quite starkly.

A further element which then needs to be added into the picture is the nature of the intervention by the Community in those policy fields where it has a role to play. This also varies substantially from case to case. One distinction made in the E.E.C. treaty is that between areas where common policies are to be applied (such as agriculture, transport, competition between firms in different member countries, and external trade) and those where co-ordinated or harmonised policies are to be sought. The first category implies at least the possibility of a rather far-reaching degree of integration; the second points rather to looser forms of organisation—though in practice the distinction between them tends to be rather blurred.

There are also very substantial differences between the degree of Community intervention with regard to the regulation of economic competition as between different sectors. While there is a very high degree of intervention in agriculture—to the extent, for instance, of regulating prices for most commodities—the activity of the Community in the industrial sector has for the most part been limited to creating the Common Market, seeking to harmonise certain aspects of competitive conditions, and applying a number of rules to the conduct of firms. Even in the case of the coal and steel sector where the Community requires the publication of prices it does not, except in exceptional circumstances, attempt to regulate them.

Table 3.1 THE SCOPE OF THE EUROPEAN COMMUNITY SYSTEM: 1950—1970

Key:
1. All decisions taken by national governments.
2. Only very beginning of Community involvement.
3. Both national governments and Community institutions involved, the former predominant.
4. Both involved, Community predominant.
5. All decisions taken by the Community

	1950	1957	1968	1970
External Relations Functions				
1. Military Security.	1	1	1	1
2. Diplomatic influence and participation in world affairs.	1	1	2	2
3. Economic and military aid to other polities.	1	1	2	2
4. Commercial relations with other polities.	1	1	3	4
Political—Constitutional Functions				
5. Public health and safety and maintenance of order.	1	1	2	2
6. Political participation.	1	1	1	1
7. Access to legal—normative system (civic authority).	1	2	3	3
Social—Cultural Functions				
8. Cultural recreational affairs.	1	1	1	1
9. Education and research.	1	1	3	3
10. Social welfare policies.	1	2	2	3
Economic Functions				
11. Counter-cyclical policy.	1	1	2	3
12. Regulation of economic competition and other government controls on prices and investments.	1	2	3	3
13. Agricultural protection.	1	1	4	4
14. Economic development and planning.	1	2	2	3
15. Exploitation and protection of natural resources.	1	2	2	2
16. Regulation and support of transportation.	1	2	2	3
17. Regulation and support of mass media of communication.	1	1	1	1
18. Labour—management relations.	1	1	1	1
19. Fiscal policy.	1	1	3	3
20. Balance of payments stability.	1	1	3	4
21. Domestic monetary policy.	1	1	2	2
22. Movement of goods, services, and other factors of production within the customs union.	1	2	4	4

Source: L. N. Lindberg and S. A. Scheingold. *Europe's Would-Be Polity,* New Jersey (1971) Table 3.1, p. 71.

All of this means that the policy issues dealt with by the Community cover a very wide spectrum of importance, from decisions in the agricultural field for instance, which are of major importance for the economy and budgets of the member states, to detailed provisions relating to the mutual recognition of professional qualifications the immediate economic significance of which is very limited.

The legal instruments at the disposal of the Community for taking action are similarly varied. Those provided under the two Rome treaties consist of regulations, directives, decisions, recommendations and opinions. The distinction between them has been put succinctly thus:[1]

> *Regulations* are of general application, they are binding in every respect and have direct force of law in every member state.
>
> *Directives* are binding on the member states to which they are addressed as regard the result to be achieved, but leave the mode and means to the discretion of the national authorities.
>
> *Decisions* may be addressed either to a government or to an enterprise or private individual. They are binding in every respect on the party or parties named.
>
> *Recommendations* and *opinions* which are not binding.[2]

In practice both the Council and the Commission have made an increasing use of regulations, and it is these which now account for the great bulk of Community measures, as can be seen from the data relating to 1970 (*Table 3.2*).

Regulations are self-executing: that is, once they have been agreed by the Community institutions they enter into force—once they have been published in the *Journal Officiel*—without any intervention on the part of national parliaments. Sometimes national governments find it necessary to make their own measures to ensure the detailed application of Community regulations, but this does not in any way affect the principle of their direct applicability. Most directives, on the other hand, require national legislation before they can be implemented, though in most of the original member countries, the governments do this by decrees or regulations which do not necessarily involve parliamentary scrutiny.[3] It is also likely that in Britain most directives will be

---

[1] Emile Noel, *How the European Community's Institutions Work*, Community Topics 38, European Communities Press and Information Service London (1972) p. 3.

[2] The nomenclature used in the Treaty of Paris relating to the E.C.S.C. is somewhat different. This provides for *decisions* which are binding in every respect (e.g. like E.E.C. regulations), *recommendations* which are binding as to ends but not to means (e.g. like E.E.C. directives), and *opinions* which are not binding. Most *decisions* taken in the framework of the E.C.S.C., unlike E.E.C. regulations, are directed to individuals or firms.

[3] For a succinct review of practice in the six countries see the Memorandum submitt-

Table 3.2 COMMUNITY LEGISLATION, 1970

Category	Council	Commission
Regulations	249	2 426
Decisions	71	435
Directives	25	3
Recommendations	—	7

Source: Emile Noel and Henri Etienne 'The Permanent Representatives Committee and the "deepening" of the Communities', *Government and Opposition* (Autumn 1971) p. 424 n. 1.

incorporated into the law by the procedures used for delegated legislation.[1]

DECISION-MAKING STRUCTURE

We now turn from the question of the scope and form of Community decisions to how and by whom they are taken. The most important point to be made in this context is the predominant role played by national governments—a role which has been strengthened rather than weakened as the Community has developed.

The general outline of the decision-making process can be simply stated (see *Figure 3.1*). Working within the terms of reference provided by the treaties the Commission puts forward proposals on which the Council of Ministers then decides. Two bodies are normally consulted before such decisions are taken: the European Parliament, consisting of parliamentarians from the member countries, and the Economic and Social Committee, a body representing a wide range of organised economic and social interests. This procedure applies to all major issues. Detailed administrative decisions required by the implementation of agreed policies are, on the other hand, normally taken by the Commission acting on its own within the powers given to it either by the treaties or a subsequent Council decision.

The decision-making structure has evolved to some extent over time, but not in the direction intended by at least some of the authors of the treaties. Those who wished to build up the 'supranational' elements in the system succeeded in inserting into the Rome treaties a number of

ed by the Foreign and Commonwealth Office in *Report from the Joint Committee on Delegated Legislation, Session 1971–1972*, (August 1972) H.M.S.O., London.

[1] See below, Chapter 7, pp. 174–177.

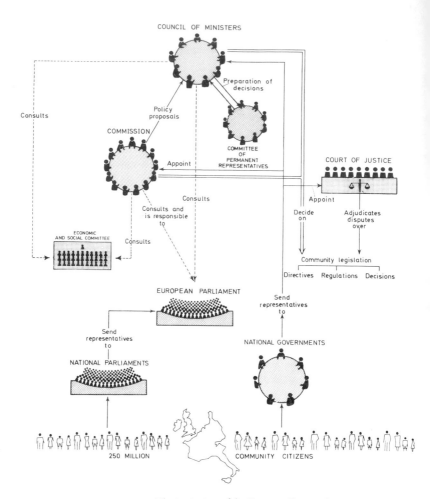

Figure 3.1 The Institutions of the European Community

mechanisms which were intended, over a period of time, to increase the authority of the Commission and the assembly. One of these was the requirement that as the customs union was gradually established over the transition period the voting procedure in the Council should switch from one requiring unanimity to one in which weighted majority votes should be used for an increasing number of issues. Whereas some 46 matters were listed in the treaty as requiring unanimity during the first stage of the transition period, this was to fall to 34 in the second stage and 27 in the third and final stages. Correspondingly the number of issues to be decided by weighted majority was to rise from about 24 in the first stage to 38 in the final stage. The basic idea was that as confidence developed between the partners they would be willing progressively to decide most issues by a majority vote rather than unanimity, and that this would gradually increase the weight of the Commission in the decision-making process. It was also proposed that once the external tariff was fully applied the Community should be financed from the proceeds of this rather than by annual contributions from national exchequers. This too was a device which it was thought would lessen the Community's dependence on national governments. Finally, to reinforce the authority of the European Parliament it was provided that its members could at some unspecified point in the future be directly elected. In short, a gradual strengthening of the nonnational elements in the institutional structure was envisaged as corresponding to a growing degree of economic integration.

In practice, however, this strategy has not worked as was intended. The Council has not so far taken action on direct elections to the assembly; it has only recently agreed to the direct financing of the Community—and then in a way which continues to give the member governments the decisive say in all major budgetary decisions; and, as a result of the 1965–1966 conflict, unanimity rather than weighted majority voting is still the rule rather than the exception. Other factors have also meant that the Commission–Council relationship has not developed as had originally been intended. Although the former body has acquired a substantial range of executive duties within the framework of the common policies agreed by the Council, it has not been able effectively to increase its authority in other ways within the Community. As a result of a 'fusion' of the executives carried out in 1967, a single Commission then took over the duties previously exercised separately by the High Authority and the two Commissions, but this did not change the situation either. As far as all major policy issues are concerned it is the member governments which continue to dominate the scene.

This dominance has been maintained not only because the national governments occupy a strategic position in the decision-making processes of the Community but also for a series of other reasons. One of these derives from the fact that although the Commission enjoys statutory independence from national governments, in the sense that it is forbidden to accept or solicit instructions from them, it is in fact heavily dependent on their goodwill. There are many reasons for this. In the first place its members are appointed by the national governments, and for relatively short periods of time (four years). At the end of that period they will only be renominated if they continue to enjoy the confidence of those governments; and as the treaty provision that each member shall be nominated by the governments acting in concert has proved to be a fiction, this means that each of them has to have retained the confidence of his own national government if he wishes to be re-elected. This is not a situation calculated to encourage a member to go out of his way to espouse views unacceptable in his national capital. When, for instance, the French president of the Euratom Commission, Etienne Hirsch, did so his term of office was not renewed. Except for those who are nearing retirement, members too are quite naturally concerned with their own careers; and in most cases preferment is only likely to come at the hands of, or with the support of, their national administrations.

As a body the Commission also lacks any substantial political resources of its own should it find itself in conflict with the governments. It has normally been able to gain the support of the members of the European Parliament, but this is in no sense a powerful body. If the Commission is to carry out the tasks assigned to it, it therefore has to seek to mobilise a winning coalition among the member governments. The temptation in such a situation is evidently that of seeking agreement on the lowest common denominator, and not to force the pace unduly.

Given these factors it is not surprising that the experience of this type of body in the Community has been rather mixed. None of them has been able to secure a substantial and permanent extension of their authority vis-à-vis the national governments. Before the fusion of the executives both the High Authority and the Euratom Commission had for some years been in decline, and although in its early years the E.E.C. Commission under Walter Hallstein seemed to be remarkably successful the single Commission which now serves all three Communities has not acquired similar prestige. At first, during the presidency (1967–1971) of the former Belgian minister Jean Rey it seemed that this might be due primarily to the presence of de Gaulle who lost no opportunity in seeking to cut the Commission down to size. But since the Hague Summit, when the general climate in the Community has been radically transformed, the experience of the Commission under Maria Malfatti and subsequently Sicco Mansholt suggests that other factors have been at work. One of these undoubtedly is the purely bureaucratic phenomenon that, as the Commission's administrative responsibilities have grown, it has tended to become absorbed in matters of detail and has had much less time to devote to major strategic issues. Its internal organisation has also failed to respond adequately to its growing range of tasks; and its collegial cohesion has been undermined both by the manner of its appointment and also its representative functions, which have meant that most of its members have spent frequent periods away from Brussels.

Two other factors have also played a significant part in undermining the role of the Commission. One is that the application of the existing treaties has revealed a number of grey areas—particularly in the field of external relations—where the respective roles of the Commission and the Council were not clearly specified. In these areas the Council and its various subsidiary bodies have boldly asserted the authority of the national governments. But even more important is the fact that in the two policy areas which are now, since the ending of the E.E.C.'s transitional period, the most crucial for the future development of the Community—economic and monetary union and political union—the role of the Commission has remained ill-defined. No new treaties have been established to regulate decision-making procedures in these areas and, once again, the vacuum has been filled by the member governments.

These have firmly asserted their own authority, by creating a series of what are in effect intergovernmental bodies to conduct studies and to make proposals. Although the Commission takes part in their work and puts forward its own views and proposals, the decision-making process which has evolved is one in which it takes a subsidiary rather than a central role. To it the name of 'concertation' has been given; this type of procedure, for which no fixed rules have been established, has come to occupy an increasingly important part in the life of the Community.

The total effect of these various pressures has been to tilt the institutional balance within the Community in a way that was admirably summed up in the report of a working group set up by the Commission to examine the enlargement of the powers of the European Parliament. Working under the chairmanship of Professor Georges Vedel, it reported in 1972 that:[1]

> The provisions and the general philosophy of the E.E.C. treaty, carrying on a trend which had already become visible in the E.C.S.C., lay down that the Council shall be predominant in taking

[1] *Report of the working party examining the problem of the enlargement of the European Parliament*, Brussels (March 1972) p. 29.

Community decisions. But practice has served only continually to increase this preponderance to such a point that the Council, acting in some instances as a Community body and in others as the States in concert, has become the sole effective centre of power in the system. This trend has certainly not had the effect of breaking the close organic connection which the Treaty sought to establish between the Council and the Commission—quite the contrary—but the collaboration between the two bodies has been marked by an increasing imbalance in favour of the Council.

The Vedel Report also noted that there had been an increasing tendency for the Community's decision-making process to consist of 'pure, diplomatic-style negotiations'; for political initiatives to originate outside the Community's institutions themselves; and for making strategic decisions to be taken in Summit meetings.

All of this may offer some considerable comfort to those, particularly in Britain, who have expressed fears about the 'surrender' of national sovereignty. On the other hand, these developments have also created a number of problems regarding the effective functioning of the Community and also its democratic aspects. These will become more apparent once we have analysed in some more detail how the various institutions of the Community actually operate.

THE COUNCIL OF MINISTERS

At the apex of the Community's regular decision-making process stands the Council of Ministers, consisting of representatives of each of the member governments. The composition of the Council varies according to the nature of the business to be transacted; for the important general issues the Foreign Ministers normally attend, their departmental colleagues dealing with business directly related to their own specific areas of competence. But frequently meetings are attended by more than one minister, which can create conflicts of competence within individual governments.

Each member country has had to set up an apparatus in its national capital to resolve such conflicts and to determine policy issues arising in the Community.[1] While in each of them it is normally the cabinet which resolves conflicts between different departments and their interests—though in France under both de Gaulle and Pompidou the head of state has been accustomed to intervene regularly in this process —each country has also had to set up an apparatus for the preparation

[1] See Helen S. Wallace, 'The impact of the Communities on national policy-making', *Government and Opposition*, (Autumn 1971).

of such decisions. Two main types of organisation have emerged. In the French case there has been a high degree of centralisation, achieved through the work of the *Secrétariat Général pour la coordination interministerielle* whose secretary has access to the highest levels in the governmental system, and whose staff is selected for its high level of competence. In the Federal Republic, however, persistent rivalry between the Foreign and Economics ministries has prevented the emergence of a similarly powerful body, and has frequently led to conflicting views being expressed in Brussels. Under Chancellor Brandt an attempt to remedy this situation was made with the appointment of Frau Focke as a State Secretary for European Affairs attached to the Chancellor's own office, a move which met with some success. Britain and the other new members are now facing the same problem of how best to organise their own governmental machinery to deal with Community matters: an issue which has already led to a great deal of departmental pushing and shoving in Whitehall both between individual departments and also within them.[1]

The definition and vigorous promotion of each national interest is a necessary element in the Community's political system, and it is the essential task of the Council to find a basis on which these conflicting interests can be reconciled. In practice discussion normally continues until general agreement is reached. Since the Luxembourg compromise of 1966 each government has maintained its right to use a veto on any issue it considers to be of vital national importance and little use has been made of weighted majority voting which is the method by which, if the treaty were fully observed, many decisions would now be taken. In the enlarged Community the votes of the various members are weighted in the following manner:

Britain, Germany, France, Italy	10 votes each
Belgium, the Netherlands	5 votes each
Denmark, Ireland	3 votes each
Luxembourg	2 votes

Out of this total of 58 votes 41 are required if a proposal is one put forward by the Commission; otherwise it can only be adopted if at least six countries contribute to the required 41 positive votes. It will be noted that this system does not allow the four larger countries to force through a decision against the others, nor equally does it permit a coalition of the smaller countries to outvote these four.

Among the Council members, the president, who is chosen by rote according to a pre-determined alphabetical list of the member countries

---

[1] See below, Chapter 7, pp. 171–174.

to serve for a six-month period, occupies a particularly important position.[1] It is upon his shoulders that the responsibility rests for maintaining the rhythm of the Council's work, and initiating and guiding the informal discussions which take place at each stage of the Council's business, and which can be of crucial importance at times of stress.

The Council and its subordinate bodies are serviced by a Secretariat —whose members are Community civil servants rather than national officials—whose own size and importance has grown with the development of the role of the Council and its associated organs. It does not formally have the right, however, of making policy proposals, active though it is in the background in clarifying issues and promoting agreement between the national representatives.

The rhythm of the Council's work imposes a very considerable strain both on this secretariat and also the individual ministers involved. In 1969 ministerial sessions (including meetings of the various Councils of Associations and negotiating conferences) took up a total of $80\frac{1}{2}$ days; the following year this rose to 91 days, of which about half in both cases were devoted to agricultural matters.[2] This meant that in the six-member Community the Ministers of Agriculture were sometimes meeting as often as twice a month, and the Foreign Ministers regularly for two days each month. It is unlikely that in the enlarged Community the burden will be reduced and, although it will be unevenly spread over the various departments of government, for some ministers it will constitute an undeniably heavy load.

Once assembled around the table the ministers, together with representatives of the Commission who take part in discussions but do not vote, are normally confronted with an agenda divided into two sections, A and B. The matters figuring in the first of these are those which have already been resolved by the Committee of Permanent Representatives[3] and are adopted without debate. This procedure was first adopted in 1962 as a result of the increasing pressure of Council business and has accounted for a growing proportion of its total output. The Council nevertheless has more than enough business to occupy itself under section B of the agenda, a substantial part of which consists normally of Commission proposals on which no agreement has yet been reached. In considering these the Council has before it a synthesis

[1] The member state from whom the president is chosen is also responsible for chairing Coreper and many of the other bodies mentioned below (see pp. 67–69) during the six-month period. This is a heavy burden for the smaller member states, but in the six-member Community it was shouldered by the Luxembourg representatives with notable success.

[2] Data given by Emile Noel and Henri Etienne, 'The Permanent Representatives Committee and the "deepening" of the Communities', *Government and Opposition* (Autumn 1971), p. 447.

[3] See next section.

of the work carried out by the Committee of Permanent Representatives indicating the major issues to be resolved. The treaty lays down that the Council can only amend a Commission proposal by a unanimous vote, but it also allows the Commission to amend its proposals up to the moment of the final vote. What in practice normally takes place is a mutual adjustment of positions with the Commission (assisted by the president of the Council) acting as broker, with the aim of arriving at a generally acceptable compromise while maintaining as far as possible the substance of its original proposal. In this process the Commission frequently produces revised proposals during the course of the discussions, though it has increasingly been confronted by a unanimous decision on the part of the member states to depart from the proposals put before them.

Quite frequently, however, an issue is referred back to the Permanent Representatives for further consideration. This may be necessary because one or more of the member governments insists on maintaining its position; because some technical aspects need further study; or simply because the issue is not considered ripe for resolution. In the past there have been many occasions when a cluster of individual decisions on which decisions have been deferred have only been taken after a package deal has been constructed offering a balance of advantages over a set of issues. The construction and successful negotiation of such package deals has often involved the Council in marathon sessions stretching over periods of several days—or even a succession of meetings spread over a period of weeks—at the end of which, perhaps because of mutual exhaustion, the neccessary decisions have at last been reached, after much manouvering in the corridors, or in the privacy of the president's office, in the early hours of the morning.

Some British voices have already been raised against this technique of decision by attrition, but it will be surprising if habits acquired over the past 20 years will now be discarded. Indeed, during the negotiations for membership Mr. Rippon showed that he too was prepared to sit through the night in order to obtain a decision. The strain on individual ministers can, however, be considerable and some way will undoubtedly have to be found in the future to ease the burden on the Council while maintaining its responsibility for decisions on major policy issues.

THE COMMITTEE OF PERMANENT REPRESENTATIVES

Already at an early stage in the development of the Coal and Steel Community the ministers found the need for a body of senior officials to prepare their meetings and deal with routine business, and in the

Rome treaties it was agreed that the Council's rules of procedure might provide for 'the establishment of a committee of representatives of Member States'. It was left to the Council to determine the tasks and competence of such a body. But that was all, and it was not until the treaty dealing with the merger of the executives was agreed in 1965 that formal recognition was given to a body which by that time had emerged as an extremely important part of the Community's institutions. This was the Committee of Permanent Representatives —usually known in Community circles as Coreper[1]—consisting of one senior official, having ambassadorial rank, from each of the member states.

The tasks of this Committee, as specified in that treaty, are to prepare the work of the Council and carry out the latter's mandate. These two short phrases hardly do justice to the very wide range of functions which the Permanent Representatives now perform, nor indeed to their political significance. To deal with the volume of business which is now their concern each of them now has a high-powered staff consisting of senior officials from a variety of their home departments;[2] and the Committee itself has spawned an extensive range of specialised committees, working groups and ad hoc task forces. In these, many home-based civil servants also take part, flying in and out as required. The rhythm of work is intense, as can be judged from the figures shown in *Table 3.3*.

Table 3.3 MEETINGS OF PERMANENT REPRESENTATIVES AND ASSOCIATED BODIES, 1969 and 1970

No. of days in:	1969	1970
Sessions of the Permanent Representatives' Committee	129	153
Meetings of experts and other committees	1 417$\frac{1}{2}$	1 632$\frac{1}{2}$

Source: Emile Noel and Henri Etienne, *op. cit.*, p. 447.

Not all Commission proposals pass through the Committee of Permanent Representatives—agricultural matters, for instance, are dealt with by a separate Special Committee on Agriculture which has jealously guarded its own autonomy—but the great bulk of them are dealt with by Coreper. It is its task to scrutinise them in the light of the different national positions as well as the views of the European Parliament and the Economic and Social Committee (though the latter two are much less significant in their deliberations than the former). The

[1] *Comité des Representants Permanants.*

[2] The size of the delegations varies: that of the Federal Republic was the largest in 1971 with 45 members. The British delegation is now of nearly comparable strength.

preliminary stages of this process are carried out in specialist sub-committees, the Permanent Representatives themselves reserving their own energies for the resolution of major political issues once the technical aspects have been clarified. Representatives of the Commission's staff take part in all these discussions, and between them and those representing the member states an intensive negotiation takes place, in which the Commission has to exercise a fine judgment whether or not, and how far, to revise its original proposals in the cause of reaching agreement.

It is in such discussion, often extending over weeks and months, that the really hard grinding work of decision-making is carried on. But the Committee of Permanent Representatives has also steadily acquired a range of additional functions, not least those concerned with the conduct of the Community's external relations. These include the preparation of Council directives to the Commission for trade and tariff negotiations; drawing up general directives for the Community's position in meetings of the various Association Councils—and leading for the Community when these Councils meet at ambassadorial level; preparing the negotiations for the renewal and amendment of the relevant association agreements; and conducting on behalf of the Community its contact meetings with representatives of the countries of Latin America. The Permanent Representatives have also become a forum where nominations to the Commission are discussed, as well as the choice of its president; and during the period leading up to enlargement it was also they who formed the members of the 'interim committee' which was set up by the Community to allow for consultations on current issues with the countries who had signed the treaty of accession. Loyalty has developed within the group, more striking in some ways than that achieved by the Commission. Without this there is no doubt that the Community would have had much more difficulty in sustaining the strains which have been imposed upon it. Critics of the system nevertheless point to the fact that many decisions are now being taken by what is essentially a bureaucratic body and that the Community's institutional structure, which was devised with a different type of development in mind, provides insufficient opportunities for the scrutiny and criticism of their work.

ORGANS OF CONCERTATION

This criticism also extends to the plethora of specialised high-level committees which have grown up over the years and which report direct to the Council of Ministers. These include the Monetary Committee, the Medium-term Economic Policy Committee, the Short-term

Economic Policy Committee, the Budget Policy Committee and the Committee for the Co-ordination of Short-term Economic and Monetary Policy (which was set up in 1972). Composed of very senior national officials together with representatives of the staff of the Commission, their task is to prepare those ministerial meetings at which problems of economic and monetary co-operation are to be discussed. In these committees the initiation of policy proposals is shared by all the participants rather than being the exclusive right of the Commission, so that their proceedings are much more like those of an intergovernmental system than the original Community method of a dialogue between the Commission and the Council.

Another, and more recent, innovation has been the establishment, under the chairmanship of the President of the Council, of a Standing Committee on Employment, composed of national ministers, the Commission and both sides of industry. This is a consultative body whose establishment has not impaired the formal decision-making powers of either the Commission or the Council. But given the nature of its composition it may well come to play a determining role with regard to policies in this area. In institutional terms it appears to represent a further erosion of the Community's original decision-making procedures.

A great deal of argument has also developed about the institutional structures and methods to be employed in other relatively new policy areas, including those concerned with industrial and scientific policy. While the Commission has been urging that Community-type procedures should be used, with, for instance, consultative bodies to be attached to itself, some of the member states have shown a marked preference either for intergovernmental types of organisation, or for the creation of mixed committees reporting to and being directly responsible to the Council itself. Such discussions have blocked progress in several spheres, and are a further indication of how in many important respects the institutional development of the Community is still very much open to question.

THE COMMISSION

While the Commission, as a result of these pressures operating on the institutional structure of the Community, has certainly not fulfilled the expectations that some placed in it—and which others feared—it nevertheless continues to fulfil a range of crucial functions. These are particularly important with regard to the day-to-day running of the Communities, where it plays a predominant role. And alongside this executive function it also performs three others which are essential to maintain the momentum of their work: policy initiation, mediation between conflicting national interests, and a general supervisory function with regard to the implementation and respect of the treaties.

The Commission currently consists of 13 members each nominated by the member governments for a term of four years.[1] The four larger countries have each two of their nationals as members, the remainder one each. They do not sit, however, as representatives of their countries; on assuming office they are required to take an oath that they will neither seek nor accept instructions from any government or other body, and will perform their duties 'in the general interest of the Community with complete independence'. Collectively the Commission is responsible to the European Parliament by whom it can be voted out of office on a motion of censure if this is supported by two thirds of those voting and a majority of the total membership. The Commission has a staff of Community civil servants which in 1972 numbered some 5000 and which is currently being expanded, particularly in the lower administrative, executive, clerical and linguistic grades, to meet the needs of the enlarged Community. It is organised in a number of General Directorates *(Directions Générales)* corresponding with the various policy sectors with which it is concerned, together with various specialised services. Each individual member of the Commission is responsible for one or more of the General Directorates, the practice of the High Authority in having several members sharing responsibility for the major policy areas through a system of working groups having been discarded.[2]

A substantial part of the work of several of the General Directorates is now concerned with the routine administration of the Community's policies, and in particular of the common agricultural policy. Most of the regulations enacted by the Commission in recent years, for instance, have been concerned with agricultural matters. The implementation of this particular policy also involves the Commission in

[1] The composition of the Commission which took office in January 1973, on the enlargement of the Community, is as follows:

President: Francois Xavier Ortoli (Fr.)

Vice-Presidents: Wilhelm Haferkamp (Ger.); Patrick Hillery (Ire.); Carlo Scarascia Mugnozza (It.); Henri Simonet (Belg.); Sir Christopher Soames (U.K.).

Members: Albert Borschette (Lux.); Ralf Dahrendorf (Ger.); Jean-Francois Deniau (Fr.); Finn Olav Gundelach (Den.); Petrus Lardinois (Neths.); Altiero Spinelli (It.); George Thomson (U.K.). (In April 1973 M. Claude Cheysson (Fr.) replaced M. Deniau on the latter's appointment to a post in the French government.)

[2] For a discussion of the implications of this, see Emile Noel, Speech to the Società Italiana per L'Organizzazione Internazionale (9 March 1972) reproduced in *Europe Documents*, No. 677 (15 May 1972) published by the Brussels-based private news agency, *Agence Europe*.

very detailed day-to-day decisions with regard to the management of the markets for the individual products. To assist it in this task a Management Committee has been set up for each of the main groups of products, consisting of officials of each member states under the chairmanship of a senior member of the Commission's staff. It is with these bodies that the Commission discusses the action it proposes to take, the institutional arrangement allowing it both to maintain close contact with national interests and at the same time a considerable degree of freedom. When a draft measure is submitted to a Management Committee its national members express their opinion on it by means of a vote which is weighted as in the Council of Ministers. Unless there is a weighted majority against the proposal the Commission is entitled to carry out its proposals; in the case of a hostile majority the issue can be taken to the Council of Ministers which has the right within one month to reverse the Commission's decision. In practice, however, very few issues are taken to the Council and the system gives the Commission a large measure of effective authority in the actual operation of the various marketing arrangements.

Several of the other common policies involve the Commission in detailed administrative action directed to ensure that individual governments and companies comply with the Community's rules. A particular case in point is its activity with regard to competition policy. This involves it in a great deal of detailed administrative work, which includes the registration of agreements between firms in different countries and decisions on whether or not such agreements are in conformity with the Community's rules of competition. This has now become a major activity in its own right. The Commission has had to deal with 36 000 registered agreements. It has gradually been establishing a body of principles on the basis of which it can deal with the various types of agreements as well as taking action against those which it considers inadmissible. In several cases this has led not only to the imposition of substantial fines, but also to subsequent litigation in the Court of Justice.

The execution of common policies also involves the Commission in the administration of several types of funds. The most important of these is the Agricultural Guidance and Guarantee Fund which in 1972 had a budget of $3526 million, the bulk of which went to cover market support costs. In addition, it administers Euratom's research and training programme (about $90 million per annum), the European Social Fund (now running at just over $100 million per annum from Community funds), and the European Development Fund for the Community's overseas associates (currently $1000 million for the five-year period 1971–1975).

The administration of the various safeguard clauses has also been entrusted to the Commission: most of those in the E.E.C. treaty were only valid up to the end of the transition period (that is, until the end of 1969) but other types of waivers and exceptional measures continue to be required, not least those which have become necessary as a result of the impact of currency fluctuations on the marketing and price mechanisms of the common agricultural policy.

Alongside this work the Commission is also responsible for the elaboration of policy proposals for submission to the Council. This involves a lengthy and complex set of procedures. An individual General Directorate once given the responsibility for drawing up a proposal will undertake discussions with a wide range of interests—including informal sounding of national administrations and relevant Community-wide interest groups—before preparing a draft for the Commission. This will also have to be scrutinised by its legal services before it is formally placed on the agenda for one of the Commission's weekly meetings. These are prepared by members of the *cabinets* (private offices) of the Commission. At this stage an effort will be made to clarify the technical aspects of the proposal, and also to reconcile what may be the divergent positions of the various General Directorates. It is at this level, too, that detailed scrutiny will be given to the less important issues which, due to pressure of business, are dealt with by a written procedure.

The Commission itself can, and frequently does, reach its decisions by majority vote, though as in other Community institutions strenuous efforts are normally made to arrive at decisions which command the assent of all its Members. How smoothly the Commission operates depends a great deal on the personalities of its Members, and also the effectiveness of its president, who is nominated by the member governments for a two-year term.

Once a proposal has been agreed by the Commission its major task is then to seek support for it in the European Parliament and the Economic and Social Committee, and to defend it in the lengthy process of scrutiny to which it will be subjected by the Permanent Representatives and—if agreement on it has not been reached at this stage—by the Council itself. It is during this phase of decision-making that the Commission exercises its mediatory and brokerage functions, and if necessary adjusts its proposals to this end. As the strength of the national element in the decision-making process has increased this has become a more and more arduous part of the Commission's work which in the case of an individual proposal may be spread out over a period of months or even years.

A further function performed by the Commission is that of acting as a watchdog over the correct implementation of the treaties, and ensuring that all concerned carry out the obligations deriving from them.

This function it performs in the following way:[1]

> Where the Commission concludes that the Treaty has been in-
> fringed—which it may do either on the strength of an investigation
> by its own officials, or at the instance of a government, or following
> complaints from individuals—it requests the state in question to
> submit its comments or counter-arguments within a specified period
> (usually a month or a month and a half). If the member state allows
> the arrangement complained of to continue and its comments do not
> cause the Commission to change its minds, the Commission issues a
> reasoned opinion with which the state must comply by the date set;
> if the state fails to do so, the Commission may refer the matter to the
> Court of Justice whose judgement is binding on both the state and
> the Institutions.

In 1970 the Commission instituted proceedings for infringement in
50 cases, and decided to refer two to the Court. In the great majority of
cases the infringments of which the Commission has complained have
been of a technical nature, and related to the detailed application of the
customs union. Sometimes they have arisen because of disagreement
between the Commission and a member state on the exact meaning of a
regulation or a directive; in other cases, and this seems to have been
particularly true of a number of complaints lodged against the Italian
Government, because of bureaucratic slowness in taking action
required by Community decisions. Typical cases have involved dis-
criminatory national taxation on individual products, a number of
which have only been resolved by recourse to the Community's Court
of Justice.

This aspect of the work of the Commission in ensuring the observance of the treaties in an impartial manner is not one which normally
attracts much publicity. It is nevertheless an important part of its functions which, taken together, are an essential element in the functioning
of the Community. The question of how its role may develop in the
future is still very much an open question. Some continue to see it as
the nucleus of a future federal government; others share very strongly
the views of President Pompidou that this is not feasible or desirable.[2]

> Some people imagined (after the war) that Europe could be organ-
> ised around a number of technical organisations, of commissions,
> which would be a kind of prefiguration of a European federation.
> Times have changed. Europe can only mean building, on the basis
> of what exists, a confederation of states . . . The idea of achieving

[1] Emile Noel, *How the European Community's Institutions Work*. Community Topics
38, European Communities Press and Information Service, London (1972) p. 4.

[2] Press conference, 21 January 1971.

confederation on the basis of technical organisations, of commissions, is an illusion that has already been swept away by the facts. The government of Europe can only arise out of the gatherings of national governments, joining together to take decisions that are valid for all.

The issue remains open. It is one to which we shall return having first completed this review of the Community's existing institutions by examining the role played by its two major consultative organs, the European Parliament and the Economic and Social Committee.

THE EUROPEAN PARLIAMENT

Before a Commission proposal is discussed in the Council of Ministers it is sent to the European Parliament for its opinion. It will be clear from the proceeding discussion, however, that the body does not perform a legislative function comparable with that of national parliamentary bodies. What role then does it play in the Community?

To begin to answer this question it is necessary first of all to trace briefly the evolution of the Community's parliament through the successive stages of its development. In the original Schuman Plan there was no mention of any such body. At an early stage of the negotiations, however, the idea of a Parliamentary Assembly was put forward to provide a representative element in the institutional structure. As it emerged in the Treaty of Paris, the Assembly—consisting of 78 delegates appointed by the parliaments of the member countries—was much more akin to an assembly of shareholders than a normal parliamentary body. It was to meet once a year, receive an annual report from the High Authority and to have the right, if a censure motion on the report was supported by a majority of its members and two-thirds of those voting, to force the resignation of that body. The High Authority was not normally required to consult it before taking a decision: this consultative function was to be exercised by a committee consisting of producers, workers, consumers and dealers. In other words the High Authority's relationship with the Assembly was conceived very much like that of the board of a company, left to conduct the affairs of an enterprise and required only to report once a year on how things were going. Unlike a normal body of shareholders, however, the Assembly was not even given the right of electing the new board if it disapproved of the actions of the High Authority: this was a task reserved for the member governments. Nor was there any suggestion that in such a case, or indeed at any point, was the approval of the Assembly required before the governments' nominees could take office.

The initial parliamentary element in the E.C.S.C. was therefore extremely slender. And although the treaty contained a provision that its members might be directly elected by a procedure to be determined 'by each of the respective High Contracting Parties there was no suggestion when the treaty came into effect that any of them proposed to take action on these lines.

It is hardly surprising that when the Assembly met in September 1952 (it became known as the 'Common Assembly' in the expectation that it would also serve the E.D.C.) its members set to work to enlarge their functions as far as possible. This they did with a fair measure of success, because the High Authority rapidly realised that the body offered it the possibility of much-needed political support. The annual session was split into several sessions; recourse was had from time to time to extraordinary sessions as provided for in the treaty; and a series of committees was set up to enable the Assembly to maintain continuity in its work and regular scrutiny of the activities of the High Authority. Between the two institutions a close working relationship was established. The High Authority consulted the Assembly about its policies and proposals; its presidents also voluntarily adopted the habit of making a policy statement to the Assembly on their assumption of office. The development of the relationship was much aided by the fact that those who became members of the Assembly were for the most part ardent supporters of integration. The Communist parties of France and Italy, who were at this stage bitterly hostile, were both excluded by the method of election to the Assembly adopted by the national parliaments in those two countries, and those who were not interested in the Communities rarely bothered to seek election to it. It rapidly became therefore an institutionalised pressure group of European enthusiasts, cheering on the High Authority. There was only one occasion when a vote of censure was seriously threatened, and that by the socialists who wished to see the High Authority following a more active social policy. Some significant differences of emphasis emerged between them and the majority of Christian Democrats, but both were firm in their support of integration as such. The Assembly had in the meantime decided to sit in plenary session by party affiliation rather than by alphabetical order or national delegation, and in this and other ways the institution began to acquire the appearance, if it still lacked the real substance, of a genuine European parliamentary body. In 1958 it was able to congratulate itself—and not improperly—on a real measure of achievement since it first came into being.[1]

---

[1] Pierre Wigny, *L'Assemblée Parlementaire dans l'Europe des Six*, Luxembourg (1958).

It nevertheless required a certain amount of pressure on its part to prevent those responsible for the Rome treaties setting up separate assemblies for each of the new Communities. As it was, a more rational solution prevailed, and the membership of the Common Assembly was enlarged to enable it to serve as the assembly for all three. It then consisted of 142 members divided as follows:

Germany, France, Italy	36 seats each
Belgium, the Netherlands	14 seats each
Luxembourg	6 seats.

Subsequently the members of the parliament themselves decided to give the institution the title of 'European Parliament': a step taken initially by the Dutch and Germans, and followed somewhat later by the Francophones and the Italians.

The new treaties themselves accepted the type of de facto relationship that had developed between the High Authority and the Common Assembly by providing that where either of the Commissions were required to present proposals to the Council the parliament should be consulted before a decision was taken. They also relaxed the provisions relating to a vote of censure, no longer tying this to a discussion of an annual report. They did not, however, increase the Assembly's legislative or budgetary powers, and while including a provision for eventual direct elections in the treaties and asking the assembly itself to draw up proposals for this, they made no commitments as to when—if ever —this provision was to be activated. So while there was some progress in comparison with the Treaty of Paris, the substantive role accorded to the Assembly was only a pale shadow of a genuine European Parliament.

Since that time the Council has continued to keep a tight rein on the Assembly both in terms of its powers and the method of its election. It is only recently, following the Hague Summit and the subsequent agreement reached by the Council on a new system of financing the Community from its 'own resources' that it has been given a modest increase of its own with regard to the budget.[1] It has therefore had an almost exclusively consultative role within the institutional structure. Similarly, although the Parliament duly approved a set of proposals which it drew up in 1960 providing for the direct election of its members, the Council has so far taken no action on them. Nor has anything so far been done at the national level to implement various schemes which have been put forward in the individual member parliaments for the direct election of individual national delegations. Its members have therefore continued to be elected by each national parliament, each of

[1] See below, p. 81 and pp. 91–97.

which has adopted its own procedure for the purpose.[1] One significant development was the admission in 1968, for the first time, of Communist parliamentarians from Italy, a delayed consequence of the *apertura a sinistra* in that country. Its seven representatives promptly took an active part in its proceedings, providing—along with the 14 Gaullists —a new sort of opposition within the parliament and a very healthy reminder of the political realities with which the Community has to deal.[2]

In the enlarged Community the number of members of the European Parliament has been increased from 142 to 198, the national representation being as follows:

Britain, France, Germany, Italy	36 members each
Belgium, the Netherlands	14 members each
Denmark, Ireland	10 members each
Luxembourg	6 members

They are nominated by the member parliaments according to a procedure determined by each member state. In the British case the delegation consists of 18 Conservatives, 2 Liberals and 1 Cross-Bench Peer —with 15 places reserved for the Labour Party, which has so far refused to be represented. Enlargement could lead to a substantial shift in the relative strengths of the various party groups within the Parliament, the socialists now being potentially the largest single group with 58 seats (once the Labour Party is represented) rather than—as was the case throughout the period 1950–1972—the Christian Democrats whose total is now 55 seats.

The internal life of the Parliament revolves very largely around its political groups, the minimum number for the constitution of a formally-recognised group having been lowered from 17 to 14 under pressure from the Gaullists (and in spite of a great deal of resistance to the recognition of a group all of whose members were nationals of the same country). Formal constitution as a group is of considerable importance as it gives access both to financial and other resources (including office space) from the Parliament for group activities, (though the Italian Communists who are under the minimum number have been given some assistance) and also leverage in elections to the officers of the parliament. These consist principally of a president and eleven vice-presidents. Collectively these constitute the *Bureau* which is responsible for the administration and staff of the Parliament and the organisation of its work.

[1] For details, see Henri Manzanares, *Le Parlement Européen,* Paris (1964) pp. 54–57.

[2] For an account of the P.C.I.'s representatives first two years in the European Parliament see Giorgio Amendola, *I communisti e l'Europa,* Rome (1971).

The headquarters and secretariat of the Parliament are located in Luxembourg, but its plenary sessions—which in recent years have increased to a total of about 45 days divided into 10 or 11 sittings—are held both there and Strasbourg. Originally all of them were held in the latter place, in the building used by the Council of Europe, partly because the French Government was anxious to have one Community institution meeting on its territory, and partly because the Six collectively wished to make a gesture towards that wider Europe of which the Council was the primary symbol.[1] The inconvenience of constantly moving there has however led to the present situation in which five or six of the longer sessions, each lasting a week, are held in Strasbourg, while the remaining shorter sessions (two to three days each) take place in Luxembourg.

These plenary sessions represent only a part, however, of the total work load of the members which for an even moderately conscientious parliamentarian now occupies about 100 days each year. The balance is made up by meetings of the various committees of the Parliament of which there are now some 300 meetings each year. It is here that the substantive work of the Parliament is done, the individual committees covering the various functional areas of the Community's activities (agriculture, transport, foreign trade, etc.). Once a proposal has been transmitted by the Council to the Parliament it is passed on to one or more of these committees which then appoints a rapporteur to draft a report and an opinion on it. This is discussed initially in the committee itself, and having been approved, is then placed on the agenda of a plenary session. When this in turn has deliberated, the report is transmitted back to the Commission and Council.

While this activity of submitting reports on proposed legislative acts is the main staple of the Parliament's activity, it has also developed a series of techniques for scrutinising the work of the Commission and Council. One of the most effective of these is the written question to which a written reply is required. In the parliamentary year 1969–1970 for instance, 477 of these were addressed to the Commission and 30 to the Council. Oral questions are also put from time to time, but are used much less frequently: in 1969–1970 only 15 were put to the Commission.

The frequent presence of members of the Commission at committee meetings is also another way in which the Parliament is able to inform itself—and to exercise some influence upon—the activities of this body. Relations with the Council of Ministers have always been much more distant, and a source of irritation and frustration to the members of the Parliament. The Council is under no obligation to inform the

[1] The annual joint session with the Consultative Assembly of the Council of Europe, normally held in the autumn, originated from the same desire.

Parliament of the action it has taken (if any) on the opinions it has submitted, and the Parliament for its part has virtually no political leverage on the organ where final policy decisions are taken. Since 1959, however, an annual colloquy has been held in November with the Council which has enabled the parliamentarians to meet the ministers face-to-face. From time to time ministers have also come to make statements at plenary sessions. The amount of information they have been willing to provide has, however, been rather less than the members of the Parliament will have been able to glean from newspaper reports or the extremely well-informed pages of the daily bulletins issued by *Agence Europe*.

In spite of the essential weakness of its position in the decision-making processes of the Community the Parliament has undoubtedly exercised some influence upon them, though the extent of this influence is extremely difficult to gauge. The main thrust of its work has been to encourage the Commission and its predecessors in their activities and to support the on-going process of integration. During the sixties for instance it added its voice in favour of an acceleration of the time-table for the customs union, encouraged the member states to pursue their negotiations for a treaty on political union, pressed them to activate plans for closer cultural cooperation (including the establishment of a European university) and welcomed the Commission's 1965 proposals for direct funding of the Community from customs duties and levies. The majority of its members went on the record on successive occasions in favour of an enlargement of the Community, though the arrival of Gaullist members introduced a minority which faithfully reflected de Gaulle's views on this issue. On individual issues, however, the Parliament has not simply acted as an approving chorus for all that the Commission proposed. This was notably the case with regard to its original proposals for the introduction of a value-added tax, which it thought much too cumbrous. On this occasion it rejected the Commission's proposal, and found itself in agreement with the Council whose eventual decision was in line with the views expressed in that parliament. A similar criticism was made of the Commission's proposals for opening up tenders for the public sector: on this occasion the Commission itself modified its proposals.

On the critical issue of agricultural policy the Parliament itself has usually been divided. Its agricultural committee has tended to support an even more protectionist policy and higher prices than those put forward by the Commission, while the trade committee has advocated a distinctly more liberal approach. The result has been a series of compromises which have reflected differences of opinion more effectively than they have influenced the policy-makers.

For parliamentarians accustomed to see some end-product for their labours, and to be in direct face-to-face contact with governments, the Strasbourg experience has undoubtedly generated a great deal of frustration. So too has the fact that the normal cut and thrust of political debate between those supporting and opposing a government has largely been absent, at least until the arrival of the Gaullists and Communists. At the same time the work load generated by the parliament has undoubtedly in many cases tended to cut members off from their own national political scene, in some cases to the detriment of their own political careers. Their debates are rarely reported at any length in the press, and they have no clear body of constituents to whom they can report or for whom they can perform services. In the circumstances it is surprising that the European Parliament has found as many of its members willing to devote time and effort to its activities as in fact has been the case: men and women who have continued not only to attend its meetings but also to carry on what for a long time had appeared to be a hopeless campaign to increase its powers and to give it, by means of direct elections, a more effective link with the citizens of the Community.

Since the Hague Summit some new perspectives for the work of the Parliament have at last begun to emerge. These have taken the form, in the first place, of a series of revisions to the three treaties providing for a modest increase in the budgetary powers of the Parliament in the context of a change in the ways by which the activities of the Community are financed. Essentially this change means that it will now no longer have to rely on annual contributions from national governments, but will derive its income from the proceeds of the external tariff, the levies on agricultural imports, and a small part of the value-added tax. By going over to this system, however, the last vestige of control exercised by national parliaments over the finances of the Community will be removed: the Council therefore recognised the need to give the Community's own parliament some greater voice in budgetary matters. The ministers nevertheless showed themselves determined to keep a very tight rein on the Parliament in this sphere, and the new arrangements have been bitterly criticised by the majority of the members of the Parliament. It is easy to appreciate the reasons for their discontent when the details of these new arrangements are examined.[1]

There are some who nevertheless believe that they may provide a springboard for a more substantial degree of parliamentary control in due course, and the Commission has supported the Parliament's own claim that they give it the right to reject the budget as a whole. The

---

[1] See below pp. 91–97, and also *The European Communities' Own Resources and the Budgetary Powers of the European Parliament. Selected Documents*, Secretariat of the European Parliament, Luxembourg, 1973.

Commission, for its part, also took the initiative in 1971—on the proposal of Altiero Spinelli, a convinced federalist—in asking the Vedel Committee to put forward proposals for strengthening the Parliament's role in general within the Community's structure. The report it produced argued strongly that the question of increased powers should be considered separately from that of direct elections, and that action on the first should be undertaken irrespective of any changes in the mode of composition of the Parliament. Having thus broken through the familiar chicken and egg argument, it then went on to propose that additional powers be given to the Parliament in two stages. In the first of these it suggested that it should acquire the right of co-decision with the Council in certain policy areas (essentially those concerned with changes in the treaties, the admission of new members, the conclusion of association agreements and the ratification of international agreements concluded by the Community), and a suspensive veto in others. In the second stage the right of co-decision should be extended to both categories of decisions. Whereas the suspensive veto would require the Council to reconsider those matters on which the Parliament expressed dissent (but without giving the Parliament the final say), the right of co-decision would involve positive parliamentary approval before Council decisions were implemented.

These proposals were designed to give the Parliament some legislative teeth and with them were associated a series of other suggestions designed also to strengthen its role. These included parliamentary ratification of the nomination of the president of the Commission (whose term, it was suggested, should be increased from two to four years), and closer organic links with national parliaments. On the question of direct elections, the Vedel Committee underlined the need to set a time-table for their introduction, suggested that at least in the first instance they should not be made dependent on the introduction of a uniform electoral system throughout the whole of the Community, and expressed its support in the meantime for the unilateral introduction in individual member countries of direct election of their own delegation to the parliament.

Several of the ideas contained in this report were taken up by the Commission and submitted as part of its proposals for the October 1972 Summit meeting in Paris. Several reforms, it argued, could be introduced without any formal revision of the treaties. These included parliamentary approval of the Council's nominee as President of the Commission, and a 'second reading' procedure under which the Parliament would have an opportunity to discuss a Council decision in those cases where it had not followed the opinion of the European Parliament. Other and more radical changes, which would require a revision or extension to the treaties, should—the Commission argued—be introduced at the latest by 1975. These should include the power of final decision in budgetary matters, and certain types of legislation (such as legislative harmonisation), and the right to participate in a significant way in all general legislation. Direct elections should also be introduced by 1980 at the latest.

The Parliament, for its part, also adopted many of the Vedel proposals in its resolution for the Summit agreed at a plenary session in July 1972. It, too, sought the introduction of a 'second reading' stage, a suspensive veto (to operate for at least a six-month period if no agreement was reached with the Council), the two-stage introduction of powers of co-decision to be extended eventually to all major legislation, and a firm commitment by the government to the introduction of direct elections.

Several of the member governments, in their own submissions for the Summit, also urged that more powers be given to the Parliament, the Dutch in particular underlining that unless more democratic control were provided the whole of the Community's institutional system might forfeit popular support. In short, as the Community neared enlargement, the question of the future role of the Parliament was being raised with increasing insistence as a central issue for the development of the Community's political system.[1]

THE ECONOMIC AND SOCIAL COMMITTEE

Very few of these documents, however, made any reference to the other main consultative body established by the treaties: the Economic and Social Committee. The forerunner of this body was the 51-member Consultative Committee attached to the High Authority of the Coal and Steel Community, which was set up to represent the interests of producers, consumers and dealers within the industries affected by its activities. In 1957 the Economic and Social Committee was set up to serve both Euratom and the E.E.C., consisting in this case of 101 members drawn from 'various categories of economic and social life, in particular representatives of producers, agriculturists, transport operators, workers, merchants, artisans, the liberal professions and of the general interest'.

The creation of these bodies derived from a view, held more strongly in continental Western Europe than in Britain, that representation of socio-economic interest groups ought to be built into the formal institutions of a political system to complement that of the general body of individual citizens provided, through the channel of political parties,

[1] See below, Chapter 4, pp. 110–113.

in the conventional type of parliamentary assembly. Such representation had in fact been introduced in most of the six countries either between the two world wars or in the immediate post-war period—the one notable exception being the Federal Republic. In all cases they had been given a consultative role with the aim of allowing the expression of the views of interested parties to be made available to governments during the legislative process. During the negotiation of the Rome treaties the need for a comparable body for the new Communities was urged very strongly by the Benelux countries. The Federal Republic, however, was equally strong in its opposition; what emerged eventually was a very emasculated version of what had originally been proposed.

In the first place the treaties provided that membership of the body would be determined by the Council of Ministers. Lists were to be presented by each Member state containing twice as many nominations as places available, the national quotas being fixed as follows:

France, Germany, Italy	24 seats each
Belgium, the Netherlands	12 seats each
Luxembourg	5 seats

The Council, after certain consultations, would then nominate the requisite number of members, each of whom would serve a four-year term.

In the second place, the Council's unanimous approval was to be required for the Committee's rules of procedure; and the Committee was given no right of initiative. It was merely to be consulted by the Council or the Commission in the specific cases provided for in the treaty. (In the case of the Euratom treaty, perhaps because of a drafting oversight, no provision was made for any consultation on the part of the Council.)

Like the Assembly, but even more so, the Committee was therefore assigned a very marginal role. The trade unions, who had originally pressed hard for the inclusion of such a body, were extremely dissatisfied with the treaty provisions, partly because they had wanted a straight employers–workers composition, and partly because it was evident that the ministers had assigned it to a very subordinate position in the institutional arrangements. Nor were the early stages of the development of the Committee at all encouraging. There was nothing at all for it to do during the first year, while the Euratom and E.E.C. Commissions were working on their initial sets of proposals: and then when finally a draft regulation was sent to it, it was a highly technical proposal for the establishment of basic norms for the protection of the health of workers in the nuclear industry. Faced by the prospect of underemployment, the Committee, through its president and officers, then made strenuous efforts to persuade both the Councils and Commissions to give it more work. For the most part they were happy to comply, and as the years have gone on, it has in fact been asked to give its opinion on the great majority of issues which have also been submitted to the European Parliament.[1]

As a result of the entry of the new member countries, the size of the Economic and Social Committee has now been increased from 101 to 144, and divided as follows:

Britain, France, Germany, Italy	24 members each
Belgium, the Netherlands	12 members each
Denmark, Ireland	9 members each
Luxembourg	6 members

The internal organisation and mode of work of the Economic and Social Committee has several parallels with that of the parliamentary assembly. It is run by an Executive Bureau, consisting of a president and two vice-presidents, and 13 members, and has evolved three groups, rather on the lines of the party groups in the assembly, consisting respectively of the workers' representatives, employers' representatives and those representing 'the general interest'. Detailed initial consideration of the proposals which come before it takes place in specialised working sections (equivalent to the parliamentary committees) which usually in turn set up small working groups to help the rapporteur to draft his report. These reports, once approved by the appropriate specialised section, are then discussed in plenary sessions which take place roughly once a month. These however, are held in private with the members sitting in rows (by alphabetical order) facing the presidential tribune. For a long time the Council opposed the publication of the Economic and Social Committee's Opinions; in practice, however, interested parties could always obtain them, and in recent years, the Council has relaxed its attitude on this issue.

One of the problems of this body, which is endemic to this type of institution, is its extremely heterogeneous composition. The most homogeneous group is undoubtedly that of the trade unions, mainly because the Free and Christian Unions are relatively well organised at the Community level, and co-operate closely in all major policy issues. The 'general interest' group is made up, however, of very disparate interests which have little in common on most issues.

A second problem, connected with the first, is the need the Committee has always felt: to try and arrive if at all possible at a consensus

---

[1] There has in fact been a certain amount of rivalry between the two institutions, though a working rule has now been established that the Economic and Social Committee sends its opinions to the Parliament in time for the latter's debates.

in order to maximise its chances of influencing policy. This has led, however, to compromises being reached at a very high level of generality on many issues and to the production of reports and opinions which are more notable for their length than the clarity of their views. This was notably the case in an early report on the Commission's proposals for the common agricultural policy, a massive document which, however, showed only too clearly the division of opinion between the agricultural producers and the other members of the Committee. Usually these socio-economic interests prevail over national divisions, though there have been some cases where this has not been so. All the Dutch representatives, for instance, voted against the Commission's proposals for a tax on fats, and the Italian delegation against its regional policy proposals, on the grounds that they failed to take sufficiently into account the needs of the Mezzogiorno. On other occasions the search for a consensus has proved quite abortive. This was notably the case with the Commission's proposed regulation on competition when the Committee split evenly for and against the compulsory registration of agreements.

As with the Parliament, the Economic and Social Committee enjoys much closer relations with the Commission than it does with the Council. Members and officials of the Commission frequently attend and speak at its sessions and undoubtedly take careful note of what is said. From their point of view, support from the members of the Committee is a potential resource which it is useful to obtain if possible, and whose direct opposition to a proposal is to be avoided if its chances of success in the Council are to be maximised. The latter body, however, takes a much loftier view of the Committee's proceedings. Although it has relaxed its original tight-fisted attitude with regard to its activities, it refused until recently to allow the Committee a right of initiative to discuss whatever it wishes,[1] and its methods of work mean that the ministers themselves are rarely directly aware of what opinion the Committee has given on any given subject.

In fact, the most important contribution to the work of the Communities made by the Economic and Social Committee lies outside the sphere of legislation. Its primary value lies in the opportunity it gives to the representatives of a wide range of socio-economic interest to meet each other in a Community context and to compare views on the current work of the Communities. This is not an unimportant function as it brings together many men (and to a much lesser extent, women) who are themselves prominent in the national life of the member states, and makes them aware of the relationship of their own activities to the on-going process of integration.

[1] This right was finally granted at the Paris Summit, see Appendix, p. 196.

COMMUNITY INTEREST GROUPS

As far as their impact on decisions is concerned, however, most of the members of the Committee have at their disposal far more effective channels of pressure and influence. These are provided both by the national interest groups to which they belong, and also the Community-level groupings of such bodies which have been established. Of the latter, there has been a great proliferation, their total now numbering over 400. The need for such organisations derives from the fact that each individual social or economic interest group—whether farmers, trade unionists, chemical producers or midwives—has been confronted by new problems, as a result of the creation of the Community, which can only be resolved by cross-frontier groupings of the national bodies which exist to promote and represent such interests. Many of them were set up in the early years of the E.E.C. as a defensive measure on the part of such interests—particularly industrial manufacturers—who wished both to have a means to regulate their own internal problems and also to make their views known to the Community's institutions. The Commission's own attitude was often a catalyst for the formation of trans-national groupings, as at an early stage it refused to deal directly with individual national groups. This was partly a matter of convenience; evidently if it could ascertain the views of a particular category within the Community by one set of talks rather than by five or six different discussions, it would save a great deal of time; but it was also a matter of deliberate political strategy. The Commission felt that the formation of such groups would positively aid the process of integration, by bringing together national leaders and providing a forum in which their attention would be focused on problems at the level of the Community as a whole. In many cases it was therefore the Commission which took the initiative in suggesting the formation of a new group. It also subsequently took some part in shaping the nature of the organisations which emerged through its decisions whether or not to accept a particular group as the valid exponent, for its purposes, of the views of a particular category.

Among the most important groups which have emerged are those representing such major socio-economic categories as the agricultural producers: *Comité des Organisations Professionnelles Agricoles* (C.O.P.A.); the industrial federations: *Union des Industries de la Communauté Européenne* (U.N.I.C.E.); the public sector: *Centre Européen de l'Enterprise Publique* (C.E.E.P.); and the two major trade union groups: the *Confédération Européene des Syndicats Libres dans la Communauté*[1] (affiliated to the International Confederation of Free Trade Unions,

[1] As a result of re-organisation following enlargement, this has now become the *European Trade Union Confederation*.

I.C.F.T.U.) and the *Confédération Mondial du Travail* (formerly the Christian Trade Unions). Alongside them are many other groups representing either large sectors of industry (the steelmakers, chemical producers, textile manufacturers, the rubber industry, etc.) or specific producer groups (sanitary ware, refrigerators, perfumes, beer, and so on) together with the liberal professions (technical professions such as surveyors, architects and engineers; the medical professions—doctors, dentists and midwives, for instance; and the legal profession—lawyers and barristers) and miscellaneous groups such as booksellers, various types of periodical publishers, and family interests.

In some of these cases, there had been little or no contact between the individual national organisations within a particular sector prior to the establishment of the Community; in others, however, wider—if very loose—European organisations had been established as a result of the activities of the O.E.E.C. The emergence within such bodies of a more restricted group à Six was not infrequently a source of some tension, though some interests—the engineering industry is a case in point —preferred to maintain a wider framework. The typical initial form of organisation was a *Comité de liaison* or *comité de contacte*, with the functions of a secretariat being performed by the various national members in rotation, and meetings serving mainly for the exchange of information. From the beginning, however, certain of these groups gave themselves much more ambitious titles, such as *fédération* or *union*, and there has been a general tendency for their internal organisation to become stronger as both their range of activities and their mutual trust have increased. Typical of such development was the decision of the agricultural producers (C.O.P.A.) to elect a president in the mid-1960s (having previously worked with a different chairman for each meeting), the setting up by brewers of a full-time secretariat based in Brussels at the same period, a general increase in the number of such full-time secretariats, and—more recently—the adoption by both the major trade union groups of new constitutions for their respective organisations.

Like the Community itself, however, these bodies are faced by the problem of reaching a consensus between their own members, and in this their achievement has been very uneven. For most of the period of the formation of the common agricultural policy, for instance, the members of C.O.P.A. were quite unable to agree other than on the most generalised policy statements; the industrial producers (U.N.I.C.E.) split down the middle on the issue of the compulsory registration of agreements between companies in different countries; and the Free Trade Unions, otherwise notable for their degree of cohesion, had great difficulties in persuading their most important member, the D.G.B., to accept the principle of medium-term planning within the Community. In almost every way the internal life of these groups has been a microcosm of the difficulties encountered by the Community's own political system, with individual national interests only slowly giving way before the need to arrive at a common position.

These difficulties in resolving their own internal conflicts of interest have undoubtedly reduced the influence exerted by such groups on the policy-making processes within the Community, though as time has gone on some at least of these tensions have been reduced, either by the Community institutions themselves taking action, or through the greater willingness of the members of such groups to reach compromise solutions. They have certainly not lacked, however, means of access to the Commission. The most valuable of these is provided by the intensive informal contacts which take place daily in Brussels, though these are frequently supplemented by more formal occasions either in the form of direct discussions with members or the staff of the Commission or participation in the many consultative committees which it or the Council have set up. By the time a proposal reaches the Economic and Social Committee, therefore, both the Commission and the relevant interest groups will be well aware of their respective positions—and the major battles will have been fought. The formal procedures in the Committee do nevertheless offer a further opportunity for a particular interest to state its view, and to seek allies for it if this is found to be necessary.

Beyond that stage in the decision-making process, it becomes much more difficult for the Community groups as such to press their case. The Committee of Permanent Representatives, for its part, neither invites nor welcomes their intervention, and the members of the Council itself have generally followed a similar policy. From time to time, however, the President of the Council has agreed to meet a trade union delegation, for instance, before a particular session to hear their views. They, and others, have also resorted occasionally to sending telegrams to the Council during its sessions to reiterate their position; these are normally circulated to all members by the Council secretariat, though the effect is unpredictable. At this final stage in the making of a decision an individual national group may have some greater hope of exercising influence over its own government, though there have been many instances where even the strongest of them may have failed to gain their objectives because of that government's need to reach a compromise with its partners. The way in which Erhard finally had to back down in late 1964 on the promises he had made to the *Bauernverband* (the German farmers' organisation) over the level of the common grain price is one outstanding case in point.

To the question of how much influence is exerted on Community decision-making by such groups there is no simple answer. It is virtually impossible to reconstruct the whole complex of factors that go to make up the various pressures and forms of influence exerted as a policy proposal makes its long and tortuous journey from a first tentative draft on the desk of a Commission official to a Council decision. And even when it is clear that a great deal of influence has been exerted by the fact, for instance, that some 14% of the Community's labour force is in agriculture, and for the most part poorly paid and discontented, the resulting policy cannot be simply equated as a success for the farmers' groups. Most of the members of C.O.P.A. would have much preferred it if there had been no common policy for agriculture at all, and that power had remained in the hands of individual governments. Similarly, although it is easy to assert that the Community's policy has been shaped in a way to benefit the large industrial producers within the Community, their perceptions of their own interests have by no means always coincided with the policies proposed by the Commission, and within their own ranks there have been constant disputes and disagreements. Protection for the coal industry, for instance, has run counter to the interests of the oil industry; a lowering of tariffs on imported wood pulp has pleased those companies with subsidiaries in Canada or Sweden but has displeased the Community's own wood-pulp producers; the brewers have been at loggerheads between themselves over whether or not the German insistence that only their own recipe for beer—based on the use of barley—should be used as the basis for 'Community' beer. On virtually every issue there has been a complicated pattern of competing interests, both within a particular sector or product group and between it and others.

Moreover, it is far from certain even when a particular interest appears to have influenced policy successfully that it will necessarily prove as advantageous to it as it appears at first sight. In spite of the high level of protection for the Community's farmers, for instance, their numbers are still rapidly declining, and their incomes failing to keep up with other sectors. And as far as industry is concerned, many now lament that the real beneficiaries of the Common Market appear to be American rather than European producers.

There can, and often is, therefore a considerable disparity between the apparent strength of the institutional presence of particular interests in the Community context and the total impact of the process of integration on those interests. The balance with respect to almost any group within the Community is extremely difficult to strike, and can only be a matter of subjective judgement. One of the weakest groups in organisational terms in the Community has always been, for instance, that representing the consumers—and it is one of the few that has collapsed.[1] The interests of consumers certainly have not been the primary consideration in the common agricultural policy. Yet living standards have risen quite markedly in the six countries since the Community was created, and the prices of at least some consumer durables have undoubtedly been kept down under the impact of increased competition. However one judges the situation in this particular case, it is important to bear this type of consideration in mind: the formal policy decisions of the Community only provide the framework for the economic and social development of society, and their intentions may either be fulfilled or negated by the response given to them by forces operating beyond the immediate control of the Community's institutions and political system.

FINANCE

We have now examined the work of the main institutions which are involved in the process by which the Community arrives at its decisions. Before turning briefly to describe the ways in which such decisions are implemented and subjected to judicial review, it is convenient at this stage to discuss the Community's budget and how it is financed.

For the calender year 1972 the budget totalled $ 4177 million (about £1700 million), of which no less than $ 3526 million was accounted for by the Agricultural Guarantee and Guidance Fund (F.E.O.G.A.). It is the mounting cost of this agricultural policy which is mainly responsible for the very rapid increase in the Community's expenditure in recent years: from a modest $ 44 million in 1959 it rose to $ 1043 million in 1968, $ 2585 million in 1970 and $ 3462 million in 1971.

Unlike the Coal and Steel Community, whose operations have always been financed from a levy on its producers, Euratom and the E.E.C. were initially financed direct by annual contributions from each national exchequer. The level of these was fixed according to a key laid down in the treaties. This system, accompanied by arrangements for the funding of the Agricultural Guidance and Guarantee Fund, continued in force until the end of 1970. Since then, however, a new set of arrangements has come into force, as a result of a treaty signed in April 1970, which are designed to lead, after a transitional period lasting until the end of 1974, to a situation in which the Community budget is wholly financed from its own resources, consisting of the proceeds of the common external tariff, the agricultural levies imposed on imports of foodstuffs from non-member countries, and a part of the proceeds of the value-added tax which is due to be adopted in the meantime by all

[1] See Paul Kemezis, 'A fairy godmother for the consumer?' *European Community* (September 1972).

the member countries. In the period up to the end of 1974, each member country is to pay in its receipts from the agricultural levies, and a proportion of its receipts from customs duties. This proportion will rise so that in 1974 it will amount to 87½% of the total sum collected in duties and levies by each member. The balance will be made up by direct contributions from each national government, calculated according to a fixed key. Special arrangements have, however, been made for the new members, which in Britain's case means that the total obligation will be limited to 8·64% of the overall budget in 1973 and 10·85% in 1974. This limitation will also apply during the first three years of the new system when the Community is financed wholly from its own resources, at the end of which—in 1977—Britain will be contributing 18·92% of the total budget. According to figures given in the 1971 White Paper—which have however been criticised by the Opposition as being far too low—Britain at that stage will be making a net contribution of £200 million to the Community budget (see *Table 3.4*).[1]

Table 3.4 THE COMMUNITY BUDGET 1973—1977: ESTIMATED BRITISH CONTRIBUTION

(1) Year	(2) U.K. key (% of E.E.C. budget)	(3) % of key to be paid	(4) U.K. cont. (% of E.E.C. budget)	(5) Possible U.K. gross cont. (£m.)	(6) Possible U.K. receipts (£m.)	(7) Possible U.K. net cont. (£m.)
1973	19·19	45·0	8·64	120	20	100
1974	19·38	56·0	10·85	155	40	115
1975	19·77	67·5	13·34	195	55	140
1976	20·16	79·5	16·03	245	75	170
1977	20·56	92·0	18 92	300	100	200

Source: *The United Kingdom and the European Communities*, H.M.S.O., Cmnd. 4715 London (July 1971) p. 24.

The procedures by which the budget is agreed were also revised by the 1970 treaty. Although each of the three Communities has its own budget and the E.C.S.C. will continue to be financed by its own levy, this procedure is now uniform for each of them and their budgetary years have also been brought into line.[2] The procedure begins by each

[1] For a further discussion, see below, Chapter 5, pp. 145–151.
[2] Originally the fiscal year of the E.C.S.C. ran from 1 July to 30 June; all three now use the calendar year.

institution drawing up a list of its own expenditure, all of which are then grouped together by the Commission and presented as a preliminary draft budget to the Council not later than 1 September each year. If the Council wishes to alter these proposals it consults with the various institutions; by a weighted majority vote it then establishes the draft budget. This is sent on to the Assembly not later than 5 October. The Assembly then has the right to propose modifications to this draft (if it does not do so within a period of 45 days the budget is considered to have been approved). If amendments are put forward by the Assembly the Council then has a further 30 days in which to deal with them. If they do not imply an increase in total expenditure a qualified majority in the Council is required to reject them: otherwise they are accepted; but if the proposed changes would increase total expenditure they are only accepted if there is a weighted majority in the Council in favour of them. However, the Council has the right if it has either rejected or not accepted the Parliament's proposed modifications to fix, by a weighted majority, a new total for the budget.

This system, which clearly maintains final control of the budget in the hands of the Council, is not the one which either the Commission or the Parliament favoured. The former originally proposed that conflicts over the budget should be resolved by a conciliation procedure rather similar to that which used to be employed in the E.C.S.C.: the Parliament for its part sought a greater influence over the final outcome by proposing that any changes which it put forward would be automatically accepted unless there was a weighted majority (including the vote of four members of the Council) against its proposals. In the resolution which it passed on the new system, it argued that it could in effect allow a minority in the Council to prevent the adoption of budgetary proposals which are supported by the Commission, the Parliament and a majority of the members of the Council itself. The Parliament also pointed out that this could lead to an impasse in the Council for a situation could arise in which the Council would be unable to raise the necessary weighted majority for the approval of the budget.

The major objections to the new system on the part of the Parliament have, however, been focused on the system which will come into effect as from the beginning of 1975. This will coincide with the moment when the Community will be wholly financed by its own resources. On that date all customs duties and levies—with the exception of a 10% administrative fee which will be retained by national governments—will automatically be credited to the Community, along with a small part of the proceeds obtained from the value-added tax.[1]

[1] This may not exceed a 1% rate of the V.A.T.

Under the budgetary system then to be employed it is to be the president of the Assembly rather than the president of the Council of Ministers who will have the authority to declare that the budget has been approved. The procedure to be followed before this can take place is, however, very complicated and it is one which gives the Parliament effective control over only a very small part of the total expenditure. Under strong pressure from the French, the Council decided during the course of its discussions of this new system to make a sharp distinction between 'expenses arising necessarily from the treaty or decisions taken by virtue of the treaty' and other types of expenditure. In the first category are included all the costs of the agricultural policy which, together with certain other items such as the Social Fund, account for some 97% of the total current expenditure of the Community. The remaining 3%, which come into the second category, include such items as staff salaries, administrative costs (rents, heating, stationery, etc.) and expenditure on information service activities.

This distinction has the effect of very severely limiting the powers of the European Parliament under the new system. Once the Council has forwarded the draft budget it will only be able to propose 'modifications' to Category I type expenditure, and then by an absolute majority of its members. These 'modifications' will in turn only be accepted by the Council if there is a weighted majority of its members in favour. The Assembly may put forward 'amendments' to the rest of the budget (in effect, the 3% part of it covering Category II expenditure) though even these will have to be within an upper limit arrived at by a complex formula which will take into account increases in the gross national product of the member states, the average variation in their national budgets, and the increase in the cost of living during the previous year. Should the Council in its own draft budget propose an increase for Category II expenditure which is over half the agreed rate, the Parliament will be able to increase this by up to another 50% of the rate; any such proposal will still however be subject to approval by a qualified majority in the Council.

If the Council fails to accept the Parliament's proposed modifications or modifies its suggested amendments the draft budget will be sent back to the assembly. With regard to the action it has taken on the Parliament's proposed modifications to Category I expenditure (that is, the bulk of the budget) the Parliament will be merely informed of the Council's decisions. It will have no right to take further action on that part of the budget. But with regard to its amendments relating to Category II expenditure it will be able to reject any changes by the Council as long as it can raise a vote satisfying the dual criteria of a majority of its members and three-fifths of those voting. Once this vote has taken place the budget procedure is—finally—terminated.

The complexities of this procedure are such that it is difficult to know what will happen in practice. But the proposals have been strongly resisted by a large majority of the members of the Parliament, which only agreed to support them under protest. Their main concern has been with the fact that they will have no determining voice with regard to 97% of the total expenditure: the Parliament can propose changes to this part of the draft budget but the Council will be under no obligation to accept them. The Parliament has pointed out that the argument put forward in support of the distinction between Categories I and II expenditure does not have the same force in the Community context as it does at the national level. The distinction is derived from French parliamentary practice which prohibits the Assembly, in the exercise of its budgetary functions, from tampering with expenditure already committed through existing legislation. In that context such a limitation can be defended on the grounds that the Assembly itself has already agreed to such expenditure. But in the Community existing procedures give the European Parliament no determining voice in legislation. It is therefore facing a situation in which it will in theory be finally responsible for the approval of the Community budget, but in practice unable to have a decisive voice except with regard to a tiny fraction of the expenditure which figures in it.[1]

It was for this reason that the Parliament claimed, during the negotiations which led up to the Council's approval of the new system, the right to reject the budget in toto. In a series of memoranda and telegrams sent by its then president, the former Italian Prime Minister, Mario Scelba, it argued that unless the Council formally acknowledged this right the provision that the president of the Parliament should declare that the budget was finally approved would be a complete farce. The right to approve—it was argued—must also imply the right to reject. The Commission supported the stand taken by the Parliament, but the Council refused to do so. As things stand at present it is not clear what would happen if in fact the Parliament did attempt to reject the budget as a whole.

While refusing to give in on this crucial point, the Council did seek in the course of these exchanges to make various lesser concessions to the Parliament. One was a promise not to tamper with the budget of the European Parliament itself; another was a commitment to institute acceptable procedures relating to its dialogue with the Parliament on budgetary issues. Nevertheless, the great majority of the members of

[1] The report on the proposals submitted by M. Spenale on behalf of the Parliament's Finance and Budget Committee pointed out that 80% of the Category II expenditure consists of obligatory costs (salaries, etc.). In effect, therefore, the Parliament's discretionary powers will apply to only 0·6% of the total budget and even with respect to this tiny part its authority to increase expenditure will be severely limited.

the Parliament remain extremely dissatisfied with the proposed arrangements.[1]

IMPLEMENTING THE COMMUNITY'S DECISIONS

Just as the member states have retained, and also seem determined to maintain, control over the Community's budget through their grip on the decisions which give rise to expenditure, so they also have retained almost complete control over the mechanisms through which the Community's decisions are implemented. Customs duties arising out of the application of the common external tariff are, for instance, collected by national customs officials. The agricultural levies are also collected by national authorities; in Britain, for instance, the new Intervention Board for Agricultural Produce has been set up for this purpose and for the administration in the country of the other provisions relating to the common agricultural policy. Value-added tax is also applied by the appropriate national authorities (in the British case, the Customs and Excise). Social security payments for migrant workers are equally the responsibility of the relevant national ministry, and so on. All this is yet another reminder of how dependent the whole system is on the active collaboration of the national governments if it is to function effectively.

There are, nevertheless, certain elements with regard to the execution of Community rules and policies which do not depend wholly on national agencies. Euratom, for instance, has its own corps of inspectors who regularly inspect nuclear establishments within the Community countries to see that its accounting procedures applying to nuclear fuel are properly observed. Similarly, officials of the E.C.S.C. police the observance by individual firms of the Community's regulations regarding the publication and maintenance of prices. In the case of the E.E.C., its officials also have to conduct enquiries into the behaviour of companies having agreements with those in other Community countries, as well as checking the observance of the common agricultural policy.

Some minor administrative duties have also been given within the framework of the same policy to producers' groups, notably with regard to the regulation of surpluses on the fruit and vegetable market. Some rather similar tasks are also being proposed for producers' organisations with regard to the common fisheries policy.

---

[1] For a more extensive discussion see David Coombes, *The Power of the Purse in the European Communities*, P.E.P./Chatham House European Series, London (1972).

The major responsibility for ensuring the application of, and compliance with, Community rules continues, however, to rest with the member states. This is true whether the rule takes the form of a regulation issued by the Council or the Commission; a directive which only takes effect when it is incorporated in national legislation; or a recommendation or opinion, neither of which has any legal force unless a national government takes the appropriate action. Similarly, it is national courts which bear a large part of the burden of settling disputes arising from the application of the treaties, and which are contributing, with the Community's own Court of Justice, to the creation of a body of case law regarding their interpretation.

JUDICIAL REVIEW

The creation of a new dimension of government by the Community has necessarily entailed the setting up of legal machinery to ensure the observance of law and justice in the interpretation and application of the treaties. The major task in this context is performed by the Community's Court of Justice, which was originally established in Luxembourg as part of the institutions of the Coal and Steel Community, but which since 1958 has also served the other two Communities.

The task of the Court has been succinctly stated as follows.[1]

> The Court reviews the lawfulness of the acts of the Council, the Commission and the member governments in respect of their Community obligations. If an appeal is upheld by the Court the Community regulation or directive in question may be declared null and void. Appeals can also be made for failure of a government or a Community institution to act where required to do so by the Treaties. Appeals against one of the institutions can be lodged by another institution, by a government, by firms and in some circumstances by individuals.

The Court now consists of nine judges who are assisted by four advocates general.[2] All of these are appointed by the member governments for a six-year term; each three years there is a partial replacement of the Court's membership. The Court elects its own president from among the judges, and also its registrar. On some occasions it sits in plenary session, but more frequently it sits in two separate Chambers. The Court's procedure differs substantially from British judicial prac-

---

[1] Roger Broad and R. J. Jarrett, *Community Europe Today* (revised edition), London (1972) p. 125.

[2] One of the judges and one of the advocates general are British.

tice and is based to a considerable extent on that of the French *Conseil d'Etat*. It consists of four stages: written submissions, investigations, oral proceedings, and judgement. The first phase consists of an initial statement of the case of the party which has initiated the proceedings, a reply by the other side, and comments by both parties on the two documents together with a report by the judge appointed to have special responsibility for the case. It is he who advises the court whether or not an investigation is necessary. If it is decided that there should be one, this takes the form of an appearance and cross-examination of the parties, witnesses and experts, together with an inspection of documents. Unlike in British courts, however, the investigation is conducted by the Court itself rather than by counsel acting for the parties to the case.

Oral proceedings then follow, which are normally held in public. The reporting judge opens by presenting the case, summarising the arguments on both sides, and dealing with the facts as they have emerged from the earlier stages. Counsel for the two parties then make their submissions, but there is no cross-examination. It is then the task of one of the advocates general to present his own conclusions to the judges. There is no exact parallel in the English judicial system to the role he fulfils: he acts not on behalf of either of the parties or of the Community, but as an independent judicial observer acting in the public interest.

The case is then discussed by the judges in private. They reach their decision by majority vote and present it in open court; unlike in the English courts, minority views are not made known. The Court's judgements are directly applicable in the member countries, and enforceable through the national courts. Like them the Court of Justice gives a judgement concerning costs, and can grant legal aid.

The volume of cases brought before the Court totalled 813 by the end of 1971, of which 279 had been brought under the E.C.S.C. treaty and 257 under the E.E.C. treaty; 3 were under Euratom, 6 related to privileges and immunities granted under the treaties and 268 were cases brought by Community civil servants. In the early years the E.C.S.C. treaty produced many cases, a great number of which were brought by individual firms; in recent years there have however been very few cases relating to this treaty. The largest single category in those arising from the E.E.C. treaty—not unexpectedly—relate to agricultural matters; but there have also been a substantial number relating to the application of the rules of competition (several of them brought by firms seeking to annul fines imposed by the Commission), and also to the rules relating to social security for migrant workers.[1]

[1] *Fifth General Report of the Activities of the Communities, 1971*, Brussels (1972) Table 25, p. 469.

Among the cases arising under the E.E.C. treaty a substantial number (134 by the end of 1971) were requests from national courts for preliminary rulings on the interpretation of the treaties and the acts arising from them. This type of activity has become an increasingly important part of the work of the Court. It arises from the provision in Article 177 of the Treaty of Rome which states that national courts may—if they consider that their judgement depends on a preliminary ruling —ask the Court to provide it. The aim of this provision was evidently to try to ensure the uniform application of Community law throughout the member countries. One study found, however, that whereas in the period between 1958 and 1968 some 360 cases in national courts involved the application of Community law fewer than 50 opinions were handed down by the Luxembourg Court during this period. This suggests that there is still considerable reluctance on the part of national courts to make use of this procedure. It does not necessarily imply, however, that Community norms are not being respected.[1]

What is more striking, is that the judgements of the Court itself so far have always been accepted by the parties concerned. A more controversial aspect of its work, however, is the relationship between Community law and national law. What the Court has done is not only to assert the independence of the former from the latter, 'but has also asserted the supremacy of Community law over national law, not only in Community law, but in the national law itself.[2] The occasion for its most forceful assertion of this was a case which arose in Italy. A private citizen, Signor Costa, refused to pay his electricity bill (of very modest dimensions, hardly more than £1) to the state-owned electricity company on the grounds that the act of nationalisation was contrary to the E.E.C. treaty. The case was referred both to the Italian Constitutional Court and also the Community's Court of Justice. The former held that Signor Costa had no right to complain because although the E.E.C. treaty was part of Italian national law, the later law nationalising the power industry took precedence over it. The Luxembourg Court, while also denying to the plaintiff any basis for his complaint on its interpretation of the treaty, nevertheless asserted the primacy of Community law.[3]

By creating a Community of unlimited duration, having its own institutions, its own personality, and its own capacity in law . . . the

---

[1] For a discussion of this see Stuart A. Scheingold, *The Law in Political Integration,* Occasional Papers in International Affairs, No. 27, Harvard University, (June 1971) pp. 30–36.

[2] Andrew Wilson Green, *Political Integration by Jurisprudence,* Leyden (1969) p. 410.

[3] Case 6/64; *Costa v Ente Nazionale per l'Energia Elettrica* (E.N.E.E.). For more extensive discussions of this case see A. W. Green, *op. cit.,* pp. 348–387 and S. A. Scheingold, *op. cit.,* pp. 6–10.

member-states, albeit within limited spheres, have restricted their sovereign rights and created a body of law applicable both to their nationals and to themselves. The reception, within the laws of each member-state, of provisions having a Community source, and more particularly of the terms and of the spirit of the Treaty, has as a corollary the impossibility, for the member-state to give preference to a unilateral and subsequent measure against a legal order accepted by them on a basis of reciprocity . . . The pre-eminence of Community law is confirmed by Article 189 which prescribes that Community regulations have an 'obligatory value' and are 'directly applicable' within each member-state. Such a provision . . . would be wholly ineffective if a member-state could unilaterally nullify its purpose by means of a law contrary to Community dictates.

Nevertheless, this assertion has not been universally accepted, for while the French and Dutch constitutions state specifically that international agreements have supremacy over conflicting national laws, and this has also been accepted by the Luxembourg courts, the situation in Belgium, Germany and Italy is less clear. A number of recent cases suggests, however, that courts in these countries are also increasingly accepting the primacy of Community law.[1] The Court of Justice has nevertheless not sought to assert its jurisdiction in concrete factual situations. The Court has held that its role under Article 177 is limited to interpreting the treaties and assuring the validity of Community acts. So although it may declare what Community law is, and that it is superior to national law, 'it may not decide whether there is a conflict of laws in a concrete factual situation, and consequently which law shall prevail in that situation'.[2]

Given the ambiguous nature of the Community's political system it is hardly surprising to find that there are also areas of uncertainty about the jurisdiction of the Court itself where this impinges on national law, a great deal of which, including the whole of criminal law and the bulk of civil law, is of course unaffected by membership of the Community. Expert opinion is also somewhat divided about how important a role the Court has played in the process of political integration. While on the one hand it has been asserted that it has sustained and strengthened the new political system by creating a body of independent Community law, upholding the authority of the Community institutions (particularly the High Authority and the Commission), resolving conflicts between member states and applying the Community law directly to individuals, it has also been noted that it has not

[1] See *Fifth General Report of the Activities of the Communities, 1971,* Brussels (1972) pp. 435–436.

[2] A. W. Green, *op. cit,* p. 411.

been used by the member states to resolve any major dispute between them, and that while it 'has forcibly asserted federal prerogatives, (it) has been very tentative on policy questions'.[1]

[1] S.A. Scheingold, *op. cit.*, p. 26.

4 Achievements and Problems

In previous chapters the discussion has been focused on the mechanics of the Community's political system: how it has developed, the forces which have impelled it forward—and also created stress within it —and the processes by which decisions are reached, implemented and subjected to judicial review. We now have to consider what the system has achieved, how well it has performed, and how satisfactory—or otherwise—it is considered to be by those in the original member countries who have been living with it for the last 20 or so years.

The first two of these three questions are not easily answered. One initial difficulty is to disentangle the effects which can properly be ascribed to the process of integration itself from those which have been, or may have been, caused by other factors. This difficulty is compounded by the fact that the process has very wide ramifications. Like a stone dropped into a pool, the activity of the Community has generated a ripple effect, the outer edges of which merge almost imperceptibly with other elements operating both on and beneath the surface of the society of Western Europe. To attempt to reconstruct the totality of the impact of the Community would be a mommoth and, in the end, elusive undertaking. Judgements about it have therefore to be based on an incomplete set of data, and to this extent they are bound to suffer from some degree of distortion.

Coupled with this problem is the fact that such judgements are necessarily highly subjective in nature. In the debates in the British Parliament on the Community, for instance, the views of the proponents and antagonists of entry on many issues were so far apart in their assessment of its policies and impact that at times it was difficult to believe that both sides were talking about the same phenomenon. Nor is the disagreement limited, either in Britain or elsewhere, to politicians. The academic community is also divided. Nor is this at all surprising for it is difficult if not impossible to establish objective measures of many of the aspects of the impact of the process. As the purpose of this study is not to add to the polemical literature on integration, but to provide a guide to understanding the issues which it raises, the survey which follows will attempt to indicate the main issues on which the work of the Community has aroused controversy, rather than attempting to enter into the merits of the issues themselves.

FORMAL ACHIEVEMENTS

It is, however, necessary briefly first to state the formal achievements of the Community to date. Chief among these is the establishment of a customs union among its members involving the abolition of the more obvious types of obstacles to the free movement of goods and the replacement of individual national customs tariffs towards the rest of the world by a common external tariff. At the same time steps have been taken to remove many of the formal obstacles which used to exist on the movement of persons, capital and services within the Community.

In this sense a common market has been achieved; yet it is one which, while it has certainly led to a great increase in the volume of trade between the member countries, is still characterised by many distortions in competitive conditions which have been inherited from the past. Many types of non-tariff barriers remain as a result of national legislative, administrative and legal provisions which have as yet not been harmonised. Common policies have been created in a number of fields, most notably with regard to the marketing and price system for agricultural goods, but even in this case its operation has proved far from smooth and in some other fields, such as transport, only partial elements of a common policy have been manoeuvred into place. The same is true of industrial policy in general, and also energy policy. Community action with regard to regional disparities has so far been fragmentary; in this, as in social policy issues, the member governments have continued to maintain the levers of power in their own hands and —for the most part—to be reluctant to give the Community itself authority in these areas. And while the member states have lost a number of instruments which traditionally they have used to regulate their economies, the task of building up Community mechanisms for this purpose, which is the essential task foreseen in the context of economic and monetary union, is as yet only in its early stages, and even such tentative steps as have been taken have proved difficult to negotiate and subsequently maintain. With regard to the Community's external posture the record is equally uneven. The existing treaties cover only part, if a substantial part, of what normally constitutes the foreign policy of its members. They do not deal with defence and security issues. These are dealt with by individual member countries either within the framework of other organizations, and in particular Nato, or on a bilateral basis—as has been the case with the Federal Republic's *Ostpolitik*. There has been a growth of consultations within the Community on such issues, but no formal commitments for common action have been entered into.

More progress has certainly been made towards the achievement of a common posture and common policies in those economic aspects of external relations which fall within the ambit of the existing treaties. All tariff negotiations are now conducted by the Community on behalf of its members, and external commercial policy—with the partial exception of trade with Eastern Europe—is also a Community matter. Aid policies fall only partially within its ambit, but the Community has concluded a series of trade and association agreements on behalf of its members, the latter including not only that with 18 African countries (which Mauritius also joined in 1972), but also with the countries of East Africa, and—in Europe—with Turkey, Greece and Malta.

Such, in outline, are the formal achievements of the Community. A great deal has been achieved, even if the union is still partial and imperfect. Assessments of these achievements naturally vary according to the values and political affiliations of particular individuals and groups. Within the original member countries they are, not unexpectedly, generally favourable among those who have provided the Community with its main sources of support, and highly critical where their opponents—mainly the Communists—are concerned. Supporters of the Community, however, are by no means themselves uncritical of it: indeed, some of the most severe and telling of its critics are to be found precisely among those—like the group which publishes the journal *Agenor* in Brussels—whose commitment to its success has been, and remains, beyond question.[1]

ECONOMIC AND SOCIAL IMPACT

As far as the economic and social impact of the Community on the member countries is concerned, it is widely held that the creation of the Common Market has contributed to sustaining rates of economic growth, even if economists disagree on how much integration as such is responsible for this; hence it has also played a part in achieving the

[1] See Ina Selden, 'Europe's radical think tank', *European Community,* (October 1972) pp. 24–25.

'accelerated raising of the standard of living' which Article 2 lists as one of the objectives of the E.E.C. treaty. The Community is also credited with having helped to foster a more competitive economy, a more rational use of resources and the conditions under which modern industrial enterprise can flourish. On the other hand, very few even of the supporters of the Community, would claim that its agricultural policy has been a success. It has not prevented a continued relative decline of agricultural incomes, while on the other hand it has stimulated massive over-production of certain commodities and, though it has cost huge sums of money, it has signally failed so far to deal with the structural problems of the industry. And while the process of integration has stimulated further growth in already heavily industrialised and prosperous regions, it has made it more difficult for areas like Southern Italy and South-West France to catch up; morever, the Community itself has done little so far to help such regions. Similarly, while it is true that material standards of living have greatly improved, the Community itself has had only a very weak social policy and has done very little to help those in need. Marxist critics of the Community argue that this is hardly surprising as they have always maintained that the Community is essentially an instrument of the dominant private economic forces in a latter-day capitalist society whose main concern has been, and remains, to create wider and more secure markets in Europe for their products, and to secure a framework within which they can band together to resist the competitive challenge of large American corporations. The emergence of the Community according to this view is therefore a further symptom of the internal conflicts within the capitalist system which will eventually bring about its collapse.[1]

In recent years the economic philosophy and goals of the Community have also come under attack from a different quarter. One of the most significant statements in this context was made by Sicco Mansholt, a Dutch socialist member of the Commission throughout the period 1958–1972. Writing in February 1972, shortly before he became president of the Commission, he based his arguments on the forecasts of increasing world population and future pressures on the resources needed to sustain it which were prepared in a report of the Massachusetts Institute of Technology. He argued that mankind as a whole faced a looming crisis of critical proportions and that the Community should play its own part in meeting it. What was necessary was a radical re-orientation of its own policy. It should replace the goal of economic growth and its preoccupation with gross national product by a new concept: 'gross national utility', related to social welfare. In order to

---

[1] See Ernest Mandel, *Europe versus America? Contradictions of Imperialism*, London (1970).

conserve raw materials and energy resources there should be a big reduction in the production of consumer durables and steps taken to extend the useful life of such products: the environment should be safe-guarded by giving priority to those products which did not give rise to pollution and which could be re-cycled. Such measures would have to be accompanied by a substantial growth of public control over the economy, both at the national and Community level.

Mansholt's proposals promptly led to a great deal of discussion in Community circles.[1] They combined a number of preoccupations which had already become familiar enough in discussions of national policy in the late 1960s, and which had already led, both in France and Britain for instance, to the establishment of governmental de-partments designed to deal with environmental questions: but this was the first time that a leading figure had suggested that the Community itself should radically revise its own economic philosophy and policies.

Mansholt's arguments also raised the issue of the Community's rela-tions with the rest of the world, and in particular the developing coun-tries. This theme was also familiar. Community spokesmen have defended its record by reference to the low level of its external tariff on raw materials and industrial products; its liberal trade policies; the fact that the Community's trade with the outside world, including that in agricultural products, has steadily risen; and the measures it has taken, within the framework of the African Association in particular, to offer preferential access to its markets and aid for the development of the economies of its partners. In 1971 they were able to add that the Com-munity had been the first among the developed countries to respond to the call made at the United Nations Conference on Trade, Aid and Development (U.N.C.T.A.D.) for the institution of a scheme of generalised preferences for the products of the developing countries.

Critics of the Community's posture argue on the other hand that its agricultural policy implies a substantial diversion of resources in favour of inefficient European producers; that its various preferential arrange-ments run counter to the general principles of the General Agreement on Trade and Tariffs (G.A.T.T.); that the African Association is a thinly disguised prolongation of former colonial ties of dependence; and that, in short, the Community is a rich man's club following poli-cies which either fail to give sufficient help to the developing world or are positively inimical to its interests.[2]

[1] Including a riposte from a Vice-President of the Commission, Mr. Raymond Barre. See *Europe Documents* No. 665 (28 February 1972) and No. 686 (22 June 1972) Agence Europe.

[2] See, for instance, David Wall, 'Trade Issues for the Developing Countries' in *Britain, the E.E.C. and the Third World*, Overseas Development Institute (London 1971).

POLITICAL IMPACT

The volume of argument on these lines about the Community's economic and social aspects has grown steadily through the years as the question 'What sort of Europe?' has been put with increasing insistence.

The debate has also extended to its more specifically political aspects, including military and security issues which as we have seen are not at present covered by specific treaty commitments. The major issues here are the future pattern of the Community's relations with the superpowers; its impact on relations with the rest of Europe, and in particular Eastern Europe; whether or not it should have its own army and defence policy (and if so, what its attitude to the possession of nuclear weapons should be); and whether it should seek to have a common posture towards such areas as the Middle East and on such issues as the forthcoming European security conference. With regard to these questions the arguments have developed less around what the impact of the Community has already been—for the good reason that the Community as such has not a common policy—than about what future common action it might take.

From our point of view there are two important points to be noted in these arguments about the Community. The first is that implicit in them is the view, which is now generally accepted both within and outside the Community, that it is already, and even more so potentially, a very important element both for the future development of European society itself and also as a factor in the relationships between Western Europe and the rest of the world. Secondly, it is recognised by everyone that what determines the content of the Community's actions is the constellation of political forces within it. What has been created is a new framework for the economic and political relationships of its members, and a new instrument for their collective policies towards the rest of the world. But the uses to which this instrument is put are wholly dependent on the attitudes and policies of the predominant political forces within it.

Similar considerations apply to the Community's own political system, the nature and possible future development of which have also given rise to sustained debate and argument. In structural terms the most striking feature of this system is its hybrid nature. It contains a number of features that differentiate it quite sharply from classic types of intergovernmental organisations, yet it is clearly not a federal system. The search for an appropriate nomenclature has been lengthy and so far fruitless. We can agree with the view expressed by Emile Noel that 'it is perhaps safest to be non-commital and leave it to future historians to fit the system into one or another of the international law-yers' categories, ourselves saying simply that it is a "Community" System'.[1]

As we have seen, the member governments have maintained effect-ive control over all the major levers of power within the system, while building up a very extensive and increasingly intensive network of mutual obligations towards one another and accepting corresponding constraints on their own freedom of action. At the same time they have also gradually adopted a range of norms regulating their behaviour within its institutions and procedures for the discussion and settling of policy issues. They have also agreed on, and have been notable in their continuing acceptance of, procedures for the applications and execu-tion of those decisions (not all of which are under their own direct con-trol), as well as methods for the adjudication of disputes by both the Community Court and national judicial bodies, and the imposition of sanctions in the case of non-observance of the treaties and the decisions which have flowed from them,

An undoubted merit of the system is that it has proved capable of producing decisions, and of pushing forward the realisation of the pro-gramme of economic integration laid down in the treaties. As one Dutch observer has remarked: 'The best thing that can be said about the present political institutions of Europe is that they have worked. And that is saying a lot.'[2] In the process the system has undoubtedly had a very important impact on the relationships between its member states. It has certainly made a major contribution to the creation of de facto solidarity in economic matters which was the primary objective of the original Schuman Plan. A crucial part of this has also been the establishment of a quite new pattern of relationships between France and the Federal Repulic. Hostility and fear have to a large extent been replaced by partnership, and—as the authors of the Schuman Plan also hoped—war between them has become 'not merely unthinkable but materially impossible'. This also applies to the other members of the Community. Other factors have undoubtedly contributed to bring about this situation—described by some political scientists as a 'plural-istic security community'—but it is difficult to believe that it could have been established so rapidly or so securely without the help of the machinery of the Community. At all events, in comparison with the past this is a major transformation of the West European political scene. The importance of this is not diminished by the fact that the new pattern of Franco–German relations has now become so much accepted

[1] Emile Noel, *How the European Community's Institutions Work*, Community Topics 38, European Communities Press and Information Service, London (1972) p. 1.

[2] Henri Faas, 'Safeguarding Democracy in a New European Government', *The Times*, (9 August 1972).

that fears of renewed conflict, inherited from memories of the past, have faded almost into oblivion in the course of the past 15 years.

If the achievement of this type of peaceful relations is one aspect of a successful process of political integration, the establishment of new patterns of loyalty and a sense of a shared political community—mutual political identification—is another. In this context progress has been more uneven. So far the Community has certainly enjoyed, as we have already seen, a very widespread degree of passive support on the part of the mass of the public of the original six member countries. This has been directly related to their desire to see an end to threats of renewal of conflict within Europe, and their expectations of improved living standards. Nor has there been any sign of resurgence of an old-style nationalism: attitudes held by young people have consistently demonstrated the weak appeal that this now has. This may well be due to factors other than—or in addition to—the existence of the Community, but nevertheless is an important background factor for its future development. Nevertheless, a much more critical set of attitudes to the Community has recently become apparent, particularly among the more politically active elements in this young generation. Those on the Left clearly regard the Community as a vehicle for the promotion of the interests of an essentially capitalist and materialistically orientated society, and for a set of values which they reject.[1]

Even among those who do not share these views there are two aspects of the Community's political system which are frequently criticised. One is its inefficiency, the other its lack of democratic safeguards. The first type of criticism is mainly confined to those with a close practical knowledge of the day-to-day operation of the system. They focus their attention on the complexity and slowness of decision-making procedures in the Community: the fact that as it has evolved, more and more bodies have been created in which the same arguments are repeated ad nauseam; that the continued insistence on unanimity for all major decisions prolongs this process and slows down the rate of decisions; that the system has been overloaded to the point at which the Council and its various organs are unable to cope with the flow of proposals from the Commission,[2] and that there is no mechanism to rescue proposals on which deadlock has developed. As the Vedel Committee reported:[3]

It has been seen that the automatic and at times nonchalant search for unanimity leads the Council into jams and deadlock. It is not the

[1] See Ronald Ingelhart, 'Changing Value Priorities and European Integration', *Journal of Common Market Studies* (September 1971).

[2] In mid-1972, for instance, the Commission complained that there were some 140 of its proposals which had not yet been considered by the ministers.

[3] *Op. cit.*, p. 45.

> Council's uncontested right to make decisions which is in question here. It is its capacity to take decisions and its responsibility for these decisions. The real problem is not caused by the Council refusing or amending Commission proposals but by the fact that these proposals are bogged down endlessly in minor procedures or silent inertia which dilute responsibilities and discourage initiatives.

The committee concluded this section of its report with the rather despairing comment that 'it will be seen that solutions are hard to find and that there is no panacea, but at least something will have to be done'.

The second type of criticism, which is much more widely and vehemently voiced, relates to the weaknesses of the parliamentary elements in the system, both at the national and Community level. While national parliaments have to a large extent lost their powers of decision and scrutiny with regard to those matters now being decided within a Community framework, there has been no corresponding gain on the part of the European parliament. Moreover, in the present system the individual citizen has no opportunity for active participation in its affairs, his political rights still being firmly confined within the boundaries of the individual member states. So at a time when many are urging the desirability of increased political participation the citizens of the Community find themselves confronted with an even more remote level of government and a net loss in their opportunities for participation.

The remedies which have been proposed to meet these criticisms are related to a continuing division of opinion within the Community about where power should lie within it, and how its political system should develop. This division was already apparent at the time of the formation of the first Community when some saw it as the means for rebuilding and strengthening the nation state, while others viewed it as the means by which power could—and should—gradually be transferred away from national governments to a new centre of political authority on a European scale.[1] The arguments between the two sides became particularly acute during the time de Gaulle was in power when he ruthlessly pursued a strategy based on the first view. His opponents, in seeking to defend the system agreed in the treaties, were forced to react rather sharply although very few of them were federalists.

The latter have always been in fact a rather small minority within the Community, though their views have been influential. The solution they propose to the twin problem of efficiency and democracy is,

[1] See L. N. Lindberg and S. A. Scheingold, *Europe's Would-be Polity*, New Jersey (1971) Ch. 1.

in outline, familiar. They argue that power should be transferred to an independent Community executive deriving its authority directly from the citizens of the member countries, and being responsible to a directly elected Community parliament. Views about how and when this radical transformation should take place vary, as do those relating to the method by which a Community government should be elected and the precise nature of its relationship with the parliament. And while there is a large measure of agreement among federalists that there should be a wide measure of devolution of power downwards, from national governments to regional and local authorities (as well as upwards to a Community authority), some go so far as to propose that the basic political unit should become the region rather than the nation state.[1]

Nevertheless, the main direction of the changes they would like to see is clear enough, and federalists can claim for their strategy the support of some of the original authors of the treaties, and a number of the commitments which the member governments assumed when they signed them including, for instance, the introduction of direct elections.

Their opponents do not necessarily dissent from the view that at some point in the future a federal form of organisation may be appropriate. They do, however, strongly deny that the conditions for this exist at present. In their view the only legitimate source of power in the Community is the individual nation state. This offers the only deeply-felt focus of political loyalty as far as the European citizen is concerned. According to this view, discussion about a federation is pointless at the present time, as is the attempt 'to construct ambitious superstructures that would lack foundations'.[2] Equally any structure that was not based on a consensus of national views would fail and so the veto must remain. According to this view therefore, the major task in the coming years is to concentrate on improving the machinery through which the member governments can more effectively concert their policies. President Pompidou, who is currently the major spokesman for this type of view, at one point suggested that one way to do this would be to appoint a minister responsible for European affairs —the suggestion apparently being that in the short-term such ministers would shoulder the major burden of the work of the Council of Ministers, and eventually evolve towards a confederal executive body. Later, however, he said that this 'was not for the immediate future'.[3] What he appears to have in mind, however—and the proposal for a political

---

[1] See Denis de Rougemont, *Lettre Ouverte Aux Européens* (Paris 1970).

[2] President Pompidou, speech at a luncheon in honour of the Federal German Government, 6 July 1971.

[3] Press conference, 21 January 1971; *The Times* (12 May 1972) p. 14.

secretariat fits in with this strategy—is that the institutional structures for the new areas of integration should be essentially intergovernmental in character and should be built up alongside, but separate from, the existing institutions within which—at the same time—the predominant role of the national governments should also be reinforced. Eventually the former might subsume the latter, with the role of the Commission being restricted to essentially administrative tasks connected with the day-to-day running of the Common Market.

A not dissimilar view of the future institutional strategy of the Community was published in the summer of 1971 by Ralf Dahrendorf, the distinguished German sociologist and in addition a member of the Commission. In two articles in *Die Zeit*[1] published anonymously, he launched a frontal assault on what he called 'the first Europe'—which was the one inherited from the early days of the movement towards integration and characterised by what he stigmatised as a 'certain institutional dogmatism' divorced from political realities. He contrasted this with 'the second Europe' which was begining to emerge with a new set of institutions on the model of those constructed by the Davignon Committee for the pursuit of political union, and which gave the national governments the central role. This, in his view, was the right way forward; he supported the idea of the appointment of Ministers for European Affairs who would take over the primary tasks of the work of the Council of Ministers, and suggested that as far as the Commission was concerned it should abandon its ambitions of being a government 'in spe', and that it should be reduced in size to a president and two or three members. He thought that alongside the Commission serving the existing Communities similar bodies might be created for other areas of policy. He also took issue with those who urged direct election for the European Parliament: this he said would change absolutely nothing at all: it was 'a luxury which for the time being one can do without'.

These two sets of views represent the major alternative institutional models which have emerged within the Community. This was clear from the various papers submitted by several of the national governments for the 1972 Summit meeting, as well as from suggestions put forward from other bodies and individuals. However, the majority of the political elite within the original six member countries would prefer—at least for the immediate future—various intermediate types of solution.[2] On the one hand, most of the proposals laid stress on the

[1] 'Wieland Europa' *Die Zeit* (9 and 10 July 1972).

[2] Various of these proposals are to be found in the *Europe Documents* series published by the private news agency Agence Europe. See in particular Nos. 666. (Luxembourg), 680 (Commission), 681 (Netherlands), 682 (Belgium), 683 (Italy) and 690 (European Parliament), published between March and July 1972.

need to streamline the working of the Council and its various associated bodies; suggestions included that of giving a more positive role to the president of this body (possibly making it a full-time job), imposing various types of time-limits on the decision-making process, making a clearer distinction between major and minor items of business, and increasing the use of abstention in those cases where a clear majority view has emerged in the Council, rather than insisting on positive unanimity. On the other hand, there was also a strong insistence that the role of both the Commission and the Parliament should be strengthened so that the original institutional balance between the 'national' and 'Community' interest could be restored. Equally, this band of opinion was anxious that established Community procedures should also be used for the pursuit of economic and monetary union, and that a clear treaty base for this should be established. And while no-one (not even the Commission itself) suggested that the Commission–Council dialogue was appropriate at this stage for the coordination of foreign and defence policy, they stressed that any political secretariat that was established should be tied in with the existing institutions, and that the Foreign Ministers should be required to report on their activities in this sphere to the European Parliament.

These preparatory papers, while demonstrating a very considerable degree of consensus on these short-term measures, diverged quite markedly on the further development of the system. While the European Parliament, for its part, reiterated its desire to see a fully-fledged European government being established with the national governments being represented in a *Chambre des Etats*, alongside a popularly elected Parliament, and the Italians that they would like eventually to see a federal system also, most national views were more reticent—the governments being clearly anxious not to provoke a major conflict with the French in particular. In fact, very little progress on these institutional issues was made at the Paris Summit, though a series of deadlines was established by which action—for the most part of an unspecified type—was to be taken. As with so many other issues, this is one with which the enlarged Community will now have to deal.

Part Two The Enlarged Community: Political Perspectives

5 Political Characteristics of the Enlarged Community

The addition of three new members—Britain, Denmark and Ireland —has made a very considerable difference both to the geographical extent and other aspects of the size of the Community. With a total population of some 250 million people it is now of a scale to bear comparison in many respects with both the United States and the Soviet Union. With regard to trade it is indeed a far more important element on the world scene than either of them, accounting for about 40% of both imports and exports (see *Table 5.1*).

From our point of view, however, it is the political characteristics of the new Community which are of primary importance. In this context the initial questions to be posed are how far, and in what ways, the enlarged Community differs from the original six-member Community, and whether or not its pursuit of integration is as a consequence likely to be more or less difficult than in the past.

BACKGROUND CONDITIONS

Our starting point for an analysis of this aspect of the new Community is provided by the factors identified in Chapter 2 as being the most relevant to an understanding of the dynamics of the process. The first of these factors, it will be recalled, consists of those major structural features of society which together compose the background conditions which are likely to exert an influence on the development of the new group's efforts to integrate.

The most apparent and indeed obvious change in this respect is the enlarged geographical scope of the Community. It now includes the

Table 5.1 THE ENLARGED COMMUNITY: COMPARISONS WITH THE UNITED STATES, THE SOVIET UNION, AND JAPAN*

Totals	E.E.C.	U.S.A.	U.S.S.R.	Japan
Population (millions)	252 609	205 395	242 768	103 540
G.N.P. ($ 1000 m.)	626·0	991·1	288†	196·1
Imports (% World total)	39·7	13·7	4·0	6·5
Exports (% World total)	40·3	15·5	4·6	6·9
Cereals: production average 1968–1970 (1000 t.)	90 476	192 966	160 145	1 742
Meat: production 1969 (1000 t.)	16 267	23 227	9 250	1 136
Milk products: 1969 (1000 t.)	97 153	52 707	81 500	4 513
Primary energy: total production (1000 tec.)	500 113	2 151 397	1 386 090	71 392
Primary energy: internal consumption (m. tec.)	1 233·1	2 250·6	1 230·0	379·6
Petroleum products (1000 t.)	498 634	565 488	n.a.	159 689
Electrical energy: gross production (kWh)	856 613	1 738 142	740 926	350 590
Steel production (1000 t.)	138 073	122 120	116 000	93 322
Motor vehicle producton: passenger cars + commercial vehicles (1000s)	10 894	8 283	1 168	5 289
Rail transport: passenger km. (millions)	154 184	19 568	261 300	n.a.
Merchant shipping: 1.7.1970 (1000 t. gross)	57 370	18 463	14 832	27 004
Motor vehicles in use: 1.1.1971	54 515	89 861	1 700	8 779
Passenger cars (per 1000 pop.)	218	432	7	85
Television receivers (1000s)	57 515	81 000	30 744	21 879
per 1000 population	229	399	127	214
Telephones (1000s)	50 206	115 222	12 000	19 899
per 1000 population	211	567	50	194

Source: *Basic Statistics of the Community 1971*, Commission of the European Communities, Brussels (1972).

*Figures refer to 1970 unless otherwise stated.

†'Net material product': roughly equivalent to the total yearly production of goods and services, and not strictly comparable with G.N.P.

Table 5.2 THE TRADE OF THE ENLARGED COMMUNITY: TOTAL IMPORTS BY AREA OF ORIGIN (1970)

	Total Imports ($m)	Origin								
		Community		E.F.T.A.		U.S.A.		Rest of World	
		($m.)	(%)	($m.)	(%)	($m.)	(%)	($m.)	(%)
Ger.	29 814	13 233	44·4	4 464	15·0	3 293	11·0	8 824	29·6
Fr.	18 992	9 256	48·9	1 980	10·5	1 896	10·0	5 790	30·6
It.	14 939	6 146	41·2	1 588	10·6	1 543	10·3	5 662	37·9
Neths.	13 393	7 483	55·9	1 498	11·2	1 308	9·7	3 104	23·2
Belg.} Lux.}	11 353	6 683	58·9	1 196	10·5	995	8·8	2 479	21·8
The Six	88 422	42 800	48·4	10 725	12·1	9 335	10·2	25 862	29·3
U.K.	21 723	4 373	20·1	3 374	15·5	2 815	13·0	11 161	51·4
Ireland	1 569	259	16·5	933	59·5	110	7·0	267	17·0
Denmark	4 385	1 457	33·2	1 808	41·2	327	7·5	793	18·1
The Nine	116 128	48 890	42·1	17 201	14·8	12 287	10·6	38 080	32·8
U.S.A.	39 963	6 612	16·6	3 812	9·5	—	—	29 539	73·9
U.S.S.R.	11 739	1 170	10·0	619	5·3	115	1·0	9 835	83·7
Japan	18 881	1 117	5·9	762	4·0	5 564	29·5	11 438	60·6

Source: *Basic Statistics of the Community 1971*, Commission of the European Communities, Brussels (1972).

greater part of Western Europe, and membership covers most of the countries in the area. Moreover the new Community has already concluded association or other agreements with almost all who remain outside, including six of the original members of the European Free Trade Association—Austria, Finland, Iceland, Portugal, Sweden and Switzerland—who now have an industrial free trade area with the Community. It is expected that in due course Norway will also enter into a similar arrangement. The new members have, for their part, subscribed to the agreements concluded earlier by the Six providing for association agreements with Greece, Turkey and Malta, and a trade agreement with Spain.

The process of enlargement has therefore removed one important weakness of the original Community, for although there may be problems for the Nine in their relations with some of the surrounding countries in Western Europe, it is rather unlikely that the degree of strain arising from these will be in any way comparable either in intensity or duration to that which the Six experienced with regard to the issue of British membership throughout the greater part of the sixties. There could be problems should France press for a closer relationship with Spain, as President Pompidou has urged from time to time; though on this question France is likely to be isolated as long as the present regime in that country persists. The fact that only one of the Scandinavian countries has become a full member is likely to prove less of a problem for the Community than for the Nordic countries themselves: the material interest of Denmark in remaining a member is so strong that it is very unlikely that her neighbours would be able—even if they sought to do so—to weaken her attachment to it. Indeed, the pressures are likely to operate in the opposite direction, and particularly with regard to Norway whose rejection of membership may prove to be a temporary rather than a permanent decision.

Another positive element in the situation is that the new members share many of the major characteristics of their partners. They have absorbed the same cultural heritage; their level of economic development is roughly comparable (though Ireland constitutes a partial exception to this, which has been recognised by special concessions for the transitional period): they certainly share with the original Six a similar set of economic and political values, and each have a well-established system of representative and parliamentary government. The level of their transactions with the Six is also high. As far as trade is concerned (see *Tables 5.2* and *5.3*) there are certainly a number of important disparities, particularly with regard to the much higher current level of exchanges between the original members of the Community compared with the flows between them and the new members, and also the very much greater dependence by Britain on trade with the

Table 5.3 THE TRADE OF THE ENLARGED COMMUNITY: TOTAL EXPORTS BY AREA OF DESTINATION (1970)

	Total Exports ($m.)	Destination							
		Community		E.F.T.A.		U.S.A.		Rest of World	
		($m.)	(%)	($m.)	(%)	($m.)	(%)	($m.)	(%)
Ger.	34 189	13 726	40·2	7 734	22·6	3 124	9·1	9 605	28·1
Fr.	17 739	8 661	48·8	2 325	13·1	954	5·4	5 799	32·7
It.	13 210	5 673	42·9	1 827	13·8	1 354	10·3	4 356	33·0
Neths.	11 767	7 290	61·9	1 775	15·1	506	4·3	2 196	18·7
Belg.} Lux.}	11 595	7 950	68·6	1 224	10·5	696	6·0	1 725	14·9
The Six	88 500	43 300	48·9	14 885	16·8	6 633	7·5	23 681	26·8
U.K.	19 351	4 209	21·8	3 064	15·8	2 258	11·7	9 820	50·7
Ireland	1 035	120	11·6	700	67·6	104	10·1	111	10·7
Denmark	3 290	746	22·7	1 639	49·8	263	8·0	642	19·5
The Nine	112 176	48 375	43·1	20 288	18·1	9 259	8·2	34 254	30·5
U.S.A.	43 226	8 423	19·5	4 506	10·4	—	—	30 297	10·1
U.S.S.R.	12 800	859	6·7	733	5·7	64	0·5	11 144	87·1
Japan	19 318	1 303	6·7	1 112	5·8	6 015	31·1	10 888	56·4

Source: *Basic Statistics of the Community 1971*, Commission of the European Communities, Brussels (1972).

rest of the world. The latter phenomenon in particular has important policy implications for the new Community, but for the rest the most significant feature is that all its members are important trade partners for each other.

The social transactions within the group are also at a high level, not least in terms of tourist flows. The impact of the mass media, particularly television, is also very important in this context, the volume of mutual information being transmitted and received in recent years having risen enormously. These countries have also taken part alongside the Six in the work of many widely-based European and international organisations, both governmental (including the O.E.E.C. and the O.E.C.D. and the Council of Europe) and otherwise.

These countries are certainly not strangers to their new partners or to each other. Nevertheless the balance sheet is not wholly positive. One important consideration is the fact that all the new members belong to the north western seaboard of Europe: this implies both a shift in the overall geographical balance of the Community (though this is likely to strengthen, rather than weaken the claim of Brussels to remain the site of the headquarters of its institutions), and the admission of a group of countries whose attitudes, traditions and habits differ perceptibly from those of its more southerly members. This is not in itself necessarily a very important phenomenon, for the original Community had no great difficulty itself in bringing together in a close working relationship those from the Mediterranean and more northerly parts of Western Europe. It is, however, given more significance by the fact that the *lingua franca* of all the new members is English. This is certainly a cause of concern to the French, who fear that it will bring in its train a serious threat to the current predominance of that language as a *langue vehiculaire* in the day-to-day work of the Community; it is an intensification of the pressures already being exercised more generally on the purity of French—which are already apparent in the widespread intrusion of English expressions and the neologisms of *franglais*, and, in a more diffuse way, the dangers of a heightening of the cultural challenge currently being presented by the Anglo-Saxon world.

These fears were already sufficient for them to have exercised President Pompidou during the course of the negotiations and for Mr. Heath to have attempted to placate them by promising that the British civil servants sent to work on the Community institutions would be required to have a competent grasp of French. But the dangers from the French point of view are real enough, especially as the Dutch and the Germans, together with the Flemish members of any Belgian group, are likely to prefer working in English as a second language rather than French. Even the Italians cannot be altogether counted on to support the Francophones, for although French is certainly at present the most widely-known second language in Italy there are elements of cultural and political stress in the relations between the two countries which, combined with rather strong Anglophile elements in sections of the Italian elite, tend to result in a knowledge of English having a higher social cachet—as well as more utilitarian value—than a knowledge of French.

It is difficult to judge at this stage how far and in what ways this element of cultural and linguistic tension in the situation is likely to impinge on the process of integration itself. But it is unlikely to disappear, and will undoubtedly be a disturbing factor in the relationship between France and Britain which—for other reasons—is unlikely in any case to prove easy.

In any case, this cultural and linguistic element is only part of a much more significant change in the Community: the fact that a new major power has been added to the original members, and has been required to accept the bargains and rules made by those members in their own interests. This means that not only has the original balance of power within the Community been profoundly altered, but also that the new Community will have to adjust itself to the interests and demands of this substantial new member. Whereas the Six refused to contemplate any major changes in their policies during the negotiations on accession, it is quite clear that the Nine will have, over a period of time, to adjust them in order to establish an acceptable equilibrium between the various interests of the members of the new Community. There are, as we shall see, a number of existing Community policies which any British government is bound to seek to change or adjust: British membership has also brought with it the challenge of a greatly enhanced role for the Community in the world at large.

These are very significant changes: while in many respects the new Community is much stronger than that of the original Six, there is no doubt that the fact of enlargement has also brought with it a whole new set of problems, and ushered in a major new phase in its development.

DEMANDS

The second element in our analysis is that concerned with the likely future strength and direction of the demands for integration within the new Community. In this respect the fact that Britain and the other applicants persisted so long in their policy of seeking to join, in spite of their prolonged and uncomfortable sojourn for over eleven years in the ante-room of the Six, is in itself impressive evidence of the strength of the pressures generated in these countries to enter and take part in the process. Nor is this consideration greatly weakened by the fact that the smaller countries only decided to submit their applications once Britain herself had decided to apply, for although the prospect of British membership was certainly the most important single consideration in the determination of their government policy, it was apparent in the subsequent debates in these countries that this was certainly not the only reason for their doing so.

The general lines of the arguments used in favour of membership were those already familiar within the Six themselves, with the additional element of fears about the consequence of remaining outside. In all cases there was a strong emphasis on the expectations of economic benefits, with British statements in particular rather ruefully reflecting on the failure of Britain outside the Community to keep pace with the rates of growth which the latter had achieved. As the July 1971 White Paper, issued when the bulk of the negotiations had been successfully concluded, argued in introducing the economic case for membership.[1]

> The central question here is how membership of the Community would affect the structure of our economy and so the prosperity of our people. For many years we have faced familiar problems: difficulties with the balance of payments, a disappointing record in industrial investment, and an inadequate rate of economic growth. The result is that we have begun to drop seriously behind other countries, and particularly the members of the Community, in attaining a higher standard of living.
>
> The Government believes that membership would provide the most favourable opportunity of achieving the progress which we all desire.

We can expect, therefore, that all of the new members will be as anxious as the Six have been to take steps to develop the Community as an instrument of sustained economic growth and higher living standards. We can also expect, however, that they will have different attitudes as to how this can best be achieved, both in terms of the priorities they will attach to particular policy areas and also the content of individual policies. In the next chapter we shall analyse this in some greater detail: here it is sufficient to underline the fact that the economic structures and problems of the new members are likely to lead to some quite sharp divergences of policy on a wide range of issues concerning both the implementation of the existing treaties and also the new policy areas which will be involved in the process of achieving an economic and monetary union.

[1] *The United Kingdom and European Communities*, H.M.S.O; Cmnd. 4715, London, pp. 11–12. This document contains a useful summary of the Government's case for membership (pp. 7–17).

One significant additional feature of the Community is the pressure that can be expected to develop for it to create the machinery and policies for it to play a more prominent role in the world at large. The major thrust for this is likely to come from Britain where the protagonists of membership have consistently laid great emphasis upon this aspect of integration. Successive prime ministers, for instance, have all stressed this aspect of British expectations with regard to the enlarged Community,[1] and official presentations of the case for entry always laid great stress on the same point, as have prominent members of both political parties. Two examples will suffice to show how pervasive an impulse this is: one from an article by Mr. Duncan Sandys, the other from a speech by Mr. Roy Jenkins—two men whose views on other matters are usually poles apart:

> A united Europe will have to concern herself not just with the affairs of this continent, but with the problems of the world as a whole . . . in future Europe will have to shoulder world-wide responsibilities, and make her own contribution to world-wide peace and stability.[2]

> The new Europe has not yet matched her wealth by her inspiration or her influences in the world . . . If we can make European unity an accepted force not only for European but for world progress, then we shall indeed be fulfilling a new leadership role.[3]

A similar view was also voiced by *The Times* on the morrow of the conclusion of the decisive agreements in Luxembourg on 23 June 1972, which paved the way to the signature of the Treaty of Accession. In its first leader on that day, under the heading 'The mid power of the world' it declared:

> Britain's joining will not simply provide Britain alone with partnership. With other new members Britain will make the European Community itself much stronger and more of a force in its own right among the great world states.

It is quite clear from these and similar pronouncements that many of the leading protagonists of entry among the British elite see this as the

---

[1] See, for instance, Harold Macmillan, *Britain, the Commonwealth and Europe,* London (1962), p. 7; Harold Wilson, House of Commons, 2 May 1967; and Edward Heath, *Old world, new horizons* (Godkin lectures, 1967), London (1970), ch. 3.

[2] Duncan Sandys, 'The political case', in *Europe: the case for going in,* London (1971), p. 134.

[3] Roy Jenkins, 'Europe past and future': Speech at Aachen on receiving the Charlemagne Prize (11 May 1972).

response, at last, to Dean Acheson's quip that Britain had 'lost an empire but not yet found a role'. Although at the time the remark triggered off an angry set of protestations, it was in fact acute and accurate: what is now apparent is that a country which was until recently a genuine world power still preserves among its political leaders in strong measure the urge to continue that role in a new guise, that is, as a leading member of the Community.

It will be surprising, therefore, if Britain does not seek to inject a new urgency and thrust into the rather desultory progress the Community has so far made in equipping itself to perform such a worldwide role. Whether there will be as much enthusiasm for this among the other new members as in Whitehall is rather doubtful. The smaller countries concerned cannot be expected to share the same set of attitudes as a country which has for so many centuries been accustomed to stride about the globe: they for the most part have been content to occupy a more modest stage. There was a period in Irish post-war history when it sought, as an uncommitted country, to play a larger role but enthusiasm for this has waned since its troops found themselves involved in Congolese affairs on behalf of the United Nations. So that while the government in Dublin has signified its readiness to work with its partners towards the achievement of political unification, the *White Paper* it published in January 1972 added: 'It should, however, be emphasised that the treaties of Rome and Paris do not entail any military or defence commitments', and Mr. Lynch was careful to assure his party that any military commitment would first be submitted to a referendum.

The other smaller countries in the Community are also likely to look with considerable hesitation at any prospect of being thrust back into the front line of world affairs in the wake of the eager British, especially if this were to have significant financial implications. The French and the Germans—particularly the former—are unlikely to have such strong inhibitions, but in their case the question then arises if the type of world role they conceive for the Community coincides with that of the British. In practice the situation is likely to be even more complicated with different groups in the various countries taking up a variety of positions on the options which are likely to present themselves.[1] A great deal will therefore depend on the constellation of power in the Community at any given time whether agreement can be reached on specific measures and specific policies to give substance to the British desire to see the Community play a significant and positive role on the world scene.

On the whole the situation the Community is likely to face is there-

[1] See Chapter 6.

fore one of a high initial level of demands, encompassing a very wide spectrum of its activities. Unless it fails in some dramatic way to satisfy at least the more pressing of these during the interim period (due to be completed at the end of 1977) during which the new members will be adjusting to the customs union and common agricultural policy, there is a good prospect that this level will be sustained throughout the seventies. The problems likely to arise are on the one hand overloading of the system, which may not be able in a satisfactory way to respond to the sheer volume of demand (we have already seen the difficulties the six-member Community has had in processing the demands it has experienced) and on the other from the divergent nature of at least some of the demands made upon it. In either case output failure could lead to negative feedback or 'spillback' processes developing; that is, a failure to fulfil expectations and a weakening or withdrawal of support from the Community. At all events, it is clear that very heavy pressure will be exerted on the Community institutions in the coming years, and on the leaders whose task it will be to guide it through the shoals which lie ahead.

SUPPORTS

In considering the strength, distribution and nature of the support for the enlarged Community we need first to examine the situation in the new members' countries and then turn to the situation with respect to the group as a whole.

As far as the new members themselves are concerned there has been far more, and far more prolonged, public discussion of the pros and cons of membership than ever took place in the Six themselves. This has meant both that the elites supporting membership have had to work harder, and over a longer period of time, to mobilise the necessary support for entry than was the case on the continent— particularly in the countries where referenda were held on the issue—and also that the prolonged debate has led in several cases to a marked polarisation of attitudes to the Community. This is most marked in the case of Britain itself, where both the major parties and even the Liberals have been divided on the issue.

The distribution of support within the new members is therefore at present very uneven. As far as popular opinion is concerned one guide is provided by the votes recorded in the referenda. In the case of Ireland there was an overwhelming favourable response. Both the Government party, Fianna Fail, and the main opposition party, Fine Gael, campaigned in favour of entry. There was a high (70%) turnout at the polls, with the following result:

For entry   1 041 890 votes (83%)

Against   211 891 votes (17%)

The overwhelmingly favourable response surprised even the most optimistic expectations of the protagonists of entry: as one commentator wrote: 'Never since independence 50 years ago had the people spoken with such unanimity and such unity of purpose, so often sadly lacking in Ireland's troubled history.'[1] The result reflected the strong desire of the Irish to escape from their very heavy degree of economic dependence on Britain, their fears for their agricultural markets if they remained outside and also—more positively—their sense of commitment to Europe nurtured by the Catholic Church.

In comparison with the overwhelming support expressed by the Irish for membership, that obtained in the referendum held in Denmark —though still substantial—was markedly lower. This was held a week after the Norwegians had rejected membership by a vote of 53% to 47% following a campaign marked by violent opposition against entry led by a combination of those groups in society who feared for their own material interests—in particular the farming and fishing communities —backed up by a substantial body of radical students who attacked the Community for being a materialist and capitalist venture. In the Danish case this type of ideological opposition was also voiced by a section of the younger generation, but did not find such ready allies, Danish farmers and industrial interests being acutely conscious of serious problems they would face if the country rejected membership. Given a strong lead by its Social Democrat government, the country voted by 63·5% to 36·5% in favour of entry.

Britain was the one country among the new entrants where the issue of entry was not submitted to the test of a referendum. During the passage of the European Communities Bill, the leadership of the Labour Party, rather hesitantly[2] proposed that there should be either a referendum or a general election to enable the public in general to have a voice in the decision whether or not to join the Community, but the government refused and succeeded in defeating the proposed amendments to the Bill. Much play was, however, made with a statement made by Mr. Heath that the government would only contemplate joining if it was assured of 'the whole-hearted consent of the British parliament and people'. This, the Opposition argued, he had certainly not secured.

The evidence of the public opinion polls supported this view. A survey undertaken on behalf of the European Movement in the spring

---

[1] Joe Carroll, 'Ireland's landslide for Europe', *European Community* (June 1972).

[2] Mr. Wilson himself had earlier argued strongly against holding a referendum on the issue.

of 1971 showed that five out of every ten electors said that they would be disappointed if Britain joined, only three said they would be pleased and two were undecided.[1] Later, at the time of the decisive vote in Parliament in October that year a Gallup Poll showed a not dissimilar situation in reply to a straight question on whether respondents were in favour or against joining, only 32% of the sample recording a favourable response as compared with 51% against and 17% 'don't know'. Subsequently, in July 1972 and in reply to the same question the response was only marginally more favourable: 36% for entry, 51% against and 13% undecided.

This level of opposition to entry appears to have been higher than at any point during the 11 long years during which Britain had sought to join.[2] During the 1961–1963 negotiations opinion had fluctuated quite markedly, with the numbers expressing approval for membership were the government to decide to enter moving between 38% at the time of the application to negotiate, to a peak of 50% in November 1962, then dropping back to 41% in January 1963. Those opposed to entry had, over the same period, risen from 22% to a peak of 34% in August 1962, subsequently falling in January 1963 to 30%. Throughout these first negotiations there was, however, a large body of 'don't knows', rarely less than 30% of the sample. During the second abortive attempt by the Labour government to enter into negotiations, an attempt backed by the Conservative opposition and sanctioned by a massive majority in the House of Commons in May 1967 of 488 to 62, the percentage of the uncommitted dropped to under 20% while those in favour (which at the end of 1966 had risen to as many as 65–67%) hovered around the 40% mark. Those registering disapproval, who throughout 1966 had remained less than 20% of the sample, increased to 34% at the time of the parliamentary vote.

The general level of support for entry negotiations was markedly higher during this second attempt than on the first occasion, the main reason being the favourable attitude taken by the Labour government and its impact on the party's supporters. The change in the party's attitude when out of office after June 1970 and subsequently being faced by specific terms for entry can be assumed to have had a considerable impact, and to have contributed to the rise in those opposed to membership. At all events, and with all due allowances having been made

[1] Barry Hedges and Roger Jowell, 'Britain and the E.E.C.', *Report on a Survey of attitudes towards the European Economic Community*, Social and Community Planning Research, London (July 1971).

[2] The data available for the earlier periods are not strictly comparable as the formulation of the questions asked varied from time to time. For a discussion of the period 1957–April 1967, see Henry Durant, 'Public opinion and the E.E.C.', *Journal of Common Market Studies* (March 1968), also *ibid.* (September 1966).

for the difficulties of interpreting the data, one must conclude that when the crunch came only about a third of the British population, taken as a whole, was positively in favour of joining.

This, however, is only a very crude yardstick by which to judge the level of support for the Community among the general public in Britain. The yes/no/don't know categorisation offers a very simplified picture of what is a very complex pattern of attitudes. A more detailed analysis showed, for instance, that only 30% of those polled considered the issue to be very important; 33% thought it moderately important; and 13% were unconcerned about it. Among the last group there were far more opponents of entry than in the other two groups. The conclusion drawn from this was that: 'The ranks of opponents of entry are very much swollen by the inclusion of a large number of people who are comparatively indifferent to the whole issue. If these are discounted, support and opposition are evenly balanced. But the more serious opponents who are left after discounting this group are perhaps more emphatic in their opposition than supporters are in their advocacy of entry.'[1]

The same poll also found that those who seemed more knowledgeable about the Community tended to be more favourable to entry than those who were not; that the under 30's were more favourable to entry than older people; and that among the various socio-economic groups the professional and managerial groups were much more in favour than manual workers.[2] When the nature of expectations and fears about entry were probed both this and another poll[3] found that a substantial majority believed that the short-term impact would be unfavourable. The main concern was higher prices. In one sample 67% thought that membership would have this effect; in another as many as 81%. The main positive benefit, on the other hand, which was expected was improved prospects for the British economy over the longer term. Economic considerations, both negative and positive, appear to have loomed much larger in people's minds than any political arguments, though when confronted with the proposition, 'If we stay out of Europe, Britain will have less and less influence in the world', 42% expressed agreement. An equal percentage, however, offered no opinion—which suggests that this aspect of entry, so important to sections of the elite, was rather obscure for much of the population.

If we now compare attitudes in Britain towards the Community

[1] Barry Hedges and Roger Jowell, *op. cit.,* p. 58.

[2] Barry Hedges and Roger Jowell, *op. cit.*, p. 73. The sample taken of the professional group was very small but its results are confirmed from other sources. See, for instance, Henri Durant, *op. cit.*, for the situation in 1967.

[3] Gallup Poll No. 135 (October 1971). For a detailed analysis see Uwe Kitzinger, *Diplomacy and Persuasion*, Ch. 12 and Appendix 3, London (1973).

with those on the continent at the level of mass public opinion we are immediately confronted by the very big gap which separates the two sides of the Channel. Dramatic evidence of this was provided by an opinion poll undertaken by a group of major European newspapers in the early part of 1970 based on a representative sample totalling 11 695 people in the seven countries.[1]

In the first place, this showed that there was a very high level of support on the continent for the entry of Britain, in marked contrast to views in Britain itself:

Q: Are you for or against the entry of Britain into the Common Market?

	Belg.	Fr.	Ger.	It.	Neths.	Lux.	(E.E.C.)	U.K.
For	89	86	91	85	90	92	(88)	23
Against	11	14	9	15	10	8	(12)	77

But perhaps even more important for the future of the enlarged Community are the results obtained in answer to other questions which probed attitudes to the political future of the Community, for here again the same gulf emerged in respect of three significant themes:

Q: Are you for or against the evolution of the Common Market towards the political construction of the United States of Europe?

	Belg.	Fr.	Ger.	It.	Neths.	Lux.	(E.E.C.)	U.K.
For	86	86	88	90	79	93	(87)	38
Against	14	14	12	10	21	7	(13)	62

Q: Are you for or against the election of a European Parliament by direct universal suffrage—that is, of a parliament elected by all the citizens of the member countries?

	Belg.	Fr.	Ger.	It.	Neths.	Lux.	(E.E.C.)	U.K.
For	83	80	88	90	74	88	(85)	31
Against	17	20	12	10	26	12	(15)	69

Q: Do you accept that there should be, above the government of your country, a European government responsible for common policies in the fields of foreign affairs, defence, and economics?

	Belg	Fr.	Ger.	It.	Neths.	Lux.	(E.E.C.)	U.K.
For	73	64	75	83	61	57	(72)	27
Against	27	36	25	17	39	43	(28)	73

These figures are one measure—however crude—of the very real distance that separates British and continental opinion as a result of the

[1] The details which follow are taken from a report on the findings of this poll published by the Directorate General for Press and Information of the Commission of the European Communities: *Les Européens: Oui à l'Europe*, Brussels pp. 11–13 (May 1970).

long years during which Britain has been a spectator of, rather than a participant in, the work of the Community. It can hardly be expected that the gap will be speedily closed, and it may well provide a source of real difficulty in the new Community.

As within the Community itself, however, the critical role will be played by the political elites in the various countries. Here the British scene is characterised by a very marked divergence between those who have supported and those who have opposed entry: a divergence which has led to an increasing polarisation of attitudes. But unlike the situation with regard to mass opinion, it is within the British elites that the pro-Community group has asserted its ascendancy, and indeed it is due to its sustained and strenuous efforts that membership was achieved. The process by which this group was formed and achieved its victory was lengthy and complex, and there is no space here to deal with it in detail. But the critical turning point was certainly the decision of the Macmillan government in 1961 to jettison previous British policy towards the Community, and to apply to join—a decision which provided the bulk of the coalition which eventually saw the European Communities Bill safely through Parliament. This coalition included a significant group—including some of its most distinguished leaders —of the Labour party, and a majority of the Liberals. Outside, in the country, it was supported by the overwhelming majority of business and industrial leaders (including the Confederation of British Industry), the National Farmers Union (which by 1970 had dropped its original objections to entry), and a substantial element of the press and those working in the mass media, and a strong (though by no means unanimous) body of academic opinion. This coalition pursued the quest of membership through the long years of waiting in the ante-room of the Community with remarkable persistence, sustained by a revivified British section of the European Movement. The critical moment came in the House of Commons on 28 August 1971. On that occasion the voting was as follows:

	For entry	Against	Abstentions
Conservatives	282	39	2
Labour	69	198	20
Liberals	5	1	—
Others	—	6	—
Total	356	244	22

Although the opposition to entry in the Conservative parliamentary party included a number of prominent men—not least Mr. Enoch Powell—they were too divided on other issues to form a coherent group which could pose any major threat to the leadership under Mr. Heath which pursued its objective with ruthless determination. One can safely assume, therefore, that as long as the party remains in power it will be firmly committed to membership of the Community. We can also assume that those seventy or so members of the Labour party who defied their own party Whips to vote with the government in October 1971 will also remain committed to the same policy.

For a number of years this group—then headed by Mr. George Brown—was in the ascendancy during the period when the party was in office. It was under their impulsion that the decision was taken in 1966 to seek to reopen negotiations, and their conviction which subsequently sustained Mr. Wilson's government through the rebuff it suffered at the hands of de Gaulle. On that occasion, at the end of 1967, the government persisted in its policy of seeking entry and, had it not been for the defeat which it sustained in June 1970 at the general election, it would have been a Labour government that negotiated the terms of entry.

Once the terms became known, however, those members in both the parliamentary party and its National Executive who had always been opposed to membership took the offensive again. In spite of the fact that it was generally agreed that the terms actually negotiated by Mr. Heath were much the same as those which a Labour government would have obtained, strong pressure developed in the party to reject them. Mr. Wilson himself bowed to this pressure leaving his deputy, Mr. Roy Jenkins, in a very exposed position. The latter did not, however, resign until the parliamentary party decided in spring 1972 to seek a general election or a referendum on the issue: at that point several of the other prominent pro-Europeans in the party also resigned their Front Bench positions, and some others were relieved of them. Mr. Michael Foot, who had always been prominent among those opposing entry, became one of the party's chief spokesmen in the House of Commons, together with Mr. Peter Shore, and Mr. Douglas Jay—who had been dropped from the Labour cabinet because of his opposition to the 1967 bid—was also restored to favour.

Although some of the pro-marketeers remained on the party's national executive, the policy statement which emerged from it in the summer of 1972 was quite uncompromising.[1] It asserted that once returned to power a Labour government would renegotiate the terms of entry with the aim of obtaining major changes in the common agricultural policy, newer and fairer methods of financing the Community's budget, the rejection of any proposal for fixed parities, the retention for Parliament of 'those powers needed to pursue effective regional, industrial and fiscal policies'; an agreement on capital movements to protect the British balance of payments and full employ-

[1] 'Labour and the Common Market', *Labour's Programme for Britain*, London (July 1972).

ment policies, and measures to safeguard the economic interests of the Commonwealth and the developing countries. The party, it said, would also oppose any harmonisation of the V.A.T. which would require Britain to tax necessities; and would insist that the cost of structural policies for agriculture be met from national rather than Community funds. If negotiations with these objectives were successful, the party would put the issue of continued membership to the electorate either at a general election or through a referendum. If 'the expressed approval of the majority of the British people' was obtained, it would then be willing to play its full part in the Community. On the other hand if negotiations were not successful 'we shall not regard the treaty obligations as binding upon us. We shall then put to the British people why we find the new terms unacceptable, and consult them on the advisability of negotiating our withdrawal from the Communities'.

This statement was the outcome of a hard-fought battle between those in the national executive of the party who wished to see it oppose entry on any terms and others, including Mr. Wilson, who wished to maintain at least some elements of consistency in their policy and to retain some freedom of manoeuvre for the future. But before it had been submitted to the annual conference of the party in October 1972 the fragile compromise was threatened by a surprise decision of the T.U.C. at its own annual congress to oppose the *principle* (rather than the terms) of membership—a decision taken by a vote of 4 892 000 to 3 516 000. Mr. Wilson had to fight hard for the National Executive's statement and for the rejection of a motion which proposed to follow the line taken by the T.U.C. In the end the latter was rejected by a small majority (3 076 000 to 2 958 000) while the official policy was confirmed by a substantial majority of 3 407 000 votes to 1 802 000. At the same time, however, another resolution proposed by the Boilermakers' Union was also passed by a vote of 3 335 000 to 2 867 000 which demanded that a future Labour government should not take part in the Community's institutions or contribute to its budget unless and until satisfactory terms had been renegotiated. While the debate revealed a solid core of minority support in the party for membership, it also showed the depth of hostility to the Community among a section of its leadership and firmly committed a future Labour government to seek a renegotiation of the terms of entry.[1] In the short term it also led to a decision by the party's national executive not to send a delegation to the European Parliament.

If we now turn to the scene in the continental core of the Community the immediate prospects in terms of support are undoubtedly much brighter. There has been no sign of a slackening in this respect among

[1] For a further discussion of the party's position, see below, Chapter 7, pp. 181–184.

the dominant political elites, and the attitudes displayed by the mass of the general public remain firmly in favour of the pursuit of integration. There are, however, some elements of uncertainty in the situation. One of these arises from the emergence of a new set of values associated with a post-industrial society which in some important respects are, or could be, in conflict with some of the major components in the Community's current value system. The evidence for this comes primarily from studies of patterns of attitudes among the younger generation, which has led to the suggestion that 'the motives which were successful in *launching* European integration may be in a relative decline'.[1] This does not mean that there is any sign of a revival of nationalism. On the contrary, there is evidence to support the hypothesis that potential support for supranational institutions is likely to grow over the years. But among the younger generation a higher priority is now being given to a range of what have been called 'post-acquisitive' values: that is, attention is now being directed at a range of problems concerning the quality of life—such things as environmental questions and opportunities for increased participation—rather more than the purely economic goals of the past. The strength of these new pressures was clearly apparent in the Norwegian referendum, where the violent opposition of many students to membership administered a sharp jolt to those within the Community who had not appreciated how radically its image had changed over the years. The same set of attitudes is also a marked feature of left-wing student opinion in Britain towards the Community. In their case, as in Norway, opposition to its value system was the main reason for their wishing to stay out. Within the original member countries student attitudes are no less critical and have led to an increasing degree of hostility towards its policies and institutions. Should the Community fail to respond it could easily be faced with a widespread withdrawal of support on the part of the younger generation. Nor are students alone in their discontent, as Sicco Mansholt's vigorous criticism of its goals and policies has shown.[2]

It may well be, indeed, that the widely based consensus that sustained the six-member Community is beginning to break up, and that the type of options which the new Community is now facing will lead to an increasing polarisation of attitudes. The emergence of a more sharply-defined socialist position with regard to it is certainly now apparent, and this development could well be speeded-up once the British Labour Party focuses its attention on the problems of membership.

It will indeed be surprising if in the coming years a much more

[1] Ronald Inglehart, *op. cit.*, p. 36.
[2] See above, pp. 105–106.

vigorous political battle does not develop around the whole direction that the Community should take. In many ways it will be a healthy sign, for it will be a recognition of the necessity of political choice and that the issues which the Community raises are matters of critical importance. It could, nevertheless, make the task of the leaders of the Community more difficult, especially if the spread of their own views is such as to lead to fundamental divergences on basic policy issues.

LEADERSHIP

It will already be apparent from the preceding discussion that the pressures on those who exercise leadership in the enlarged Community will be intense. A high but in many cases divergent pattern of demands, coupled with the probability of a British government determined to assert its own interests within the Community (a determination arising in part out of the internal political situation) will produce a situation requiring skill and ability if it is not to lead to serious stress. To this another factor has to be added: the fact that in the coming years the Community will be faced by issues which impinge directly on the heartland of national sovereignty. So the task will not be easy.

Nor will it be eased by the fact that there are now nine rather than six members around the Council table, especially as each of them will no doubt wish to maintain the right of a veto on issues which they consider to be of vital national interest. In addition, there are also certain structural features about the relationships between the nine which are likely to produce their own problems.

There is, in the first place, the fact that there are now four rather than three major units in the Community. This, at all events, is the formal situation which has been recognised in the Treaty of Accession: this gives equal numerical weight in voting and other respects to Britain, France, Germany and Italy. The crucial set of relationships is likely, however, to be that formed by the triangle of Paris, Bonn and London. For unless these three are able to reach agreement it is difficult to see how progress can be made; just as in the negotiations on entry the support of both France and Germany was critical for the admission of Britain.

There are likely, however, to be many tensions in these relationships. The French and British, for instance, have always been rivals and have rarely found it easy to work together even when formally they have been allies. There is an element of mutual admiration in their relationship, but also tensions which arise from the fact that they are both proud countries with their own traditions, language and culture. As one of the polls mentioned earlier discovered, these tensions are deeply rooted in popular attitudes. In reply to a question about which countries in the Community were the easiest, and which were the most difficult, for the British to get on with, France emerged as by far the most difficult. The complete rank order of preferences is shown in *Table 5.4*.

In the context of their Community relationship there will undoubt-

Table 5.4 BRITISH ATTITUDES TO OTHER EUROPEANS, 1971

	Easiest to get on with %	Most difficult (%)
Netherlands	66	3
West Germany	49	27
Belgium	37	16
Italy	12	51
France	12	75
Luxembourg	11	8

Source: Barry Hedges and Roger Jowell, Britain and the E.E.C., *Report on a Survey of Attitudes Towards the European Economic Community*, Social and Community Planning Research, London (July 1971)

edly be many elements of tension, quite apart from the cultural and linguistic elements to which reference has already been made. In the first place the French will not speedily forget the long years when the British stood aside and hoped that the Six would fail, nor the British that it was a French government which for so long subsequently barred their way into the Community. And if one examines a series of specific policy issues, there are a number on which the two countries are bound to have divergent interests.[1]

With regard to relations with the Federal Republic, the experience of the original Community suggests that as far as France is concerned these are unlikely to be altogether smooth; the British on the other hand are unlikely to suffer from the same complexes which operate in Paris with regard to Bonn, though on some issues—and perhaps most notably in the case of the common agricultural policy—there will be important differences of interest to be reconciled.

For all three countries there will be difficulties in deciding on the most appropriate strategy within the Community. During the negotiations, for instance, it was apparent that Mr. Heath had decided to give priority to his relations with President Pompidou on the assumption —which was no doubt correct—that a special effort had to be made with regard to a country whose political leaders had up to that point been the main obstacle to British entry. He knew he could count during that period on the understanding of Chancellor Brandt. It could, however, be very dangerous in the future if the two countries

[1] See Chapter 6.

sought, or were believed to be seeking, to create a Franco-British diarchy within the Community. This would arouse intense suspicion and hostility among all the other partners. The same would be true of any other combination of two out of these three member states, and hardly less so in the case of an attempted dominant triumverate. The more acceptable situation would undoubtedly be one in which the major countries participate in ad hoc coalitions according to their interests with regard to particular issues. This in fact was the pattern during the more productive phase of the original Community —though it will require great skill and tact on the part of all concerned to conduct the affairs of the enlarged Community on this basis.

Power relationships within it will undoubtedly be more complicated by the fact that the smaller countries are now in a numerical majority. On the whole it looks unlikely that their interests on most issues will be such as to allow them, even if they thought this desirable, to operate as a bloc: the Benelux countries within the original Community only rarely found sufficient common purpose to do so, and they have had a far more intimate relationship over the years than the three new smaller member countries. An alternative strategy for these states might be a policy of seeking an understanding with one of the larger powers, but this is unlikely to be acceptable as it would imply a type of satellite status. They too, therefore, are likely to prefer ad hoc coalitions maximising as far as possible such common interests as they are able to identify within the group of smaller countries.[1]

Confronted by a Community in which the dominant mood is that of an assertion of national interests, it is possible that these countries will find at least one point of common concern: namely, a reinforcement of the role of the Commission. Such a strategy could offer them the possibility of building up a certain countervailing authority to set against that of the larger countries. But this is likely to be a long-term rather than immediate goal, and one which it may be difficult to secure.

Apart from these structural factors in the situation affecting the leadership function in the Community there are a number of others which also have to be taken into account. One of these is the stability or otherwise of the various national political systems and their governments. In the short-term the risks of any major upset seem relatively slight. The political regimes of the member countries have shown a remarkable degree of stability throughout the post-war period, and such changes as may take place should occur by constitutional means rather than by any more dramatic process. There are, nevertheless, some latent possibilities of governmental changes which could create problems. One of these is that of a return to power by the Communist par-

[1] During the negotiations and the subsequent period when Luxembourg was in the chair, Ireland for instance, sought its aid—to good effect—in resolving certain issues.

ties in Italy or France. Both have retained a strong electoral appeal and in France the party has now concluded an agreement with the socialists for a joint programme.[1] In Italy the ending of Socialist participation in government which occurred in the summer of 1972 could also lead—if this party remains out of power—to a renewal of close links with the Communists. In both countries it is unlikely, however, that the Communists would gain sufficient support to be able to form a government without their socialist allies; this fact, together with the evolution which has already occurred in their policy towards the Community, suggest that their participation in a governmental coalition would not necessarily have any dramatic effects on it.

At the present time it seems even more unlikely that any of the member states will face the danger of a coup leading to the installation of a regime—on the Greek model—which would be unacceptable to the other partners. The fact that in more than 20 years the Community has not so far had to face this type of problem does not mean, however, that it could not arise at some point in the future. If, for any reason, there should arise an issue of this sort to cast doubt on the acceptability of one or more of the members to the others, there is little doubt that the Community would come to a halt, and might be threatened by disintegration. For the foreseeable future however the climate in this respect appears to be set fair, for although it would be an overstatement to characterise the members of the Community simply as one happy family, such stresses as exist are well below the level of tolerance which it is reasonable to expect. The only partial exception to this is the situation in Northern Ireland, which could provide a continued source of tension between Britain and the Republic. Its impact, grave though it is on the people of Ulster themselves, is however likely to be localised as far as the affairs of the Community itself are concerned. Governmental instability, on the other hand, is a factor which could have an impact on the exercise of leadership in the Community. The conduct of Italian policy has suffered a great deal from this over the years, even if governmental posts have been filled by a relatively restricted number of individuals who disappear and then reappear in Brussels wearing a different ministerial hat.

The most crucial factor of all, however, may well be the capacity of the individual leaders of the major countries to establish harmonious relationships with one another. This was a fundamental factor in the early success of the six-member Community; the relationship between Adenauer and de Gaulle was hardly less so at a later stage. The understanding between Pompidou, Brandt and Heath also provided the

[1] The renewed strength of this left-wing coalition, and the much weakened position of the Gaullist majority, were both apparent in the French general election of March 1973.

necessary underpinning for enlargement. As the role played by Summit meetings has steadily increased, so the purely personal elements in the relationships between those who take part has also assumed even more significance. Here there are far too many uncertainties for any forecasts to be made: it is however a reassuring sign that at present there is not visible even on the horizon a figure of the stature of de Gaulle whose dramatic style created so many difficulties for his partners. The current leaders of the Community all practise a much more pragmatic style of bargaining, and it is this which is likely to maximise the chances for the Community of resolving in a relatively amicable way the divergent interests with which it will have to deal.

6 Policy Issues

We now turn to a consideration of the major policy issues which the new Community will be facing in the coming years; the main interests which are likely to be involved in the discussion of these issues; the extent to which these will be convergent or divergent, and the nature and level of the stresses which may consequently make themselves felt.

One important initial point should be made in this context: although the new members were required to accept the existing policies and rules of the Community as the price of entry, it is quite clear that the bargains which were struck between the original Six members will necessarily have to be modified to accommodate the interests of the newer members, and above all those of Britain herself. These adjustments can be expected to occupy a great deal of the time and energy of the new Community during the five-year transition period: it will at the same time be confronted with a substantial range of new policy issues arising from the fact of its enlargement. In the following pages the aim is to review the major fields with which it will be concerned.

ECONOMIC AND MONETARY UNION

There can be no doubt at all that a central set of issues will be those arising from the Community's declared intention of seeking to achieve an economic and monetary union by 1980. To understand the importance of the questions likely to arise in this context we first need to examine why the Community has now set itself this new task, and what it implies. The answers to both these questions were given in the report of the high-level committee set up under the chairmanship of the Luxembourg prime minister, Pierre Werner, which was presented to the Council and Commission in 1970.[1] The report began by observing that the advances which had been made up to that point towards economic integration—primarily the customs union and the common agricultural policy—had thrown into relief 'the marked differences existing between the member countries in the realization of the objectives of growth and stability' and that these differences threatened to produce serious disequilibria in the Community as a whole if the economic policy of its members was not to be effectively harmonised. This need was all the greater because, the report said:

> The increasing interpenetration of the economies has entailed a weakening of autonomy for national economic policies. The control of economic policy has become all the more difficult because the loss of autonomy at the national level has not been compensated by the inauguration of the Community policies. The inadequacies and disequilibria that have occurred in the process of realisation of the Common Market are thus thrown into relief.

Underlining the limitations and failures of the attempts which had been made up to that point to coordinate the economic policies of the member countries, the Werner report also highlighted the fact that industrial, business and financial interests had, by contrast, adapted themselves to the enlarged market. Although this had had some positive repercussions it had also produced, for instance, speculative movements of capital of enormous proportions which had exacerbated the difficulties which individual governments had had to keep control over economic development. The achievement of an economic and monetary union was therefore necessary in order 'to realise an area within which goods and services, people and capital, will circulate freely and without competitive distortions, and without thereby giving rise to structural or regional disequilibrium'.

The report then went on to spell out the major elements in such a union:

> Total and irreversible mutual convertibility of currencies free from fluctuations in rates, and with fixed exchange rates, or, preferably a single Community currency.
> The creation of liquidity throughout the area and a centralisation of monetary and credit policy.
> Monetary policy towards the outside world to be decided at the Community level rather than by national governments.
> A unification of the policies of member states with regard to the

---

[1] *Report to the Council and Commission on the Realisation by Stages of Economic and Monetary Union in the Community* ('Werner Report'), Brussels (1970).

capital market of the Community itself.

Decisions to be taken at Community rather than national level regarding 'the essential features of the whole of the public budgets, and in particular variations in their volume, the size of balances and the methods of financing or utilising them'.

Regional and structural policies which 'will no longer be exclusively within the jurisdiction of the member countries'.

'A systematic and continuous consultation between the social partners' (e.g. representatives of major economic and social interests such as industrial federations, trade unions, etc.) at the Community level.

In spite of the very wide-ranging nature of these objectives the report nevertheless considered that the objective of economic and monetary union was 'realizable in the course of the present decade, provided the political will of the member states to realize this objective, solemnly declared at the Conference at The Hague, is present'. Nevertheless, it went on to say that it could only be achieved gradually, and suggested that there should be three stages, the first of which should cover the period from January 1971 to December 1973.

What in effect the report did was to sketch out—subsequently in considerable detail—a whole new programme of further economic integration, far more extensive than that originally set out in the Rome treaties and penetrating much deeper into the heartland of national sovereignty. For what it envisaged as the ultimate goal was a situation in which, for instance, major budgetary decisions would be taken in Brussels rather than the individual national capitals; the member countries would lose their freedom to establish and change exchange rates for their national currencies both within the Community itself and with regard to the outside world; those currencies themselves might be replaced by a common Community currency; and such issues as targets for rates of economic growth, levels of employment and credit policy would be decided by the Community institutions and not by individual member countries.

All this meant that the stakes involved in membership of the Community were to be greatly raised, and the importance of the political decisions to be taken very much increased. It is hardly surprising therefore that although the goals set out in the Werner Plan were accepted in 1970, progress towards them up to the point of enlargement was very tentative and hesitant. Nor is it at all surprising that in that period major differences of opinion emerged about the strategy to be pursued as well as the nature of the initial steps to be taken. The most serious difference in this context has been the insistence on the part of the Federal Republic that further economic coordination should precede progress towards monetary union while the French government has consistently pressed for the opposite strategy. The major reason for this is that France is anxious to assert the monetary cohesion of the Community vis-à-vis the United States and to use it as a bargaining weapon with regard to the dollar and as a means of achieving those reforms in the international monetary system which it wishes to see, while the Germans—who, for strategic reasons are more cautious in their relationship with the United States—fear that the cost of maintaining fixed parities within the Community would fall essentially on their balance of payments.

The British, for their part, have shown much more sympathy with the German position than that of the French, if for somewhat different reasons. As a country very heavily dependent on trade and anxious to sustain its volume of exports, Britain has had on several occasions to have recourse to devaluation as a means of correcting its rising domestic costs; to lose this instrument of managing the economy—one of the few which is left to it—could have serious consequences. On this many academic economists agree with the position taken up by the Labour party;[1] and not only because of the potential impact of fixed exchange rates on levels of economic growth and employment, but also because of its equally important effects, in the absence of countervailing policies, on the economically weaker regions in the country.

The difficulties of the situation from the British point of view were underlined by the decision taken by the government in July 1972 to allow the pound sterling to float in spite of its earlier commitment to the Community to keep exchange rate fluctuations with regard to the other Community currencies to within a band of 2·25%. Even with the support being offered to sterling by these countries there was a sudden and powerful wave of speculation which caused an immediate drain on the British reserves: and this time the government was not willing, unlike the Labour government until its own decision to devalue in 1967, to see Britain's international indebtedness rise in order to maintain the existing parity of the pound.

British policy with regard to economic and monetary union is likely, therefore, to give a much higher priority to measures designed to co-ordinate economic policies more effectively—and in particular to measures to deal with regional imbalances—than to those designed to lead to the achievement of a common currency. It will also be seeking —and in this case the other members certainly share its concern —common action to curb inflation. It remains to be seen, however, whether the Community as such will be able to devise any effective measures to deal with this major problem in the light of the fact that

[1] See, for instance, Peter Coffey and John R. Presley, *European Monetary Integration*, London (1971) chs 6 and 7.

not only are economists divided amongst themselves about the appropriate measures to take within an individual country, but also because of the structural differences between the economies of the various member countries.

At the same time the Community will also be faced by another critical issue: the future of sterling. When the negotiations began it was widely believed that this problem would at that stage already prove to be a major stumbling block, as it was known that the French in particular were extremely reluctant for the Community to be saddled with the problems of one of the world's two major reserve and trading currencies. In practice, however—and much to the surprise of most observers—the issue was speedily disposed of as a result of the understanding reached between Mr. Heath and President Pompidou. This took the form of a very generalised statement of intentions made by the British which Mr. Heath reported to the House of Commons in these terms.[1]

We have said three things to the Community. We have said that as members of the enlarged Community we would play our full part in the progress towards economic and monetary union. That was confirmed in my talk with President Pompidou and in my statement to the House. We have said that we are prepared to envisage a gradual and orderly rundown of official sterling balances after our accession. We have said that after accession we would discuss measures by which a progressive alignment of the external characteristics of sterling with those of other Community currencies might be achieved.

He then emphasised that there had been agreement between President Pompidou and himself that 'no country's vital interests would be overruled by other members', and that the British had laid down conditions on their side with regard to the reduction of the sterling balances: in particular the protection of the interests of the balance holders and the avoidance of unacceptable burdens on the British balance of payments. He also underlined the enormous complexity of the problems involved with regard to sterling; reiterated that no commitments had been made with regard to the method of dealing with the problem, or its timing, and that the Six had accepted that 'we shall be ready to discuss the whole subject in a fully Community spirit, without preconceptions or prejudices about how to deal with the problems'.

[1] On 10 June 1971. The full statement is given in the White Paper (1971), paras. 125–128.

How exactly the problem is to be dealt with may prove to be a matter of very considerable dissension. The simplest solution would undoubtedly be for sterling's reserve role to be merged in a new European currency. There are, however, likely to be serious objections to this: there is little enthusiasm among the other member countries for the Community to develop a reserve currency, not least because it might well prove to be an element of instability affecting the whole of the Community's economy. An alternative would be to find a solution to the sterling problem through the internationalisation of sterling debts on a wider basis, involving the Group of Ten and in the framework of the International Monetary Fund. This, however, would involve very wide-ranging issues involving the whole of the international monetary scene and its reserves, and would in particular require reaching agreement with the United States. Neither solution is likely to be easy or swift to obtain, yet the problem is one which will have to be tackled and resolved if the Community is to be able to make progress towards its goal of economic and monetary union.

The importance and difficulty of the issue were both underlined in the early part of 1973 when, as a result of yet another bout of pressure on the dollar and massive flows of hot money into the Federal Republic, six of the Community countries agreed on a joint float—but with sterling (and the lira) excluded from the joint arrangements. The British had laid down extremely tough conditions with regard to support for sterling which had not been acceptable to their partners. As long as these guarantees are not forthcoming it will be extremely difficult for genuine solidarity in the monetary field to be created.

At this stage, when the Community is only in the foothills of its long climb towards its objective, it is impossible to forecast the exact configuration of the difficulties which lie ahead, much less how successful the Community will be in meeting them. What is certain is that this wide area of policy-making is likely to prove as crucial to the new Community in the seventies as agricultural policy was for the Six in the previous decade. Powerful interests are involved; there are likely to be marked divergencies in the specific policy objectives being pursued by individual countries—yet at the same time many opportunities for bargains to be struck between them. And like the earlier quarrels over agriculture this is also a topic which raises, but in a more acute form, issues concerning the institutions of the Community. As the Werner Report pointed out, economic and monetary union can only be successfully achieved if there is a transfer of decision-making from national governments to Community institutions. On this it added:[1]

These transfers of responsibility represent a process of fundamental

[1] *Werner Report*, p. 12.

political significance which implies the progressive development of political co-operation. Economic and monetary union thus appears as a leaven for the development of political union, which in the long run it cannot do without.

This is a theme to which we shall return further on. We first, however, need to examine a number of other policy areas which are likely to assume importance in the life of the new Community.

AGRICULTURE

Among the major policy areas, agriculture is certain to be prominent. One of the reasons for this is that three of the original member countries—France, Germany and Italy—still have a substantial agricultural population in spite of the flight from the land which has taken place over recent years. In 1970 there were still 2·4 millions employed in agriculture in the Federal Republic, almost 2·9 millions employed in France and over 3·6 millions in Italy. Together these three countries will still account for the bulk of the agricultural population in the new Community—almost nine millions out of a total of eleven millions. They are bound therefore to maintain a keen interest in agricultural policy, as will also be the case for Ireland which has well over a third of its labour force still employed in agriculture, and Denmark, where although the agricultural work force is lower both in absolute numbers and as a percentage of the total work force its future is nevertheless a matter of major national concern.

The British, for their part, will have an equally keen interest, though for rather different reasons. Their concern will be primarily as the Community's major food importer which, as a new member, will have to adjust not only to a new system of agricultural protection, but also a substantially higher level of prices for most agricultural products. At the same time it will also become a major contributor to the Community's budget, some 81% of which currently consists of the costs of the common agricultural policy.

Opponents of British membership have consistently and forcefully argued that adaptation to the Community's existing common agricultural policy will have disastrous effects on the country's economy as well as involving the United Kingdom in shouldering a wholly disproportionate net contribution to the Community's budget. As Mr. Douglas Jay has argued.[1]

---

[1] Rt. Hon. Douglas Jay, M.P., 'The Economic Burden of Entry' in Douglas Evans (ed.) *Destiny or delusion: Britain and the Common Market*, London (1971) p. 15.

Quite apart from any statistics, the reason why this country would suffer such huge losses is simple and clear. We import about 20% of our national income, including about half our food and most of our raw materials. We pay for this by exporting manufactured goods competitively all over the world. Joining the Common Market in its present form means fundamentally that we would buy our food from dear sources instead of cheap; that we would raise our export costs over the whole of British industry; that we would lose preference and free entry right for our exports in a far larger area of the world than that in which we should gain; and that we would have to pay a huge sum of our own budget revenue across the exchanges to the Common Market authorities.

In the same article Mr. Jay calculated that the total additional burden on the British balance of payments due to membership would amount to between £1 250 and £1 500 millions a year. This would be made up of £600 millions from direct food and agricultural costs; £600–650 millions from the net worsening of visible trade in non-food products; and £200 millions on capital amount.[1]

The T.U.C., in the estimates it made in 1971, also took a very gloomy view of the balance of payments situation, even if its calculations were noticeably less horrific. On its most unfavourable assumptions the total burden would be £855 millions a year by 1980, made up of £555 millions representing the net British contribution to the Community's budget plus the additional costs of food imports; £200 millions relating to trade in non-foodstuffs; and £100 millions on capital account. Its considered view was that 'by the end of the decade the total balance of payments costs would be at least £460 millions per annum, and more likely of the order of £700 millions'.[2]

A Labour party report published at about the same time quoted the same figures, and added the observation that according to estimates submitted by the Treasury during the course of the negotiations Britain would, by 1978, be contributing 31% of the Community budget and receiving back only 6%. It added that 'these original estimates are now disclaimed, but no reason has been given for rejecting such assumptions'.[3]

[1] Douglas Jay, *op. cit.*, p. 24.

[2] *Britain and the E.E.C.*, Report of the T.U.C. General Council to the 103rd. annual Trades Union Congress, London (1971) p. 8.

[3] 'No Entry on Tory terms' *The United Kingdom and the European Communities*, London (August 1971) p. 8.

A wholly different picture of the situation has, however, been given by a group of economists supporting entry. The conclusion derived from their work is that 'membership is not likely to cause any difficulty for the British balance of payments up to 1978' and that the cost in 1980 was likely to be less than £175 millions a year.[1]

The assumptions on which these calculations were made differed a great deal, of course, from those quoted earlier. In particular they took account of detailed work undertaken at Michigan State University on the impact of price levels on patterns of food consumption (which, applied to the British situation in the Community resulted in the conclusion that there would be a positive gain to the country's balance of payments rather than a loss); more favourable estimates of the 'dynamic effects' of entry on British industry,[2] and a quite different set of hypotheses regarding the evolution of the agricultural element in the Community's budget.

The government, for its part, has refused to commit itself very far. The only estimates it has published are those to be found in the July 1971 White Paper, and these offer only partial calculations relating to the balance of payments costs of entry up to 1977, and none at all for the period beyond. As far as the figures for 1977 are concerned (which were based on a 10-nation Community), these suggested a net British contribution to the budget of £200 millions and an additional £50 millions in respect of the increased costs of food imports: a total of £250 millions. It did not attempt to quantify other elements likely to impinge on the balance of payments and, having observed that the percentage of British contribution to the budget had been pegged during the negotiations for the period up to the end of 1979, it refused to speculate on what the situation might be, even with regard to this element in the situation, beyond then. 'In the Government's view', it said, 'neither our contribution to nor our receipts from, the Community budget in the 1980s are susceptible of valid estimation at this stage'. It did, however, add the observation that 'the Community declared to us during the course of the negotiations that if unacceptable situations should arise 'the very survival of the Community would demand that the institutions find equitable solutions.[3]

Subsequently the government also refused to be drawn during the debates in Parliament on the passage of the European Communities Bill. The position it then took consisted of saying (a) that no valid fore-

---

[1] John Pinder, 'What Membership Means for Britain' in J. Pinder (ed), *The Economics of Europe*, London (1971) pp. 11–13

[2] For the contrasting views on the 'dynamic effects' see the articles by John Williamson and Christopher Layton in John Pinder (ed.) *op. cit,* and by Nicholas Kaldor in Douglas Evans, *op. cit.*

[3] White Paper (July 1971) para. 96.

casts could be made, and (b) of asserting that the total balance of payments effect of membership would not be greatly different from 'the kind of random and cyclical swings which we expect to be able to handle without much difficulty in the ordinary course of events'.[1]

There is little doubt that the government's prudence on these issues in the period up to actual British entry was carefully calculated. It knew perfectly well that it would be diplomatically unwise to suggest changes in either the agricultural policy or the Community's budgetary arrangements in advance of entry: yet on the other hand neither it nor any other British government would be so foolish, as a member of the Community, to allow arrangements to persist which proved to be manifestly inequitable. The doom-laden forecasts of those opposed to entry were predicated on total British inaction should such a situation arise: a wholly unrealistic assumption. For if in fact the balance of payments situation were to prove so onerous, and the budgetary contributions so inequitable, as has been suggested, the Community would undoubtedly face a determined attempt by Britain to correct the situation, whichever party was in power.

All the evidence is that the present government is already applying its mind, and its not inconsiderable political resources, to preventing such a situation in fact arising. For the time being there are two major policy objectives with regard to the agricultural policy itself: a limitation in price increases and resistance to any substantial funds being made available by the Community for structural changes—the latter for the simple reason that Britain herself is unlikely to qualify for any significant payments in this field, yet could find herself a major contributor to any new fund set up for this purpose. If these steps, together with the attempt to persuade the Community to fund other policies where Britain stands more chance of being a net recipient of funds, do not attain the desired objective, a more drastic policy is likely to be followed. This could entail a major revision of the agricultural policy itself and also possibly the search for a new basis for the Community's budgetary arrangements. Although both objectives would have been anathema to the Six had they been raised during the course of the negotiations on entry, the situation now that the Community has been enlarged has changed significantly. Britain is now a full member, and a major factor in the Council chamber. Moreover, the agricultural policy itself is now functioning so badly—in particular since the imposition of border taxes made necessary by the spate of exchange rate fluctuations—that the need for a drastic overhaul is becoming increasingly apparent. Even the French are concerned by some aspects of the policy, and in particular the way in which it is put-

[1] Mr. Patrick Jenkin, House of Commons, 8 June 1972.

ting large sums of money into the pockets of the more affluent farmers while failing to help the poorer peasant cultivators. I should not therefore be assumed that the policy cannot be changed: on the contrary it now seems very likely that it will be.

It will be surprising if the nature of the changes made do not reflect British preoccupations, and make the earlier forecasts about effects of the agricultural policy unrealistic and alarmist. Nevertheless, some hard-fought battles can be anticipated in this sector, with the Federal Republic in particular having an interest in maintaining price levels as high as possible. In the medium to long term it is nevertheless probable that agricultural issues will cease to occupy so central a position in the politics of the Community. With the agricultural population declining so rapidly and enlargement bringing a great number of new policy questions into prominence it is unlikely that the new Community will find itself devoting so high a proportion of its time and energy to this sector as the Six themselves were obliged to do.

REGIONAL; INDUSTRIAL AND SOCIAL POLICY

At the Paris Summit it was significant, for instance, that no mention was made of agricultural policy, but a good deal of attention was devoted to other themes. Two of them were related to policy areas where Britain hopes to be able to recoup some of the funds which it will be contributing to the Community budget: regional and industrial policy.

As far as the first of these is concerned, Britain's main concern is to press for measures which will correct the dangers inherent in membership for the more peripheral regions of the country, and at the same time to obtain Community funds to revitalise the country's older industrial areas. The latter aim was already indicated in the 1971 White Paper; paragraph 139 of this document read as follows:

> In the enlarged Community, we shall be sharing experience and exploring how the institutions of the Community can help us in dealing with the process of regional adaptation to major changes in industrial structure.

Subsequently in the debates in the House of Commons on the European Communities Bill, Mr. Rippon was a good deal more blunt when he said on 24 May 1972: 'We wish to see, for example, that there is a proper emphasis on regional policy as it affects urban areas, and not simply consider the problem of the less-developed areas.'

At the Paris Summit, Mr. Heath made a determined effort to persuade his future partners of the need for such a regional policy, and succeeded in obtaining a commitment to the establishment of a Regional Development Fund to be financed in the second phase of the transitional stage of economic and monetary union from Community (rather than national) funds, and designed—among other things—to deal with those regional imbalances resulting from industrial change and structural underemployment.[1] To this extent he succeeded in one of his main objectives at the meeting, though it should be added that the French were reluctant to agree to a system of Community finance for regional policy and that all the important battles on this front still lie ahead. There will in particular be the problem of how much of the projected fund will be available for purposes in which the United Kingdom itself is interested: this is likely to generate a sharp conflict between the many claimants for the limited resources available.

Industrial policy is another area which will undoubtedly occupy a much more prominent position in the new Community than was the case in the past. Under the energetic direction of Altiero Spinelli, the Commission Member responsible for this sector since 1970, a substantial new impetus has been given to thinking about the creation of positive Community policies particularly with regard to technologically advanced industries. The need for Community intervention had earlier been strongly argued,[2] and although the specific means to achieve the desired ends have been—and remain—a matter of dispute,[3] the general need to take action on the Community level has been widely recognised. Confirmation of this was provided at the Paris Summit by the inclusion in the final communique of a section dealing with industrial, scientific and technological policy. This made reference, among other things, to the need to remove barriers hindering closer relations and mergers between firms, the opening up of public sector purchases, 'the transformation and conversion of declining industries' (a matter of particular concern to Britain), the rapid adoption of a European company statute, and a common policy in the field of science and technology. As a first step towards the attainment of these objectives the institutions are required to draw up an action programme and a detailed timetable for decision before the end of 1973.

A special section in the communique was also devoted to social policy, for which a comprehensive programme of action is again to be drawn up during the course of 1973. The aim in this case is a coordinated rather than a common policy, though certain types of action are to

[1] For full text, see Appendix, para. 5.

[2] See, for instance, Christopher Layton, *European advanced technology; a programme for integration,* London (1969). (Mr Layton, it should be noted, subsequently became *chef de cabinet* to Signor Spinelli in Brussels.)

[3] See Keith Pavitt, 'Technology in Europe's future', *Science Policy I,* 1971/72, pp. 210–273.

be financed by the Community through the Social Fund. Among the fields of activity which it is proposed to cover are employment and vocational training; improving working and living conditions; the close involvement of workers in 'the progress of firms'; Community-wide collective agreements; and measures for consumer protection.

The inclusion of these proposals was undoubtedly a reflection of the need now being felt in the Community to give it a more human face, and in particular of pressure from the German Chancellor. There are nevertheless several topics on which significant differences of view are likely to be encountered in implementing the generalised prescriptions of the Summit—not least the involvement of workers in decision-making at company level, where the German experience of co-determination is not likely to recommend itself either to the governments or trade unions of several of the other member countries.

REGIONAL, INDUSTRIAL AND SOCIAL POLICY

A great deal of time and effort will, of course, also have to be devoted to a wide range of policy issues related to the smooth working of the common market itself. This, as we have seen, exists in a formal sense, but in practice its operation is distorted and impeded by a multitude of non-tariff barriers. The process of removing these and harmonising the relevant national legislation and administrative practices is likely to be tortuous and prolonged. As the experience of the Six has shown, the task of freeing the movement of services and securing the right of establishment is in itself a mammoth task. Agreement has to be reached between the various professional groups concerned and also the national governments on the equivalence of qualifications, and also on the rules which are to be applied to the exercise of an individual activity on a Community-wide basis. Sharp conflicts between particular interests can be expected over a wide range of issues, which are likely to prove all the more difficult to resolve, if the experience of the Six is any guide, because the political pressures to resolve them are likely to be relatively weak. It is precisely this type of decision-making which has often proved the most difficult for the Community to carry out effectively, many of the Commission's proposals having become hopelessly stranded on the shoals of disagreement between the national experts summoned to discuss them by the Committee of Permanent Representatives. There is no doubt that in some cases British interests will further complicate the problem: the case of the insurance industry is one such, where the British companies will be hoping to secure a liberal type of regime for their activities against a tradition in most continental countries of a heavily-protected national insurance market.

This type of example could be multiplied many times over, and it will be a thankless and onerous task for those concerned to arrive at acceptable compromises between entrenched interests in the various member countries.

The same will also be true of those areas where the Community is committed, or is likely to seek, to construct common policies. With regard to transport, for instance, only slow progress was made by the Six in their attempt to reconcile not only the opposing interests of the rail, road and inland waterways undertakings, but also the fierce differences in attitudes to transport policy held on the one hand by the Dutch (described by one exasperated observer as believing that they had a divine right to be the transport kings of the Community), who have fought hard for a liberal type of regime, and the other members who have traditionally regarded transport policy as being secondary to other national economic and social goals. The recent—and prolonged —argument on the maximum size and weight of road vehicles is another example of the acute conflicts of interests that can be expected in this particular sector, to which the pressure being exerted by environmentalists have recently added yet another dimension. Here again the presence of the British will add both to the range of issues to be considered—shipping, for instance, may have to be brought within the ambit of the attempt to devise a common policy, as well as civil air transport—and also the acuity of the conflicting interests to be reconciled. In the same category further difficulties can be expected with regard to the common fisheries policy and also attempts to arrive at a common energy policy—an objective which eluded the Six in spite of their prolonged search.

As a glance at any recent report of the Commission will indicate, these are only a very few of the multifarious policy issues which the Community will face as it seeks to arrive at a less uncommon Common Market. For the most part, however, these are matters which should lend themselves to pragmatic bargaining and compromises which provide a reasonable spread of benefits to the various partners. That is not to say that these will be easy to achieve: the issues involved however should not occasion any serious level of stress within the Community, however loud the noises-off may be. What is more likely to happen, in those cases where major differences persist, is that the issue will be left unsettled, or only partially resolved. The evidence of the six-member Community has been that the process of integration can accommodate a fairly extensive limbo of this sort without it having any major impact on the central dynamics of the process, unsatisfactory though this may be to the interests directly concerned. This is one aspect of the 'autonomy of functional contexts' which has been mentioned earlier; in other words, neither success nor relative failure with regard to issues generally considered to be of secondary importance is likely to have a determining influence on the pace of the Community's overall development.

TRADE AND AID

Certain aspects of the external economic relations of the new Community will undoubtedly prove to be much more important in this respect. One of them of major concern not only to Britain but also the Community as a whole, is relations with the developing world. The British interest is, of course, particularly focused on the Community's relations with the developing countries of the Commonwealth, very few details of which were settled during the negotiations themselves. One major reason for this was the fact that the Community's Association Agreement (the Yaoundé Convention) with eighteen African countries and the Malagasy Republic is due to expire on 31 January 1975, and negotiations for its renewal to begin not later than August 1973. As a number of Commonwealth countries already had forms of association with the Community, and others had expressed interest in a similar possibility, it was agreed on both sides to postpone negotiations until enlargement had taken place.

Many will regard these negotiations as a crucial test of the good intentions—or otherwise—of the Community towards the developing world, and their outcome could have a significant effect on attitudes in Britain towards the new Community. It will however be a matter for the Commonwealth countries themselves in the first place to decide on what type of arrangement they wish to achieve. The formal situation is that it has been agreed between Britain and the other members of the Community that as far as the developing Commonwealth countries are concerned their interests should be safeguarded either by association arrangements comparable with those already in force or, where this for any reason is not appropriate, by some alternative solution. In the case of those independent Commonwealth countries in Africa, the Carribbean, the Indian Ocean and the Pacific:[1] there will be a choice between three options:

> An association within the framework of a revised Yaoundé Convention (involving both preferential trade arrangements and also aid from the Community).
> Some other form of association (of which one model is provided by

[1] Barbados, Botswana, Fiji, Gambia, Ghana, Guyana, Jamaica, Kenya, Lesotho, Malawi, Nigeria, Sierra Leone, Swaziland, Tanzania, Trinidad, and Tobago, Tonga, Uganda, Western Samoa, and Zambia. Mauritius made her choice in advance of British entry by acceding to the Yaoundé Convention in 1972.

the Arusha Convention concluded between the three east African countries and the E.E.C.: this provided for preferential trade but no aid).

A commercial agreement to facilitate and expand trade with the Community.

In the first instance, the main problem will be the renegotiation of the Yaoundé Convention to admit such of those African Commonwealth countries which signify a preference for this type of association (see *Figure 6.1*). One difficulty to be anticipated is that of reconciling the interests of the present (largely Francophone) associates, who naturally will wish to maintain as many of their current privileges as possible, with those of the new entrants. These two groups will no doubt expect that France and Britain respectively will support their demands and this could cause some friction between Paris and London. But it could well be that on certain issues the Francophone and Anglophone African countries will make common causes: for instance, in seeking a higher level of aid than that offered by the Community. The Commonwealth countries will also be concerned lest the British contribution to the European Development Fund—which is the Community agency through which its aid funds within the framework of the Association are channelled—will mean a loss of bilateral aid. So there are likely to be considerable cross-currents in these negotiations both within and between the two sides.

The Community for its part will also have to evolve a new philosophy with regard to the whole field of its relations with the developing countries. Whereas when the E.E.C. was first set up the African association was conceived largely in terms of a prolongation on a somewhat different basis of existing colonial relationships (the associates at that time still having colonial status) strong pressures have subsequently developed to reduce the exclusive preferential elements in it and for the Community to treat all developing countries on a similar basis, certainly as far as trade policy is concerned. Its introduction of a Scheme of Generalised Preferences (S.G.P.) in July 1971—following the resolutions agreed at the U.N.C.T.A.D. conference in New Delhi in 1968—was a significant move in this context, whatever assessment is made of the value of this scheme for the developing countries.[1] In the new Community there may be some problems in aligning the parallel British S.G.P. with that of the Community but the more important issue will be the relationship between this part of the Community's policy towards the developing countries and its trade-and-aid association with what will still be essentially an African group of states. One

[1] For opposing views on this see *Britain, the E.E.C. and the Third World*, Overseas Development Institute, London (1971). Also *European Community* (January 1972).

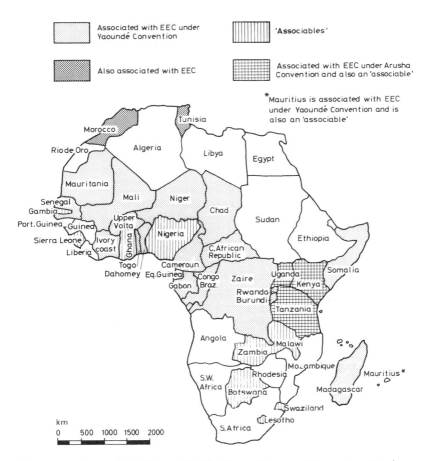

Figure 6.1 *Africa and the Enlarged E.E.C.* (*Source:* European Community, October 1972)

factor to be considered in this context is the future role of customs preferences which in practice have sometimes been found to be of only limited effect.[1]

The Community may also have to consider how far aid policy —which is still essentially a matter for individual national governments[2]—should come within the ambit of the Community's activities, and whether or not the Community as such should have a strategy of aid. As the policies of its individual member countries are markedly different, this is likely to prove a difficult discussion.

How far Britain herself may wish to push in this direction is very much an open question; what Britain will however certainly be concerned with is the Community's policy with regard to sugar imports from the Commonwealth.[3] Given the crucial importance for a number of them—particularly the Caribbean countries—of outlets for this product, both in terms of foreign exchange earnings and also employment, the negotiations will be a matter of particular concern. During the negotiations on accession this was one of the few issues on which Britain sought to obtain concessions from the Community. What it achieved was, in the first place, an agreement that the Government's contractual obligations under the Commonwealth Sugar Agreement to buy agreed quantities of sugar from these countries (and also Australia), should be respected until the end of 1974. This corresponded to the date at which Britain had the right to withdraw from the agreement. The government however also sought a Community commitment for the period beyond 1974. What it obtained was an agreement that the flow of sugar imports should then be regulated within the framework of either an association or trading agreement, together with a commitment that the enlarged Community would have 'as its firm purpose the safeguarding of the interests of the developing countries concerned whose economies depend to a considerable extent on the export of primary products and in particular of sugar'.[4] The British delegation then assured the governments concerned that this constituted 'a specific and moral commitment' by the enlarged Community.

This undertaking was however a good deal less than the British had originally hoped to secure, even if the governments of the developing countries concerned are reported to have expressed their satisfaction

[1] Gerhard Schiffler, 'Enlargement of the E.E.C. and the Community policies in the field of Trade' in Britain, the E.E.C. and the Third World, p. 57.

[2] In 1969 the countries of the E.E.C. provided $5·1 billion of aid on a bilateral basis, and only $0·1 billion collectively through the European Development Fund.

[3] The countries in question are: Antigua, Barbados, Fiji, Guyana, India, Jamaica, Kenya, Mauritius, Swaziland, Trinidad and Tobago, Uganda, St. Kitts-Nevis, Anguilla and British Honduras.

[4] White Paper (1971) para. 112.

with it. At all events the specific arrangements for trade in sugar from 1975 onwards will need to be speedily worked out, the major problem here being to reconcile the interests of the Commonwealth producers with those of the strong sugar-beet lobby within the Community itself. This problem may be eased, however, by the fact that the enlarged Community is expected to have additional sugar requirements of a volume which is about equivalent to the sugar exports of the developing countries of the Commonwealth.

Another aspect of the Community's trade policy which is of major concern to the British government will be its treatment of New Zealand dairy imports. The problem here is not that New Zealand is in any sense a poor country, but it is very heavily dependent for its export earnings on access to the British market (about 85% of her earnings on butter and cheese are accounted for in this way). Any sudden shutting off of this market could therefore cause grave problems for the New Zealand economy. During the negotiations an agreement was secured by Britain that safeguards the position up to the end of 1977.[1] It was agreed, however, that in 1976 the position with regard to butter would be re-examined, and that in the light of this review a decision would be taken 'on suitable measures for ensuring beyond 1977 the continuation of special arrangements for New Zealand butter'. Here again, the major problem will be to reconcile the interests of that country with those of the Community's own butter producers, which may prove difficult if the enlarged Community as a whole develops a surplus of production which was so persistent a feature of the six-member Community.

On all these issues Britain will have a particular responsibility in defending within the new Community the interests of other Commonwealth countries; there will however be other issues of trade policy in which, together with her partners, she will be more concerned with her own domestic interests and those of Western Europe as a whole. This will be the case, for instance, with regard to the United States, which is bound to exert increasing pressure on the Community—as it has already been doing over recent years—to defend the interests of her own producers. The future in this respect may well be rather stormy, especially if the protectionist lobbies in the United States succeed in persuading the federal government to champion their cause. But the more pressure of this sort is applied the more solidarity is likely to develop as between the members of the Community, and although there may be differences on tactics and the treatment given to individual products, this area of the Community's external trade policy is not likely to create major tensions between its own members. Nor is it

---

[1] White Paper (1971) paras. 102–110.

likely that the problem of trading relations with Eastern Europe and the Soviet Union will be the cause of any major conflict: in spite of the non-recognition of the Community by the C.E.M.A. (Comecon) countries the foundations for a common policy towards these countries have already been laid and while the current restraints on any major increase in trade are likely to persist for some time, all the members of the new Community share a common wish to work towards its expansion.[1]

The new Community will also need to develop common attitudes and policies towards other countries and problems likely to arise in the context of its external trade, for instance, with regard to Japan, Latin America, the Mediterranean countries, and such thorny issues as Middle-East oil imports. Undoubtedly this whole area of policy will assume a vastly increased importance, and take up much more time and effort than has been the case hitherto. It can hardly be otherwise given the importance of the new group on the world trading scene, which in the future will be called upon to play a major role in such international bodies as G.A.T.T., U.N.C.T.A.D., I.M.F. and the O.E.C.D. There are those who fear that the overall effect of the new Community on world trade will be very negative:[2] others on the contrary believe that British entry will reinforce the liberal trading elements—such as the Federal Republic and the Netherlands—within the Community, and lead to it acquiring a stronger sense of its world responsibilities and the adoption of the appropriate policies to foster an expansion of world trade. It will at all events no doubt take some time for the Community to come to terms with its new situation, and for the pattern of its posture to become clear. It is to be expected that on certain issues there will be quite sharp differences of view. It does not on the whole, however, seem likely that important though these issues are, they are incapable of resolution by a series of pragmatic bargains, or that they should occasion any major or prolonged rift within the Community itself.

FOREIGN AND DEFENCE POLICY

As far as its external economic relations are concerned the Community

---

[1] For a detailed treatment of this question see the companion volume in this series by Charles Ransom, *The European Community and Eastern Europe.*

[2] See, for instance, Harry G. Johnson 'The implications for the world economy', in Douglas Evans, *op. cit.,* p. 170. 'British accession to the Common Market will in all probability mean a halt to the progressive liberalisation of international trade that has characterised the post-war period, and a blockage of the only avenue by which the United States might be induced to abandon its current retreat into protectionism.'

has already both a clearly defined set of treaty obligations and an institutional apparatus which provide it with the basis to formulate policies and carry them out. Neither is the case, however, with regard to the non-economic aspects of its posture towards the rest of the world. In spite of all the discussion which has taken place about the desirability of moving towards what in the jargon of the Community is known as 'political union' very little so far has been achieved. The development of the Community has been marked by successive failures in this field, of which the abortive project for a Defence Community and the equally abortive negotiations for a treaty of political union in the early sixties are only two of the more obvious. And although the issue was raised again at the Hague Summit, the outcome of yet another examination of the problem was a very loose set of consultative arrangements consisting of twice-yearly meetings of Foreign Ministers backed by quarterly meetings of a political committee composed of senior members of the respective foreign ministries.

Foreign and defence policy-making has therefore remained in the hands of the individual member governments. The major initiatives which have been taken—whether one thinks of the French attempt to improve relations with the Soviet Union and the countries of Eastern Europe in the mid-1960s, or the Federal German government's *Ostpolitik* of recent years—have all been taken on a bilateral basis, and not within a Community framework. Nor has the fact of membership of the Community meant necessarily that these individual policies have moved closer together. The French withdrawal from the integrated military command structure of Nato in 1965 was a striking demonstration to the contrary, as was also the completely divergent reactions on the part of the French and the Germans to the American proposal which preceded that move of a Multilateral Nuclear Force with Nato. It is true that more recently the European members of Nato, other than France, have been holding informal meetings to seek to align their own positions within that organisation, but that group has been wider than the Community and these activities have had no formal connection with its activities.

The question of whether the new Community should seek to establish its own apparatus for policy-making and move towards common policies in these two fields is, nevertheless, very much on the agenda. The consultative procedures initiated—or rather revivified—as a result of the Hague Summit, have generated new pressure in this direction; the British have indicated their strong desire to see the Community playing a world role; and the Paris Summit called for proposals for improved cooperation to be presented by the middle of 1973. We need to ask therefore what the prospects of the Community extending its scope in this way are, what difficulties it is likely to encounter, and what relationship there is likely to be between its efforts in this direction and the rest of its activities.

In order to understand the nature of the problems we first need to examine some of the major characteristics of the international environment which are likely to be relevant to attempts by the Community to move into the fields of foreign and defence policy. In this context one is immediately confronted by a curious paradox. It is that while on the one hand recent years have seen a general recognition of the status quo in Europe uncertainty about the future has also noticeably increased. The inaction of the western powers when confronted with the Soviet invasion of Czechoslovakia in August 1968 confirmed their recognition of the Soviet sphere of influence in Eastern Europe; equally the Federal Republic's *Ostpolitik* has been based on a recognition of that country's post-war frontiers and the facts of life—including the existence of the German Democratic Republic—in Eastern Europe. In this sense the status quo established since the second world war seems now more generally accepted than ever before.

The lessening of tension within Europe, which has come about primarily because of the *détente* in the relationship between the United States and the Soviet Union has, however, led to a new situation and new problems. There are three aspects in particular of concern to policy-makers in Western Europe. The first arises from their fears that the United States and the Soviet Union may seek to settle European affairs over the heads of their respective allies. The growth of their bilateral relationship, of which Strategic Arms Limitation Talks (S.A.L.T.), President Nixon's visit to Moscow, and Mr. Henry Kissinger's frequent toings and froings are all significant examples, have all added point to this concern. Secondly, they are uncertain how to approach the forthcoming Conference on European Security and Cooperation which it has now been agreed should take place during the course of 1973. Originally proposed by the Soviet Union and its allies, this raises important questions relating to the future force levels in Europe, and in particular whether it will be possible to achieve—as the official policy of Nato now proposes—'mutual and balanced force reductions' in Europe, as well as possibly some new type of security arrangement accompanied by appropriate institutions.

Thirdly, and this is directly related to the second issue, there is the problem of future relations with the United States. In economic terms these are now characterised by a considerable degree of friction and a much firmer defence on the part of the United States of its own interests; strategically there is some doubt about how firm the transatlantic commitment to the defence of Europe now is. What is apparent is the strong pressure in the United States, not least as a result of its experience in Vietnam, to reduce its military commitments in other parts of the world. In the case of Europe this could well lead—and indeed there is now a general expectation that it will sooner rather than later in fact lead—to a substantial reduction of the number of United States ground troops stationed on the continent. As Senator McGovern observed during his presidential campaign in the autumn of 1972: 'If anyone had ever suggested 25 years ago when American troops first went into Europe they'd still be there in 1972 he would have been regarded as a madman'.[1] The policy he advocated was that United States forces in Europe should be cut back from their present level of about 300 000 to no more than 130 000, irrespective of any reduction in Soviet forces. The Nixon administration for its part has resisted similar pressures for unilateral force reductions, and while calling on its European allies to increase their own defence effort, has formally put its weight behind the official Nato policy of mutual and balanced reductions. Nevertheless, governments of Western Europe are uneasily aware that the nuclear umbrella under which they have sheltered may now be less leak-proof than it appeared when it was first erected, and are wondering what they should do about it.

It is hardly surprising that both perceptions of the situation and prescriptions for it vary widely. As far as the Soviet position is concerned, for instance, some underline its growing military and naval strength —the latter in the Mediterranean in particular—and the potential threat which this holds. Others, on the other hand, stress rather Soviet political objectives in Europe and see the Security Conference as a more subtle means of hastening the withdrawal of United States troops and sowing the seeds of disorder in the Atlantic Alliance. Some others, however, are tempted by the prospect of a weakening of the military alliances which have dominated Europe throughout the post-war period and believe that this could further reduce tension and lead to more European cooperation across the old frontiers of the cold war, and a liberalisation of the political regimes in Eastern Europe.

Even among those who believe that the maintenance of the Atlantic alliance is still essential for the defence of Western Europe there is uncertainty about some important issues. The one most relevant to our present theme is whether or not the new Community should assert its own 'defence personality', and if so, how. One view has always been that it would be dangerous and ultimately destructive of the alliance for it to attempt to do so, even if it took the form of the 'twin-pillar concept' in which Europe would seek to become a more equal partner with the United States.[2] Others, on the other hand, argue that West

---

[1] *The Times* (1 September 1972) p.6.

[2] See, for instance, Leonard Beaton 'The Strategic Issues' in Douglas Evans, *op. cit.* p.182: 'A united Europe will inevitably be seen by the United States as a power which could become a rival. As Europe presumed to claim equal control, especially in a crisis,

Europeans must play a greater part in their own defence if they are to maintain a credible posture and that if they can organise their conventional defence forces more effectively within a Community framework they are more likely both to be able to persuade the Americans that Europe is worth defending, and also acquire a greater say in Atlantic decision-making.[1] This view does not necessarily lead, however, to the conclusion that the Community should also seek to acquire its own nuclear capability, either based on a Franco-British weapon system or a genuine Community system—though there are certainly some (including Mr. Heath)—who suggest that this should be an eventual objective. The issue was raised by Lord Carrington at the Conservative party conference in 1972, when he argued that the new Community would eventually need to have its own nuclear capability, if smaller than that of the United States. There was an immediate protest from the Labour party: a foretaste of the battles that will certainly arise in the future should the French or British governments seek to move in that direction. Some, however, are sceptical of the Community's will or capacity to undertake any serious effort in the field of defence: they point to the fact that average defence expenditure in Western Europe is only 4% of national income, and to the many conflicting views about what—if anything—the Europeans should do to sustain a credible defence policy.[2]

Even apart from the fact that France appears to have no intention of returning into the Nato defence system, and that one of the new members—Ireland—is not a member of that organisation, there are therefore very serious problems confronting the Community should it seek to acquire a common defence policy, above all because of the very disparate views currently held on what that should consist of. There is no doubt, too, that moves in that direction would sooner or later pose in an acute form the problem of political control and require a degree of centralised authority which at the moment the Community simply does not possess.

Even more modest steps towards acquiring a common posture with regard to the United States and the Soviet Union—such as will be required in the forthcoming Security Conference—are also likely to become the subject of considerable disagreements. Some observers have concluded that only pressure exerted by some major shock—such as a massive unilateral withdrawal of United States troops—is likely to provide enough stimulus to overcome current differences of view and

---

the American fear of being committed to a conflict they could not manage would grow.'

[1] This view is strongly argued by Sir Bernard Burrows and Christopher Irwin in *The Security of Western Europe: Towards a Common Defence Policy,* London (1972).

[2] 'Malvolio', 'Perche non faremo L'Europa', *Affari Esteri* (Aprile 1972).

galvanise the Community into effective action. Others take a rather more sanguine view and, pointing to the way in which consultations have developed within the Davignon machinery and the pressure likely to be exerted by the British, believe that as the member countries acquire the habit of consulting together on foreign policy issues they will gradually be able to tackle the more difficult problems which confront them.

The difficulties which have arisen in connection with the proposed creation of a political secretariat to carry this work forward lend support to the argument of the pessimists rather than the optimists. It may well be also that the smaller countries of the Community will be resistant to being dragged in the wake of their larger partners towards common policies in these delicate fields. So the prospect of rapid developments seems rather unlikely. For the foreseeable future the most that seems likely to develop is an increased Community capacity to respond as a group to those situations which are forced upon it, particularly those arising in the context of Nato, rather than any marked capacity to take initiatives on its own. In spite of the British, it is on the whole unlikely that internal pressures within the Community will be so strong as to make progress in these policy areas the pace-maker for the rest of the Community's development. But equally, if past performance is any guide, the Community will be able to sustain even a fairly high degree of disagreement in these areas without it impinging very radically on the rest of its activities. But this is a sphere where external events could dictate the pace of events. The most likely of these—a substantial reduction of United States force levels in Europe—could well speed up the pace of developments and impose on the Community the need to respond as a group: in these circumstances, indeed, it might well find it easier to make more rapid progress towards political union than it has over the whole course of its development so far.

INSTITUTIONAL ISSUES

So far we have been examining a number of the major policy issues which will confront the new Community in terms of particular areas of its activity. But there is in addition another type of issue which it will have to face: namely, the development of its own political system and the role to be played in the future by the various institutions of the Community.

As we have already seen this theme has given rise to a great deal of discussion and argument within the Community throughout its development, and it is inevitable that this should continue as it raises questions of fundamental importance, such as where power should lie, how it should be exercised, and to whom—and by what means—those who exercise power should be held responsible. The major debate in the Community has always been between those who see it as an embryonic federal system—in which power is to be gradually transferred from national governments to an independent Community executive—and those who, on the contrary, regard it as a convenient framework within which a group of nation states can work together while each retains its essential national sovereignty.

In practice, up to now, the second view has prevailed over the first. In the short term, at least, enlargement is likely further to consolidate this situation. The great majority of British political leaders—as well as the great mass of the British public—have always expressed strong opposition to the idea of a federal United States of Europe. Mr. Gaitskell, for instance, spoke in terms of horror at the prospect:[1]

> Let us be clear what it means. It means the end of Britain as an independent nation: we become no more than 'Texas' or 'California' in the United States of Europe. It means the end of a thousand years of history . . .

Mr. Heath for his part has made his own views and those of his government clear on many occasions. He has dismissed the argument about a federal or confederal Europe as 'at best a sterile debate and at worst a positive hindrance to European progress'[2] and has served notice that neither major political party in Britain wishes to see the creation of a federal system:[3]

> Those members of the Community who want a federal system, but who know the views of Her Majesty's Government and the Opposition parties here are prepared to forgo their federal desires so that Britain should be a member and take part in political consultation and coordination with them.

The emphasis given by the government during the period leading up to accession on the availability of a veto in the Community where vital national interests are at stake was wholly consistent with this view. As the White Paper put it: 'All the countries concerned recognise that an attempt to impose a majority view in a case where one or more members considered their vital interests to be at stake would imperil the very fabric of the Community.'[4]

In this respect, the policy of the British government is wholly in line

---

[1] Broadcast on 21 September 1962. Reproduced in *The Listener*, 27 September 1962.

[2] Edward Heath, *Old world, new horizons*, London (1970) p. 56.

[3] House of Commons, 25 February 1970.

[4] White Paper (1971) para. 30.

with that being pursued by President Pompidou. On another institutional issue, however, the policies of the two governments have diverged. Mr. Heath did not support the French suggestion that the secretariat designed to hasten the achievement of a common foreign and defence policy should be located in Paris: on this matter the British aligned themselves with those other member governments who argued that it should be located alongside the other Community institutions in Brussels.

The first British nominations to the Commission—Sir Christopher Soames and Mr. George Thomson—also suggest a different approach from the French to the role of this body. These are clearly men of some considerable political standing, rather than—as French practice had preferred—appointments based on technical brilliance rather than political authority. It would, nevertheless, be rash to conclude from this that the British strategy is to build up the role of the Commission: it could more simply reflect a belief that powerful British voices should be heard at all levels of the institutional structure. The fact that the nominations were announced in advance of the meeting when the Community as a whole was due to decide on the composition of the new Commission rather suggested, indeed, that the British had adopted a no-nonsense approach to the question, but had concluded that their self-interest would be better served by a different strategy from that which had been followed by the French.

On other institutional issues the government has so far adopted a pragmatic and non-committal approach. This is particularly the case in its attitude to the future of the European Parliament. As Sir Alec Douglas-Home told the Conservative party conference in Blackpool in October 1972.[1]

We should get some practical experience of the operations of this body before putting forward ideas for any revision of the existing structure. I want to see our people inside, judging the European Parliament from inside, before we press for any particular, drastic changes.

Although, for instance, reference is occasionally made to the Anglo–Italian declaration of 29 April 1969—which according to some interpretations implied a commitment by the Labour Government to direct elections to the European Parliament[2]—there has been no suggestion

[1] Quoted in *The Times* (14 October 1972)

[2] The text of the relevant part on the Declaration is ambiguous. It reads: 'Europe must be firmly based on democratic institutions, and the European Communities should be sustained by an elected Parliament, as provided for in the Treaty of Rome.' For full text see *Electing the European Parliament,* Federal Trust, London (1972), appendix III.

that the government is currently prepared to support such a reform. Mr. Heath, for his part has made it clear that he thinks that the time is not yet ripe; and has indeed argued that the present method of indirect elections should be able to provide a sufficient base for its development: 'After all the United States Senate, probably the most powerful individual parliamentary body the world has ever seen, built up its power and influence for the first hundred or so years of its life on the basis of indirect election. The Europeans could well take heart and encouragement from this'.[1] On the other hand, both Mr. Heath and the government appear to be more willing to consider some increases in the powers of the Parliament: on its first appearance at Strasbourg the Conservative party delegation put forward a series of proposals with this aim.[2]

The official British posture on institutional questions is therefore a tentative and pragmatic one, occupying a middle ground between those who, like the Dutch for instance, wish to see the Community assume a more federal form and the French who are determined that this shall not be allowed to happen. The main question for the future is whether this middle ground between the opposing camps will remain sufficiently large for some urgently needed reforms to be made without provoking a violent storm such as occurred in 1965–1966. The issue is certainly very much on the agenda, not least because of the decisions taken at the Paris Summit. Although Dutch pressure to fix a date for the introduction of direct elections to the European Parliament was then resisted, and very few substantive decisions were taken, a series of deadlines was fixed for action on institutional issues.

In the first place the Council and Commission were asked to put into effect 'without delay' a number of measures—the content of which was not specified—to reinforce the role of the Parliament and to improve their relations with it. This presumably will mean a number of relatively minor changes which can be carried out without a revision of the treaties. Similarly, the Council is to take steps to improve its own working procedures before the middle of the year. The Commission was also asked to prepare proposals by 1 May 1973 on the whole complex of institutional issues, and the governments agreed to take a decision on these before the end of the first stage of the transitional period towards economic and monetary union.

If past experience is anything to go by the governments will pursue a highly pragmatic and piecemeal approach. On certain reforms they are likely to find it relatively easy to agree: there are a number of changes which could be made to improve the efficiency of the Council, for

[1] Edward Heath, *op. cit.*, p. 56.

[2] See Peter Kirk, M.P., 'The beginnings of a true Parliament', *European Community* (February 1973) p. 6, also *ibid*, pp. 23–24.

instance, on which no serious conflict should arise. There is also likely to be a substantial measure of support for some further increase in the powers of the European Parliament, and in particular the introduction of a form of 'second reading' procedure which would enable it to scrutinize and comment on Council decisions before they are finally enacted. It is also possible that a majority of governments will be in favour of giving the Parliament the last word in some of the less critical areas of policy-making, such as those concerned with the harmonisation of national legislation.

All these would be useful changes both in terms of efficiency and also as a means of providing greater degree of Parliamentary scrutiny over the activities of the Council. They would nevertheless keep all crucial power in the hands of the national governments. It is just possible, though less likely, that these governments will give the Parliament some say in the process of the nomination of the Commission.

There could, however, be quite sharp conflict if any government —the most likely one in this case is the French—sought to set up an institutional structure for the pursuit of economic and monetary union outside the existing structures. Equally, the pressures in some of the original member countries for the introduction of some form of direct election to the European Parliament could spark off a major clash, in which again the French government would be the main antagonist. In this case the attitude of the British could well prove to be decisive, though present indications suggest that London would not wish to be drawn into a conflict with Paris on this issue, and would be more likely to find itself on the same side of the argument.

The major question mark hanging over the system is whether in fact it will be capable of operating efficiently and whether it will be acceptable to a majority of the political elites in the member countries. The smaller countries may well find, for instance, that from their point of view the veto is a rather weak weapon and that their interests would be better defended by a more powerful Commission. And all concerned may find that frequent recourse to the veto in fact prevents the Community from reaching decisions. In other words the engine may prove too weak and the brakes far too powerful to sustain the forward movement of the vehicle. If this should happen, then the member could be faced, as were the original American colonies, with an important choice: either to insist on the maintenance of states' rights and accept a weak and ineffective form of union or swallow their national pride and build together a genuine European government. Federalists, for their part, have always argued that such a government is essential if the Community is to work: the coming years will show whether or not they are right.

TOWARDS EUROPEAN UNION

In the final paragraph of the communique issued after the Paris Summit a new objective was set out for the Community: its transformation 'before the end of the present decade and with the fullest respect for the treaties signed, of the whole complex of the relations of the member states into a European Union'. The institutions were asked to draw up a report on this subject before the end of 1975 for submission to a new Summit meeting.

What exactly was in the minds of the authors of this part of the statement, generally assumed to have been the French, is not very clear. It could amount to no more than a general tidying-up operation to take account of the various new developments which, if all goes well, will have occurred by the end of the present decade. It could, on the other hand, mean the elaboration of a new treaty which will attempt to set out both a new constitutional structure for the Community and also a set of still more ambitious objectives—for instance, in the fields of foreign and defence policy—as well as bringing others (education, would be one example) within the ambit of its work.

At all events what it suggests is a realisation that if the various heavy tasks which the 1972 Summit set for the Community are in fact carried out Western Europe will, by the end of the decade, be poised to emerge as a formal economic and political union, to take its place alongside other major powers in the world. This now is the target: what remains to be seen is whether the political will to attain it will survive the stresses which will inevitably be experienced by the Nine who have set out so hopefully in this direction.

7 Britain and the Enlarged Community

Having examined the major political characteristics of the new Community and some of the major problems it is likely to face, we now need to examine the implications of membership for Britain itself, as well as the factors which will affect the role it plays in the new Community.

There is no doubt that membership will have, over a period of time, a very considerable political impact on the country, quite apart from its social and economic repercussions. Even the current scope of the Community's activities will affect a very wide range of interests in this country, quite apart from the Government and Parliament, and the likelihood that both the scope of these activities and their intensity will grow in the future will necessarily involve more and more individuals and groups in them. In the short term, however, the political impact of membership—unlike its economic effects—will be felt primarily by the relatively restricted groups which compose the political elite of the country. It is they who are now faced by the need of adapting themselves and the institutions within which they work to a new situation. The major characteristic of this is that an important range of decisions is now being taken by the institutions of the Community rather than by the British Government on its own. It is to the problems arising from this situation to which we turn first.

THE MACHINERY OF GOVERNMENT

The need to adapt itself to the new situation falls in the first place on the government. Its primary duty is to formulate policies which it considers to represent the national interest in the context of membership of the Community; to ensure that these policies are well-argued and strongly defended in the Community institution; and that the resulting decisions are acceptable both to it and the country at large.

This task is one of considerable complexity, which requires in the first place an appropriate organisation of the government at home. This involves both ensuring that each government department is properly equipped to follow developments in the Community, and also that machinery exists to co-ordinate policy and resolve disputes between the interests of different departments. A number of important issues arise in this context. One is whether specialised structures need to be created in those departments which are heavily involved in Community business to deal with it, or whether the task of considering and formulating policy is to be spread within departments according to their existing internal functional specialisation. The distinction is between that of considering Community matters as belonging to the sphere of foreign policy rather than that of domestic policy. At this level the government appears to have chosen the latter option though views on the issue are by no means unanimous and it is still too early to judge whether current arrangements will stand the test of time.

One important effect that membership has already had, it should be noted, is to give to some departments a particularly important role in the context of Community business: this is especially the case with the Department of Trade and Industry and the Ministry of Agriculture, Fisheries and Food which are having to bear the brunt of the detailed work involved with the implementation of the existing treaties. The M.A.F.F. in particular has found its role significantly expanded in this context, given the importance of the common agricultural policy and the problems it involves in terms of detailed administration and the overall strategy of the government's policy within the Community.

The problem of the relative weight of various departments in the decision-making process has, however, been raised in a more acute form by the need to devise machinery to resolve conflicts between their various interests and to co-ordinate policy in Brussels. This, as we have seen, is a problem common to all the member governments, and has been resolved in a variety of ways.[1] In all of them a major issue has been the role to be assigned to the Foreign Ministry. In the period up to the third and successful negotiation on entry a great variety of different arrangements were made by successive British Governments:[2] during the negotiations themselves and subsequently the Foreign and Commonwealth Office shared with the Cabinet Office the primary respons-

[1] See above, Chapter 3, pp. 64–5.

[2] See Helen Wallace, *National Decision-making and the European Communities*, P.E.P./Chatham House European Series, London (1973).

ibility for this co-ordinating role. Increasingly, since membership took place, it is the latter which has assumed a primary role in coordinating policy, under the supervision of Mr. John Davies, Chancellor of the Duchy of Lancaster. With a seat in the Cabinet, he has in effect been acting as Minister for Europe, chairing the crucial meetings in London, and attending most of the Council meetings in Brussels and Luxembourg. In performing these tasks he has worked closely with the Prime Minister, so that—as far as Community business is concerned, at least —the Cabinet Office has begun to assume a role not unlike that suggested in a plan which was circulating in Whitehall in the summer of 1972 which suggested the creation of a Prime Minister's Department, with responsibilities ranging over the whole extent of governmental policy.[1] Although this proposal may not be realised in its original form —or at all—it is significant of the forces making for shifts of power within the Whitehall machine, of which the importance and volume of Community business is certainly not the least.

This business has also led to the creation in Brussels itself of a powerful team under Sir Michael Palliser, the United Kingdom's first Permanent Representative to the Community. He was appointed Head of the British delegation there early in 1972 once it was certain membership was to take place, and so was able to acquire an intimate knowledge of the working of the Community, not least through the consultative procedures which were instituted in advance of entry, well before 1 January 1973. Other senior appointments to the staff were made in the months preceeding entry with the aim of creating a skilled and knowledgeable negotiating team. As we have seen, a heavy responsibility rests on this group in the day-to-day decision-making processes of the Community. It is also the primary source of information for the home departments on the affairs of the Community, and has the difficult task of both defending national policy in Brussels and also explaining to London why compromises are necessary in the interests of maintaining the forward momentum of the Community.

As far as the general effects on the civil service are concerned, these will take a variety of forms. There will in the first place be some increase in their numbers; the government has estimated that membership will involve, over a period of time, the recruitment of a total of about 1 500 additional staff.[2] Within the service more will certainly need to have a competent knowledge of French; and for a considerable number there will be a good deal of travelling back and forth across the Channel to discuss Community business. The closer network of

---

[1] *Financial Times* (23 August 1972); *The Times* (24 August 1972).

[2] *European Communities Bill, Explanatory and Financial Memorandum* p.vi. Of this total, 500 were to be recruited before entry, the remainder 'spread over several years thereafter'.

relations which will have to be established with the other member governments will probably also mean some changes in the functions being performed by British embassies in their respective capitals: over time it will probably mean that far more direct ministry-to-ministry contacts will be established by home departments which may short-circuit some of the traditional channels.

PARLIAMENT

Although these changes with regard to the machinery of government are not inconsiderable, the impact of membership on Parliament will be very much more profound. In the first place, joining the Community has meant that Parliament was confronted during the passage of the European Communities Bill—which gave the force of law to the Treaty of Accession—with a mass of existing Community legislation which it was required to accept with only the briefest opportunity of scrutiny, little opportunity for debate, and none at all for amendment. The Opposition in particular protested vehemently about this, arguing that the Bill had been deliberately drafted in a way which prevented them from discussing the details of the 43 volumes of Community legislation; that they were prevented by a ruling of the Chair from putting many of the amendments which they wished to table; and that the Government's imposition of a guillotine during the committee stage made a mockery of the whole process.

More important for the future, however, is the fact that a substantial volume of governmental business is now being routed through the Community's institutions which means that not only that decisions are no longer being taken by the British Government but by the Community's Council of Ministers, but also by a procedure which —many fear—will prevent Parliament at Westminster from exercising any effective control over, or scrutiny of, it. Opponents of membership from both sides of the House argued during the passage of the European Committee Bill that this would gravely impair the role of Parliament. Mr. Michael Foot, for instance said:[1]

> No one can dispute the proposition that the Bill is the most deliberate proposal for curtailing the powers of this House that has ever been put before Members of Parliament . . . The passage of this Bill . . . would alter fundamentally the relationship between the British people and the British Parliament.

Others were more vehement. Mr. Raphael Tuck, for instance had

[1] House of Commons, 17 February 1972, col. 742

this to say:[1]

> This is not a free association of parties who are free to make their own rules for that association and also to enjoy its benefits. This is a shot-gun marriage in which the poor bridegroom, the United Kingdom, is going in with a gun at its back and its hands manacled and unable to make the rules for this marriage.

Mr. Peter Shore, for his part, argued that over a wide area of affairs Parliament was doomed to become 'a spectator of legislative events'; Mr. Douglas Jay, that some of the essentials of parliamentary government and basic democratic rights of the electorate were being signed away; and Sir Derek Walker Smith that there would be 'a total subordination' of Parliament with regard to Community affairs.

The Government, for its part, sought to calm these fears. Mr. Rippon assured the House on 15 February 1972 that there was nothing in the Bill which abridged 'the ultimate sovereignty of Parliament', and added this pledge:

> Her Majesty's ministers will at all times be responsible to Parliament for the action they take within the Community machine and the House will be able to bring its influence to bear by all the traditional parliamentary procedures, such as questions, Adjournment debates and Supply Days. No government would proceed on a matter of major policy in the Council unless they knew that they had the approval of the House.

Many Members pointed out nevertheless that the parliaments in the existing member countries had had great difficulties in exercising any close degree of supervision over the activities of their respective governments in the Community;[2] that once a decision had been taken in the Council there was nothing that Parliament at home could do about it; and that the budgetary arrangements were such that, as Mr. Enoch Powell observed 'We are neither to be informed in the manner to which we have been accustomed; nor are we to be allowed to debate these sums; nor are we to be allowed to vote them'.[3] Many speakers also underlined the fact that an increasing volume of Community legislation was taking the form of regulations which were directly binding once they had been agreed by the Council or Commission and would not be submitted to Parliament at all; and expressed their fears that by taking powers under the Bill to enact directives by Order in

[1] House of Commons, 17 February 1972, col. 723

[2] For a discussion of this, see Michael Niblock, *The E.E.C: National Parliaments in Community Decision-Making* Chatham House. P.E.P. European Series No. 17. London (1971).

[3] House of Commons, 8 June 1972

Council and giving powers not only to Ministers but also their departments to issue regulations 'for the purpose of implementing any Community obligation in the United Kingdom' the government would greatly restrict Parliament's capacity to scrutinise even this type of Community legislation.

In spite of the government's assurance that it would not abuse the delegated legislation procedure in giving legal force to Community directives, a great deal of anxiety remained. This was also voiced by the all-party Select Committee on Procedure of the House which in the summer issued a report which concluded that 'the entry of Britain into the Communities presents a profound challenge to many of the established procedures of Parliament which, if not adequately dealt with, could leave Parliament substantially weaker vis-à-vis the executive'.[1]

A later parliamentary report was rather more reassuring, at least as far as the volume of delegated legislation likely to be generated was concerned. A paper prepared by the Cabinet Office had shown that although during 1971 the Community had issued 2900 regulations and 410 directives and decisions, there would have been need of only some 65 instruments of delegated legislation had Britain been a member at that time. This compared with a volume of about one thousand such instruments each year already being scrutinised by the Select Committee set up for that purpose. On this basis the report concluded that the problem was not unmanageable, and that if certain procedural modifications which it suggested were adopted, Parliament should be able to maintain a watch over such legislation without undue strain.[2]

This report was concerned, however, with only part of the problem. Members of both houses have also expressed concern about more general aspects of Community business apart from the purely legislative domain. Here the initial problem is to ensure a manageable flow of information about developments and issues; a second problem is to devise structures and procedures through which Members can question ministers on matters of detail as well as providing opportunities for general scrutiny of Community policies and debates on its development. A number of suggestions have been put forward in this context, including a Select Committee of the House of Commons on Community affairs (which might operate through a series of specialised sub-

---

[1] *Third Special Report from the Select Committee on Procedure,* House of Commons, 26 July 1972, para. 9

[2] *Report from the Joint Committee on Delegated Legislation, Session 1971–1972* (August 1972) pp.xl–xliv. The Committee's recommendations included the creation of a Joint Scrutiny Committee by both Houses, a Commons Standing Committee, and additional time for discussion of contested statutory instruments by the House of Commons.

committees) or a Joint Committee of both Houses.[1]

It still remains to be seen how far Parliament will go in adapting its procedures to allow it the maximum of opportunities to keep the activities of the government within the Community context under scrutiny. There are, however, important limits to what it can achieve in this direction. Although it may be able—if its Members are well-enough informed and work sufficiently hard—to offer its views and comments on proposals emanating from the Commission, it will certainly not be able to intervene in the critical final stages of decision-making. It will not be able, either, to amend—much less reject—the regulations which emerge from this process; and the amount of freedom it will have with regard to directives is also rather slight. Westminster may be able to exercise rather more effective scrutiny over the activities of the British Government than the parliaments of some of the other member countries, but it will certainly play a much weaker role with regard to business transacted within the Community than it does with regard to purely domestic legislation. It is true that the Government will still be ultimately responsible to Parliament for its actions within the Community as for all its other actions, but detailed, day-to-day supervision and criticism will be difficult if not impossible.

Membership of the Community undeniably means that Parliament has lost some of its authority over the executive. Unless the Community were to abandon some of its present decision-making procedures and make all of its decisions dependent on ratification by national parliaments, there is no conceivable method by which that loss can be made good. Theoretically the only way by which effective parliamentary supervision can be re-established is through the European Parliament itself. A minority of members have in fact urged that greater powers should be given to that body. Many on the continent also hope that the British devotion to parliamentary processes will mean that additional pressure will be exerted from this country to achieve what they have long been urging. It is by no means certain, however, that the majority of British parliamentarians will be willing in this way explicitly to acknowledge that the British Parliament is no longer as powerful as before. As Mr. Michael Foot observed at the end of the debate on this during the passage of the European Communities Bill:[2]

> I will not lay down what I think should be the conclusion on these matters. I am not saying that I want the European Assembly to be given even greater powers and that this is one way of dealing with

---

[1] For a further discussion, see *Westminster to Brussels: the Significance for Parliament of Accession to the European Community*, P.E.P. (in association with the Hansard Society and the Study of Parliament Group), London (1973).

[2] House of Commons, 13 June 1972.

the undemocratic nature of the Brussels Commission and the operation of the Council of Ministers, because I believe that there are dangers in that proposal in the sense that the stronger the European Assembly was made, the greater would be the injury inflicted upon the rights of the British House of Commons.

This will certainly be an important issue for the future, both for the British Parliament and the European Parliament itself: so, too, is the question of how British representation in that Parliament is to be organised. At present the 36 British members are formally nominated by the Prime Minister after consultations through the usual channels —which in effect means the party Whips. These members, particularly those from the House of Commons, have however, a very heavy load of work to sustain in addition to their normal parliamentary duties. Many of the members of the Parliament from other countries have found that it is virtually impossible to combine the two, and in the British situation where each Member has a heavy load of constituency work the problem is even more acute. Many of those who have already had experience of other European assemblies—the Consultative Assembly of the Council of Europe and the Assembly of Western European Union—have already experienced this to their cost, especially in those cases where they have become chairmen of committees of those bodies.

There is a real risk in this situation that an unsupportable burden will be placed on the shoulders of a minority of Members of Parliament; that their electors will find themselves deprived of effective representation; and that only the very young or those nearing the end of their political careers will wish to go to Strasbourg. Several solutions have been put forward to this problem. One that has gained a certain amount of support is that proposed by Mr. Michael Stewart.[1] He has suggested that while a small number (four to six) of the British delegation should continue to be nominated from the House of Lords (for whose members the dual mandate poses far fewer problems), the remaining 30 or 32 should be directly elected by large regional constituencies *in addition* to the existing Members of Parliament. They would be Members both of the House of Commons and the European Parliament, but would devote most of their time to the latter. They would preferably be allowed a proxy vote at Westminster—though this is not in the author's eyes absolutely essential.

Such a system would certainly not contravene the treaties, and would indeed introduce a form of direct election to the European Parliament for which those treaties provide. A number of reservations

---

[1] Rt. Hon. Michael Stewart, 'Britain and the Assembly of the E.E.C.' in *Electing the European Parliament*, Federal Trust, London (1972).

have, however, been entered against both this plan and other proposals designed to overcome the problem of the dual mandate.[1] As yet there is no sign that either of the major political parties is willing to change the existing system of nomination. But the problem remains. It is certain to become more acute as time goes on, and pressure can be expected to mount in the other member countries for some form of direct election to the European Parliament. Apart from anything else, this would for the first time give the citizens of the Community a form of direct participation in its affairs. It is precisely the absence of such participation which many consider to be one of its weakest and unacceptable features at present. Direct elections would also provide, for the first time, an incentive for the political parties to organise themselves effectively on a Community basis, and so build up the political infrastructure of the Community. And although some believe that a more effective European Parliament would also be a more unruly assembly, others argue that it would be far more healthy to have a body where the conflicting political interests within the Community could be represented, and could bring to the attention of the public the nature of the options facing it, rather than restricting debate—as it is at present—to ministers, civil servants, and parliamentarians whose activities are largely ignored by the mass of the public.

INTEREST GROUPS

In contrast to the problems facing Parliament, those confronting bodies representing specific socio-economic interests in Britain are relatively simple. They have the same problem of organising themselves to operate with a new dimension of government represented by the Community institutions, but for the most part the channels through which they can do this had already been established and contact made with the relevant Community-wide interest groups well before entry took place. In some instances indeed, British groups had already been admitted to membership of them.

In spite of its opposition to entry, the Trades Union Congress had, for instance, long taken an active—and indeed leading—part in the European Regional Organisation of the International Confederation of the Free Trade Unions. With over 10 million members it is the largest single national trade union organisation in Western Europe, having as many members as the whole of the Free Trade Unions in the original six member countries, within which the German union—the

---

[1] See Michael Steed, 'The European Parliament: the Significance of Direct Election', *Government and Opposition*, Autumn 1971.

D.G.B.—is by far the largest with around eight million members.[1]British entry has therefore meant a major accession of strength for the free trade unions within the Community, even though the T.U.C. has so far refused to send representatives to the Economic and Social Committee. The unions of the Six, for their part, have always been among the staunchest supporters of the process of integration. When the High Authority of the Coal and Steel Community was set up in 1952 one of their leaders the Belgian, Paul Finet, became a member of it, and the coal and steel unions set up a special committee in Luxembourg to co-ordinate their action within the Community. In 1958 a new organisation, the *Seretariat Syndical Européen,* was established to perform a similar function with regard to the new Communities, and this in turn was strengthened in 1969 when it acquired a new constitution and a new name—the European Confederation of Free Trade Unions. Although the T.U.C. remained outside this body, it maintained close contact with it, and also set up in the same building in Brussels a parallel group—the E.F.T.A. Trade Union Committee—to co-ordinate action within that organisation. With the prospect of British membership, and the dissolution of E.F.T.A. itself, the need for a new body then became apparent. Although there was considerable opposition from the non-European members of the I.C.F.T.U., who feared that its creation would weaken the parent body, agreement on this was finally reached early in 1973 when the European Trade Union Confederation was set up, with Mr. Victor Feather, general secretary of the T.U.C., as its first president.

The Confederation of British Industry (C.B.I.) for its part set up its office in Brussels in January 1971 and entered into an informal relationship with the *Union des Industries de la Communuaté Européenne* (U.N.I.C.E.) of which it has now become a full member. This is the body which represents the corresponding bodies in the other member countries (though in some cases, as in Germany, there are separate bodies representing private industry and employers) and which is recognised by the Commission as the authoritative voice of private industry in the Community. A parallel (but weaker) body represents the public sector interest throughout the Community—the *Centre Européen de l'entreprises publique (C.E.E.P.)*—and a number of nationalised British industries may well become members of this body.

The National Farmers Union (N.F.U.) has also found a natural partner in C.O.P.A. (*Comité des Organisations Professionnelles Agricoles de la C.E.E.*) which, after a very uncertain start in the early years of the E.E.C., has now emerged as the main voice of the farming interests in

[1] For a discussion of the free trade union movement in the Community, see Walter Kendall and Eli Marx *Unions in Europe*, Centre for Contemporary European Studies, University of Sussex, 1972.

the Community. In this case, too, the British organisation had taken good care in the years leading up to membership already to establish close relations with this body, so that for it January 1973 offered no surprises.

Similar links have also been established by a great variety of professional associations in Britain with the relevant Community organisations which now exist for almost every conceivable type of interest. Enlargement of their own membership will, of course, mean problems for them which are similar to those which the Community institutions themselves are now having to face: a wider spread of interests, and also a strong British presence which may not always be condusive to harmonious relations. But no British interest which has not already established such links will have far or long to look to identify the appropriate Community group to join, and in most cases they will be assured of a ready welcome. It is only once inside that the real problems begin: the search for a common position on issues on which the Community is proposing to take action, and ensuring that the organisation is sufficiently well-equipped to exert pressure both on the Commission and on the relevant national governments. So although the contours and rules of the game for such groups have changed, the experience already gained by their colleague in the Six is available to the new British members, and they can be expected to adapt themselves readily to the needs of the new situation.

PARTY ATTITUDES AND POLICIES

So far in this chapter we have been discussing the domestic impact of membership in Britain; we now need to examine the reverse side of the coin and look at the impact of British membership on the Community.

As far as the original member countries are concerned, we have already seen that there was a high level of support among the general public for British entry.[1] It should be added, however, that this was accompanied by both hopes and fears. The hopes most frequently expressed were that the presence of Britain would establish a more stable political equilibrium within the Community; that it would reinforce the democratic elements within it; strengthen those wishing to see it adopt more liberal trade policies towards the rest of the world; and bring to the Community a more outward-looking set of attitudes and a keener sense of its world responsibilities. On the other hand fears were also expressed that enlargement would make the Community unmanageable; that the British would reinforce the Gaullist elements within

[1] See above, Chapter 5, p. 131.

it; and that the Community would be in danger, under pressure from London, of degenerating into a loosely-organised and ineffective inter-governmental type of organisation.

To these fears the evolution of attitudes in the Labour Party in Britain has certainly added a keener edge. For this raises the question of whether British membership may only be temporary, and whether the sort of renegotiation to which the party is now officially committed should it return to power might not prove to be disruptive of the Community as a whole. Many will therefore be casting anxious eyes on the British political scene and in particular the prospects for a return to power of a Labour Government at the next general election which has to take place not later than the early summer of 1975.

It is clearly idle to speculate at this point in time how likely these prospects are. There are too many imponderables in the situation for any firm forecast to be made. On the one hand the domestic record of the Conservative government has certainly not fulfilled the expectations which its electoral promises aroused in 1970; on the other the dissensions within the ranks of the Labour Party leadership, particularly on its European policy, have somewhat blunted its challenge to Mr. Heath. The possibility of a formal split within its ranks on this issue is certainly not to be wholly discounted, though both sides are likely to draw back from irrevocable action in this direction. Were the pro-Europeans to be driven out of the party it would lose a good proportion of its more distinguished and experienced parliamentarians, as well as an appreciable volume of electoral support. This in itself could prove disastrous at the polls. For this reason alone, a break is a rather remote possibility.

Should the party be returned to power at the next general election it is therefore probable that a Labour Cabinet would contain both those who have been in favour of entry as well as those committed to an attempt to renegotiate the terms of entry. This in itself casts doubts on whether the threats made before membership took place would actually be carried into practice, quite apart from the actual difficulties of the sort of renegotiation which was contemplated in 1972. In this context it is relevant to recall that a far more determined opponent than Mr. Wilson of the Community, General de Gaulle, found it prudent to accept the obligations of membership when he returned to power in 1958 rather than risk the isolation of his country from its neighbours. It has also to be recalled that the last time the Labour Party was in power its leadership took positive steps in an attempt to gain entry.

Another pertinent consideration in this context arises from the practical difficulties of any attempted renegotiation of the terms of entry. Theoretically such a renegotiation would involve the presentation to the Community's Council of Ministers of a series of demands accompanied by a threat that if they were not met the party would recommend to the British public that the country should withdraw from membership. A Labour Government which adopted such a posture would almost certainly discover however—and rather rapidly—that there were far more pressures operating on it to prevent a breakdown than upon those with whom it was negotiating. A failure on its part to obtain satisfactory terms would be interpreted by many at home as at least as much a reflection of its own incompetence as of ill-will on the part of its partners. And if the Government were to have to face the electorate with a proposal that Britain should withdraw it would at the same time—for its posture to remain credible —have to suggest what then would follow. Unscrambling membership would hardly be easy: decisions would have to be taken whether or not to re-instate tariffs between Britain and its erstwhile partners; about new marketing and price arrangements which would be substituted for those we had adopted into the framework of the Community's own common agricultural policy; and whether or not all the regulations and directives which by then would have been applied should all be discarded. The confusion and disruption implied by all this would be immense. Moreover some further negotiations would then be necessary with the Community. The Labour Government would probably wish to try and maintain a free trade area with it for industrial goods, but would find itself in an extremely weak position with a major sterling crisis on its hands. The prospect would be frightening, and would be such as to damage irreparably the Labour Party's electoral chances not only immediately but for many years to come.

In the light of these considerations, it is most improbable that a return to power of a Labour Government at the next general election would in fact lead to a British withdrawal from the Community. What is more likely to happen is that by the time such an election is held British influence will have already made itself powerfully felt within the Community, and in a way to meet many of the fears which the party had before entry. By that time renegotiation of the terms of entry will be clearly seen to be a pointless exercise, and that far more can be achieved through a British presence within the Council of Ministers. No doubt the leaders of the party would then be faced (should it be returned to power) with a final rear-guard action on the part of those who remain ferocious opponents of entry who would demand that the decisions of the 1972 Party Conference be implemented. The leadership would then have to explain that times had changed, and that much though they continued to object to many features of the Community, it was clear that they would have more chance of achieving the substance of their aims by remaining inside than by re-opening the question of the original terms of entry. Such a policy would also offer an opportunity to heal the breach within the party especially, as Mr. Roy Jenkins has already made quite plain,[1] those who are in favour of membership are by no means uncritical of many features of the Community.

A gradual alignment of the Labour Party's policies with regard to the Community on lines not dissimilar with those of other left-wing parties in the other member countries can therefore be anticipated with some confidence in the course of the coming years. At the same time both it and any future Conservative Government can be expected to pursue policies designed to defend British interests vigorously within the Community. How difficult a partner Britain will prove to be will depend to a considerable extent on the nature of the economic impact of membership, and how flexible the other members prove to be in meeting British interests. Even if one takes an optimistic view on both these issues, all the signs are that Britain will not be an easy partner. What assumptions then should one make about the overall prospects for the new Community?

[1] See, for instance, his speech in the House of Commons on 17 October 1972.

8 Conclusion: Future prospects

There have always been those who have considered the construction of an economic and political Community among the countries of Western Europe to be an impossible, and even absurd, undertaking. They have not been the least bit dismayed by the fact that so far their prophecies of doom have not been fulfilled. At each stage they have found new arguments to support their scepticism and disbelief. This view is, for instance, held by one British observer who has argued on the following lines:[1]

> However worthy all the 'European' projects may have seemed in the period of their being worked out, from 1948 to 1956, the change in the scale of international problems since that period has made them irrelevant to anything worth while. . . . The scale of the world's major problems is too great for them to be solved, not only by an as yet non-existent Europe, but even by either or both of the existing superpowers. . . . All need action on a world scale, and if Britain is looking for fields in which to exercise her energies and her diplomatic skills, it is there, rather than in the pursuit of the useless and dangerous European chimera, that they are needed. When shall we wake up to the fact that we are now no longer living in the forties and fifties, when the European dream seemed plausible, but many light-years later, in the seventies?

This view is not, however—as we have seen—held by any significant body of opinion within the original member countries of the Community which, having been welded together over the course of the past

---

[1] William Pickles, 'Political hopes and political realities' in Douglas Evans, *op.cit.*, p.120.

20 years by their common experience—as well as by the economic interests which now bind them together—are very unlikely for their part to abandon a construction which in their view has served them well. Whatever else happens in the new Community, it is extremely improbable that this core area will be disbanded. For if some of the original reasons for its formation no longer apply, others have come to replace them. And although it is true that many problems in the world certainly exist on a scale far wider than even the enlarged Community this is certainly not, in the eyes of the great majority, any reason for abandoning the pursuit of integration in Western Europe. Indeed the Community offers an instrument through which action may and can be taken whereas the weakness of world institutions, as the experience of the United Nations shows clearly, all too often results only in immobility and impotence.

Nevertheless, the sceptics can point to many features of the new Community which are likely to make its life difficult and its success uncertain. Chief among them are the divergent interests which its members are likely to defend; the fact that there are now nine governments around the Council table rather than six; and that all of them —notably France and Britain—insist that they should have a veto on any issue where they consider their own vital national interests to be at stake. Moreover, the level of the support for the Community among the general public in Britain is low and one of its two major parties has taken up a position which calls into question the continued presence of the country in the enlarged Community.

All these are valid sources of concern. As far as Britain is concerned, however, it has been argued that it is unlikely even in the event of return to power of the Labour Party that the country would withdraw from the Community. Nevertheless, the fact that Britain has not shared the long experience of its original members of the process and the problems of integration means that there is a considerable gap to be bridged, quite apart from the fact that, by having had to accept the rules drawn up by the Six to meet their own needs, Britain will be seeking to make changes in some sensitive policy areas. Both major parties are also clearly intent on the vigorous pursuit of what they consider to be the national interest within the Community. So Britain is not likely to prove an easy partner, even if one makes optimistic assumptions about the balance of payments effects of membership: and should these prove as negative as some expect, any British Government will be bound to seek radical remedies.

France, too, can also be expected to have an equally keen sense of her own interests and to pursue them with comparable determination. The Federal Republic, for its part, is also likely to wish to make its new-found economic and political strength felt. So at the heart of the new

Community there will be strong, and by no means always convergent, national interests to be reconciled. There are many policy issues which could quite easily become sources of considerable stress. Whether or not they will do so will depend essentially on the political leadership within the Community. It is this leadership which will decide how conflicts are handled and whether they are dealt with by processes of bargaining and discussion or by threats; whether they are contained within the normal rules of the Community game, or are allowed to escalate into crisis situations.

The availability of a pragmatic type of leadership devoted to the success of the Community over the coming years is certainly essential if the prevailing conventional wisdom, so strongly held in Britain and France about how its affairs are to be conducted, is to be vindicated. Otherwise the vigorous defence of national interests will almost certainly create a high and persistent level of stress within it which could so easily bring it to a halt amid a welter of mutual recrimination. It may be that for some years there will be still too weak a sense of genuine Community for any alternative form of government to be a viable possibility—though pressures for stronger federal elements in the system can be expected to grow and could themselves provoke tension within it.

At all events it is unlikely that the progress of the Community towards a closer economic and political union will be smooth. We can expect many more prolonged negotiations in Brussels and Luxembourg, and bleary-eyed ministers and officials emerging for air after nights spent around the Council table. There may be more walk-outs on the model of the French in 1965. There may well be periods of stagnation and immobility. On the other hand there is little to suggest the prospect of a complete breakdown, much less a disintegration of the new Community. There is too much at stake for all concerned; too many pressures impelling its members forward; and no real alternative to pursuing these new, peaceful methods of building together an effective Community.

Appendix: The Paris Summit—Final communiqué

PREAMBLE

The heads of state or of government of the countries of the enlarged Community, meeting for the first time on October 19 and 20 in Paris, at the invitation of the President of the French Republic, solemnly declare:

At the moment when enlargement, decided in accordance with the rules in the treaties and with respect for what the six original member states have already achieved, is to become a reality and to give a new dimension to the Community;

At a time when world events are profoundly changing the international situation;

Now that there is a general desire for détente and cooperation in response to the interest and the wishes of all peoples;

Now that serious monetary and trade problems require a search for lasting solutions that will favour growth with stability;

Now that many developing countries see the gap widening between themselves and the industrial nations and claim with justification an increase in aid and a fairer use of wealth:

Now that the tasks of the Community are growing, and fresh responsibilities are being laid upon it, the time has come for Europe to recognize clearly the unity of its interests, the extent of its capacities and the magnitude of its duties; Europe must be able to make its voice heard in world affairs, and to make an original contribution commensurate with its human, intellectual and material resources. It must affirm its own views in international relations, as befits its mission to be open to the world and for progress, peace and cooperation.

TO THIS END:

i The member states reaffirm their determination to base the development of their Community on democracy, freedom of opinion, the free movement of people and of ideas and participation by their peoples through their freely elected representatives.

ii The member states are determined to strengthen the Community by establishing an economic and monetary union, the guarantee of stability and growth, the foundation of their solidarity and the indispensable basis for social progress, and by ending disparities between the regions;

iii Economic expansion is not an end in itself. Its first aim should be to enable disparities in living conditions to be reduced. It must take place with the participation of all the social partners. It should result in an improvement in the quality of life as well as in standards of living. As befits the genius of Europe, particular attention will be given to intangible values and to protecting the environment, so that progress may really be put at the service of mankind;

iv The Community is well aware of the problem presented by continuing underdevelopment in the world. It affirms its determination within the framework of a world-wide policy towards the developing countries, to increase its effort in aid and technical assistance to the least favoured people. It will take particular account of the concerns of those countries towards which, through geography, history and the commitments entered into by the Community, it has specific responsibilities;

v The Community reaffirms its determination to encourage the development of international trade. This determination applies to all countries without exception.

The Community is ready to participate, as soon as possible, in the open-minded spirit that it has already shown, and according to the procedures laid down by the IMF [International Monetary Fund] and the Gatt [General Agreement on Tariffs and Trade] in negotiations based on the principle of reciprocity. These should make it possible to establish, in the monetary and commercial fields, stable and balanced economic relations, in which the interests of the developing countries must be taken fully into account.

vi The member states of the Community, in the interests of good neighbourly relations which should exist among all European countries whatever their regime, affirm their determination to pursue their policy of détente and of peace with the countries of Eastern Europe, notably on the occasion of the conference on security and cooperation in Europe, and the establishment on a

sound basis of a wider economic and human cooperation;
   vii The construction of Europe will allow it, in conformity with its
ultimate political objectives, to affirm its personality while remaining
faithful to its traditional friendships and to the alliances of the member
states, and to establish its position in world affairs as a distinct entity
determined to promote a better international equilibrium, respecting
the principles of the Charter of the United Nations. The member states
of the Community, the driving force of European construction, affirm
their intention to transform before the end of the present decade the
whole complex of their relations into a European union.

ECONOMIC AND MONETARY QUESTIONS

   1 The heads of state or of government reaffirm the determination of
the member states of the enlarged European Communities irreversibly
to achieve the economic and monetary union, confirming all the elements of the instruments adopted by the Council and by the representatives of member states on March 22, 1971, and March 21, 1972.

   The necessary decisions should be taken in the course of 1973 so as to
allow the transition to the second stage of the economic and monetary
union on January 1, 1974, and with a view to its completion not later
than December 31, 1980.

   The heads of state or government reaffirmed the principle of parallel
progress in the different fields of the economic and monetary union.

   2 They declared that fixed but adjustable parities between their currencies constitute an essential basis for the achievement of the union
and expressed their determination to set up within the Community
mechanisms for defence and mutual support which would enable
member states to ensure that they are respected.

   They decided to institute before April 1, 1973, by solemn instrument, based on the EEC treaty, a European Monetary Cooperation
Fund which will be administered by the Committee of Governors
of Central Banks within the context of general guidelines on economic policy laid down by the Council of Ministers. In an initial
phase the fund will operate on the following bases:

   Concerted action among the central banks for the purposes of
narrowing the margins of fluctuation between their currencies;

   The multilateralization of positions resulting from interventions in
Community currencies and the multilateralization of intra-
Community settlements;

   The use for this purpose of a European monetary unit of
account;

The administration of short-term monetary support among the central banks;

The very short-term financing of the agreement on the narrowing of margins and short-term monetary support will be regrouped in the fund under renovated mechanism; to this end, short-term support will be adjusted on the technical plane without modifying its essential characteristics and in particular without modifying the consultation procedures they involve.

The competent bodies of the Community shall submit reports:

Not later than September 30, 1973, on the adjustment of short-term support;

Not later than December 31, 1973, on the conditions for the progressive pooling of reserves.

3 The heads of state or of government stressed the need to coordinate more closely the economic policies of the Community and for this purpose to introduce more effective Community procedures.

Under existing economic conditions they consider that priority should be given to the fight against inflation and to a return to price stability. They instructed their competent ministers to adopt, on the occasion of the enlarged Council of October 30 and 31, 1972, precise measures in the various fields which lend themselves to effective and realistic short-term action towards these objectives and which take account of the respective situations of the countries of the enlarged Community.

4 The heads of state or of government express their determination that the member states of the enlarged Community should contribute by a common attitude to directing the reform of the international monetary system towards the introduction of an equitable and durable order.

They consider that this system should be based on the following principles:

Fixed but adjustable parities

The general convertibility of currencies

Effective international regulation of the world supply of liquidities.

A reduction in the role of national currencies as reserve instruments

The effective and equitable functioning of the adjustment process

Equal rights and duties for all participants in the system

The need to lessen the unstabilizing effects of short-term capital movements.

The taking into account of the interests of the developing countries.

Such a system would be fully compatible with the achievement of the economic and monetary union.

REGIONAL POLICY

5 The heads of state or of government agreed that a high priority should be given to the aim of correcting, in the Community, the structural and regional imbalances which might affect the realization of economic and monetary union.

The heads of state or of government invite the Commission to prepare without delay, a report analysing the regional problems which arise in the enlarged Community and to put forward appropriate proposals.

From now on they undertake to coordinate their regional policies. Desirous of directing that effort towards finding a Community solution to regional problems, they invite the Community institutions to create a Regional Development Fund. This will be set up before December 31, 1973, and will be financed, from the beginning of the second phase of economic and monetary union, from the Community's own resources. Intervention by the fund in coordination with national aids should permit progressively with the realization of economic and monetary union, the correction of the main regional imbalances in the enlarged Community and particularly those resulting from the preponderance of agriculture and from industrial change and structural underemployment.

SOCIAL POLICY

6 The heads of state or heads of government emphasized that they attached as much importance to vigorous action in the social field as to the achievement of the economic and monetary union. They thought it essential to ensure the increasing involvement of labour and management in the economic and social decisions of the Community. They invited the institutions, after consulting labour and management, to draw up, between now and January 1, 1974, a programme of action providing for concrete measures and the corresponding resources particularly in the framework of the Social Fund, based on the suggestions made in the course of the conference by heads of state and heads of government and by the Commission.

This programme should aim, in particular, at carrying out a coordinated policy for employment and vocational training, at improving working conditions and conditions of life, at closely involving workers in the progress of firms, at facilitating on the basis of the situation in the different countries the conclusion of collective agreements at European level in appropriate fields and at strengthening and coordinating measures of consumer protection.

INDUSTRIAL, SCIENTIFIC AND TECHNOLOGICAL POLICY

7 The heads of state or of government consider it necessary to seek to establish a single industrial base for the Community as a whole.

This involves the elimination of technical barriers to trade as well as the elimination, particularly in the fiscal and legal fields, of barriers which hinder closer relations and mergers between firms, the rapid adoption of a European company statute, the progressive and effective opening up of public sector purchases, the promotion on a European scale of competitive firms in the field of high technology, the transformation and conversion of declining industries, under acceptable social conditions, the formulation of measures to ensure that mergers affecting firms established in the Community are in harmony with the economic and social aims of the Community, and the maintenance of fair competition as much within the Common Market as in external markets in conformity with the rules laid down by the treaties.

Objectives will need to be defined and the development of a common policy in the field of science and technology ensured. This policy will require the coordination, within the institutions of the Community, of national policies and joint implementation of projects of interest to the Community.

To this end, a programme of action together with a precise timetable and appropriate means should be decided by the Community's institutions, before January 1, 1974.

ENVIRONMENT POLICY

8 The heads of state or of government emphasized the importance of a Community environmental policy. To this end they invited the Community institutions to establish, before July 31, 1973, a programme of action accompanied by a precise time-table.

ENERGY POLICY

9 The heads of state and heads of government deem it necessary to

invite the Community institutions to formulate as soon as possible an energy policy guaranteeing certain and lasting supplies under satisfactory economic conditions.

EXTERNAL RELATIONS

10 The heads of state or of government affirm that their efforts to construct their Community attain their full meaning only in so far as member states succeed in acting together to cope with the growing world responsibilities incumbent on Europe.

11 The heads of state or of government are convinced that the Community must, without detracting from the advantages enjoyed by countries with which it has special relations, respond even more than in the past to the expectations of all the developing countries;

With this in view, it attaches essential importance to the policy of association as confirmed in the Treaty of Accession and to the fulfilment of its commitments to the countries of the Mediterranean basin with which agreements have been or will be concluded, agreements which should be the subject of an overall and balanced approach.

In the same perspective, in the light of the results of the Unctad [United Nations Conference on Trade and Development] conference and in the context of the development strategy adopted by the United Nations, the institutions of the Community and member states are invited progressively to adopt an overall policy of development cooperation on a worldwide scale, comprising, in particular, the following elements:

The promotion in appropriate cases of agreements concerning the primary products of the developing countries with a view to arriving at market stabilization and an increase in their exports:

The improvement of generalized preferences with the aim of achieving a steady increase in imports of manufactures from the developing countries;

In this connexion the Community institutions will study from the beginning of 1973 the conditions which will permit the achievement of a substantial growth target.

An increase in the volume of official financial aid.

An improvement in the financial conditions of this aid, particularly in favour of the least developed countries, bearing in mind the recommendations of the OECD [Organization for Economic Cooperation and Development] development assistance committee.

These questions will be the subject of studies and decisions in good time during 1973.

12 With regard to the industrial countries, the Community is determined, in order to ensure the harmonious development of world trade:

To contribute, while respecting what has been achieved by the Community, to a progressive liberalization of international trade by measures based on reciprocity and relating to both tariffs and non-tariff barriers;

To maintain a constructive dialogue with the United States, Japan, Canada and its other industrialized trade partners in a forthcoming spirit, using the most appropriate methods.

In this context the Community attaches major importance to the multilateral negotiations in the context of Gatt which it will participate in in accordance with its earlier statement.

To this end, the Community institutions are invited to decide not later than July 1, 1973, on a global approach covering all aspects affecting trade.

The Community hopes that an effort on the part of all partners will allow these negotiations to be completed in 1975.

It confirms its desire for the full participation of the developing countries in the preparation and progress of these negotiations which should take due account of the interests of those countries.

Furthermore, having regard to the agreements concluded with the Efta [European Free Trade Association] countries which are not members, the Community declares its readiness to seek with Norway a speedy solution to the trade problems facing that country in its relations with the enlarged Community.

13 In order to promote détente in Europe, the conference reaffirmed its determination to follow a common commercial policy towards the countries of Eastern Europe with effect from January 1, 1973; member states declared their determination to promote a policy of cooperation, founded on reciprocity, with these countries.

This policy of cooperation is, at the present stage, closely linked with the preparation and progress of the conference on security and cooperation in Europe to which the enlarged Community and its member states are called upon to make a concerted and constructive contribution.

14 The heads of state or of government agreed that political cooperation between the member states of the Community on foreign policy matters had begun well and should be still further improved. They agreed that consultations should be intensified at all levels and that the Foreign Ministers should in future meet four times a year instead of twice for this purpose. They considered that the aim of their cooperation was to deal with problems of current interest and, where possible, to formulate common medium and long-term positions, keeping in mind, inter alia, the international political implications for and effects of Community policies under construction. On matters which have a

direct bearing on Community activities, close contact will be maintained with the institutions of the Community. They agreed that the Foreign Ministers should produce, not later than June 30, 1973, a second report on methods of improving political cooperation in accordance with the Luxembourg report.

REINFORCEMENT OF INSTITUTIONS

15 The heads of state or government recognized that the structures of the Community had proved themselves, though they felt that the decision-making procedures and the functioning of the institutions should be improved, in order to make them more effective.

The Community institutions and, where appropriate, the representatives of the governments of member states are invited to decide before the end of the first stage in the achievement of the economic and monetary union, on the basis of the report which the Commission, pursuant to the resolution of March 22, 1971, is to submit before May 1, 1973; on the measures relating to the distribution of competences and responsibilities among the Community institutions and member states which are necessary to the proper functioning of an economic and monetary union.

They felt it desirable that the date on which meetings of national cabinets were normally held should be the same so that the Council of the Communities could organize itself with a more regular timetable.

Desiring to strengthen the powers of control of the European Parliamentary Assembly, independently of the date on which it will be elected by universal suffrage under Article 138 of the Treaty of Rome, and to make their contribution towards improving its working conditions, the heads of state or government, while confirming the decision of April 22, 1970, of the Council of the Communities, invited the Council and the Commission to put into effect without delay the practical measures designed to achieve this reinforcement and to improve the relations both of the Council and of the Commission with the Assembly.

The Council will, before June 30, 1973, take practical steps to improve its decision-making procedures and the cohesion of Community action.

They invited the Community institutions to recognize the right of the Economic and Social Committee in future to advise on its own initiative on all questions affecting the Community.

They were agreed in thinking that, for the purpose in particular of carrying out the tasks laid down in the different programmes of action, it was desirable to make the widest possible use of all the dispositions of the treaties, including Article 235 of the EEC treaty.

EUROPEAN UNION

16 The heads of state or government, having set themselves the major objective of transforming, before the end of the present decade and with the fullest respect for the treaties already signed, the whole complex of the relations of member states into a European union, request the institutions of the Community to draw up a report on this subject before the end of 1975 for submission to a summit conference.

Suggestions for Further Reading

The following titles represent only a very limited selection of the mass of literature which the process of integration in Western Europe has generated: and for the most part they have been chosen from among those written in English. Many of the books cited have their own extensive bibliographies; for a useful (though now slightly dated) overall survey see Carol Ann Cosgrove, *A Reader's Guide to Britain and the European Communities*, Chatham House: P.E.P. European Series No. 14, August 1970. (Several other titles in this series are also relevant to the issues discussed in this book.)

For those wishing to follow current developments in the Community the monthly publication of the London Office of the European Communities' Information Service, *European Community*, is invaluable. This is available free of charge on application to the office at 23 Chesham Street, London, S.W.1.

The *Journal of Common Market Studies* (Basil Blackwell, Oxford), publishes current academic studies on the Community; articles on the same theme are frequently also to be found in *International Organisation*, World Peace Foundation, Boston, Mass.

GENERAL WORKS

Roger Broad and R. J. Jarrett, *Community Europe Today*, rev. ed., London (1972).

Walter Laqueur, *Europe Since Hitler*, London (1970) (Pelican Books 1972).

Roger Morgan, *West European Politics since 1945: The Shaping of the European Community*, London (1972).

P.E.P., *European Unity: Co-operation and Integration*, London (1968).

Lord Gladwyn, *The European Idea*, London (1966).

Anthony Sampson, *The New Europeans*, rev. ed., London (1968) (Panther Books, 1971).

THE POLITICAL SYSTEM

Historical Development

CAMPS, MIRIAM, *European Unification in the Sixties*, London (1967). A penetrating analysis of developments in the period 1963–1965; and *Britain and the European Community, 1955–1963*, London (1964). The standard work for this theme.

DAVIDSON, IAN, *Britain and the Making of Europe*, London (1971). A good short account of the period between 1965 and 1971.

HAAS, ERNST B., *The Uniting of Europe*, 2nd. rev. ed., London (1968). A detailed pioneer work on the E.C.S.C. and the period up to 1958.

KITZINGER, UWE, *Diplomacy and Persuasion*, London (1973). An excellent detailed study of how Britain—finally—joined the Community.

MAYNE, RICHARD, *The Recovery of Europe*, London (1970). This is particularly detailed for the period up to 1960 and a good account of the role of Jean Monnet.

SPANIER, DAVID, *Europe, Our Europe*, London (1972). A lively account, by *The Times'* correspondent, of the successful negotiations for British entry.

WILLIS, F. ROY, *France, Germany and the New Europe, 1945–1967*, 2nd. ed., London (1968); and *Italy chooses Europe*, London (1971). Two excellent studies by an American historian.

The Political Dynamics of Integration

FRIEDRICH, CARL J., *Europe: An Emergent Nation?*, New York (1969). A series of studies of the social aspects of Community building.

LINDBERG, LEON N. and SCHEINGOLD, STUART A., *Europe's Would-Be tion*, Stanford (1963). An important study, based on a detailed analysis of the E.E.C. during the period 1958–1962.

LINDBERG, LEON N. and SCHEINGOLD, STUART A., *Europe's Would-Be Polity*, New Jersey (1970). A detailed and ambitious work which aims to provide an overall theoretical framework for the analysis of the process of integration. Contains useful case-study material.

LINDBERG, LEON N. and SCHEINGOLD, STUART A., (eds.) *Regional Integration: Theory and Research*, Harvard (1971). A symposium including contributions by most of the leading neo-functionalist writers designed to evaluate 'more than a decade of intellectual effort' by academic analysts. Originally published as a special issue of *International Organisation*, Autumn 1970.

NYE, J. S., *Peace in Parts: Integration and Conflict in Regional Organisation*, Boston (1971). A comparative neo-functionalist approach to the study of regional integration.

How the system works

COOMBES, DAVID, *Politics and Bureaucracy in the European Community*, London (1970). A critical analysis of the evolution of the role of the Commission.

GERBET, P. and PEPY, D., (eds.) *La Décision dans les Communautés Européenes*, Brussels (1969). A symposium, covering various aspects of decision-making at both the national and Community level. Now slightly out-of-date, but useful case-study material.

IONESCU, GHITA, (ed.), *The New Politics of European Integration*, London (1972). A symposium, most of which was originally published in two special issues of *Government and Opposition*, July 1967 and October 1971. Contains a useful bibliography.

MEYNAUD, JEAN, and SIDJANSKI, DUSAN, *Les Groupes de pression dans la Communauté Européenne*, Brussels (1971). An extensive and detailed study of the organisation and activities of Community-wide socio-economic interest groups.

VIRALLY, M., GERBET, P. and SALMON, J., (eds.) *Les Missions permanents auprès des organisations internationales*, Brussels (1971). Includes a section on the Committee of Permanent Representatives.

WALLACE, HELEN, *National Decision-making and the European Communities*, Chatham House: P.E.P. European Series (1973). A review, based on recent research, of the organisation of national administrations in the Community framework.

Achievements and Problems

Economic and Social Issues

BUTTERWICK, M. and ROLFE, C. J., *Food, Farming and the Common Market*, London (1968).

DENTON, G. R., (ed.), *Economic Integration in Europe*, London (1969). A symposium by a number of leading experts dealing with both theoretical and sector aspects of economic integration.

OVERSEAS DEVELOPMENT INSTITUTE, *Britain, the E.E.C. and the Third World* (1971).

SWANN., D., *The Economics of the Common Market*, London (1970). A short introduction to the major economic aspects of the Community.

ZELLER, ADRIEN, *L'Imbroglio agricole du Marche Commun*, Paris (1970).

Political issues

BUCHAN, ALASTAIR, (ed.), *Europe's Future, Europe's Choices*, London (1970).

CALLEO, DAVID P., *Europe's Future*, London (1967).

PINDER, JOHN and PRYCE, ROY, *Europe After de Gaulle*, London (1969).

THE ENLARGED COMMUNITY

BOW GROUP, *Europe: Power and Responsibilities*: 1—*Institutions*, by Peter Ratzer and David Baker; 2—*Parliament: Direct Elections*, by David Baker and Barnard Brook-Partridge, London (1972).

BURROUGHS, BERNARD and IRWIN, CHRISTOPHER, *The Security of Western Europe: Towards a Common Defence Policy*, London (1972).

CHAPMAN, DONALD, *The European Parliament—the Years Ahead*, London (1973).

GASTEYGER, CURT, *Europe and America at the Crossroads*, The Atlantic Institute, Paris (1972).

GOODWIN, G., *European Unity: A Return to Realities?* Leeds (1972).

P.E.P. (in association with the Hansard Society and the Study of Parliament Group), *Westminster to Brussels: the Significance for Parliament of Accession to the European Community*, London (1973).

SHONFIELD, ANDREW, *Europe: Journey to an Unknown Destination*, London (1973). An expanded version of the B.B.C. Reith Lectures, 1972: a penetrating—if controversial—analysis of the problems of the enlarged Community.

SPINELLI, ALTIERO, *The European Adventure*, London (1972).

Index